# DEMOCRACY  IS NOT A SPECTATOR SPORT

## *the* ULTIMATE VOLUNTEER HANDBOOK

### ARTHUR BLAUSTEIN
#### WITH HELEN MATATOV

SKYHORSE PUBLISHING

Skyhorse Publishing books may be purchased in bulk at special discounts for sales promotion, corporate gifts, fund-raising, or educational purposes. Special editions can also be created to specifications. For details, contact the Special Sales Department, Skyhorse Publishing, 307 West 36th Street, 11th Floor, New York, NY 10018 or info@skyhorsepublishing.com.

Skyhorse® and Skyhorse Publishing® are registered trademarks of Skyhorse Publishing, Inc.®, a Delaware corporation.

www.skyhorsepublishing.com

10 9 8 7 6 5 4 3 2 1

Library of Congress Cataloging-in-Publication Data is available on file.
ISBN: 978-1-61608-062-4

Printed in China

For Esther and Morris

# CONTENTS

---------------------------------- ★ ----------------------------------

PART THREE: ON YOUR OWN  251

---------------------------------- ★ ----------------------------------

# Introduction:
## A Nation Challenged

Americans have been a very fortunate people. Indeed, our nation and our people have been blessed with abundant natural resources; a temperate climate; the protective geography of two oceans and friendly neighbors to the north and south; a Bill of Rights and a Constitution bequeathed to us, thanks to the genius of our founding fathers; waves of immigrants, who, fleeing religious and political persecution, as well as economic deprivation, were thankful to arrive at Ellis Island or Angel Island; and a citizenry with boundless energy, openness, and generosity. Americans have taken great pride in being the world's oldest democracy and the land of opportunity. ★

1

Yet that is not the America we know today—one that is reeling from the economic fallout from the Great Recession and the worst environmental disaster in our history; a housing mortgage meltdown, with families losing their homes; skyrocketing health-care costs; unacceptable levels of unemployment and underemployment; and an aging and broken infrastructure. If this were not bad enough, local governments, states, and cities—some close to bankruptcy and others already bankrupt—are faced with massive layoffs of teachers, police, firefighters, and human-service professionals. These are hard times, and a growing majority of Americans have been telling the pollsters, for the past eight years, that "our nation is headed in the wrong direction" and that "their children will be the first generation to do worse than their parents." Among other issues, this book will focus on two critical questions: How did we get into this mess? And what can be done to turn things around? There is a role for you in helping to reverse this downward trend.

Volunteers are needed in America today in record numbers. People are in trouble, and they are turning to voluntary organizations in their communities for help. Millions of Americans—middle-class, working-class, professional and business executives—have experienced the loss of jobs, homes, businesses, or small farm failures; they have endured personal bankruptcy, or the loss of their pensions or retirement income. And millions more are only a layoff, an illness, a divorce, or an accident away from falling into poverty. Recent studies have found that the largest increase in homelessness has been among families with children. Food banks—even in upscale suburban areas—are serving families who, a couple of years ago, were the ones doing the serving and donating of food.

The environment is in trouble, too, and environmental organizations need volunteers to be effective.

Above all, public debate on where this country is headed is in trouble. The political deadlock and poisonous partisanship in Washington does not help matters. Organizations that work

2

on public policy need volunteers to keep debate alive, to keep democracy viable, and to make a better future possible.

Voluntary efforts should not be a substitute for the government's failure to act, however. That's the great danger today, because the federal government has been cutting back on social and human services for the past thirty years, since the Reagan administration, while slashing funds for basic social service assistance to state and local governments. This could not be happening at a worse time.

Our nation is in an extremely precarious position. It looks like we could well have a double-dip recession and even stagflation for the next several years. Yet while President Obama has put forth several important initiatives—to stimulate the economy; provide needed financial aid to local government; offer loans to help small business; and extend unemployment benefits, to name a few—the Republicans in Congress have opposed him in every instance. This makes it extremely difficult to pass legislation that could alleviate the suffering that cash-strapped families are experiencing.

What is needed is a coherent and comprehensive understanding of how we got into this economic mess, as well as an understanding of the public policy initiatives—economic, environmental, and social—that it will take to ensure a necessary and healthy recovery. Yet this is not happening. Why not? There are several reasons, but initially, I'll touch on three: 1) Because of the way that economics is taught; 2) Because of the way that the mass media covers politics; and 3) Because the Republicans seem to think that it's in their political interest to oppose every necessary reform that President Barack Obama proposes.

First, the way economics is taught: This course is almost nonexistent at the high school level (a few random pages of charts and curves), and on the college level, it's far too abstract and theoretical. Thus, the vast majority of Americans do not understand how economic policy is made and how it affects them. Nowhere have the

3

mass media, politicians, experts, and our education system failed us more than in the area of economic education. It is amazing how so many intelligent people get nervous at the sound of the word "economics." What's more, the so-called experts have confused us so much that we don't even trust our common sense anymore. The truth of the matter is that we have an appallingly low level of economic literacy, with most people buying into myths rather than truths. It is for precisely this reason that likely independent voters are telling pollsters that the Democrats are responsible for our economic woes, particularly the deficits and debt, when in fact it was eight years of George W. Bush and a compliant and enabling Republican Congress that gave us these failed policies.

Next, it's important to examine the critical role of the mass media, the dominant means of conveying information to the American public. In the past thirty years we've experienced a steady and marked decline in the quality of journalism.

To a great extent, we have not had a serious national public policy debate because the mass media, with few exceptions—NPR, PBS, and some print journalism—have treated politics, as well as economic and social policy, as entertainment: a combination of hype and palliation. There's an unconscious cynicism in the way palliative the mass media have reported the previous day's happenings: OBAMA WINS or SENATE DEMS BEATEN. The political and economic life of the country has been reduced to little more than a struggle for political power, the results not unlike the score of a football game. There seems to be no higher good, no national purpose, no critical judgment. The problem is that 75 percent of the public gets its news from television and talk radio, the worst offenders. And with the advent of 24/7 cable TV, the Internet, and the blogosphere, traditional news sources have dumbed down their content in order to compete for revenue and audiences with short attention spans.

Most of us should know that our dependence on mindless, endless, irrelevant evening-news sound bites and talk-radio ranting creates the illusion that we are learning something. We are not. In the process of being bombarded by decontextualized and useless information, we lose our freedom to make genuine choices based on coherent, rational ideas about our economy and how it affects social policies and the well-being of our communities. Hype has impoverished our political debate. It undermines the very idea that public discourse can be educational and edifying—or that national public policy can grow out of reflective discussion and shared political values. This "McNews" approach has undercut our moral values and civic traditions. We have sought simplistic answers to complex problems without even beginning to comprehend our loss.

But now we're getting ahead of ourselves. A more detailed analysis, as well as a healthy antidote to media hype, is discussed in a final chapter, *The Reading Cure*.

The loss of coherent and comprehensive public discourse raises some difficult and complex questions about the relationship between policy and community service. Volunteers work in a context, and that context is shaped by America's social and economic policy. That policy, in turn, is shaped by politics in Washington, D.C.

Next, let's look at Republican opposition to Obama's policies and the political deadlock in Washington. It would appear that the GOP leadership, Mitch McConnell, the Minority Leader in the Senate, and John Boehner, the Minority Leader in the House—as well as John McCain in his primary campaign in Arizona, and Sarah Palin on the stump—are convinced that the way for their party to climb the greasy pole back to power is to attack anything Obama says and to oppose any and all legislation that the White House or congressional Democratic leadership propose. And they do so without any concern as to what is best for the country. They have opposed the economic recovery stimulus package; health-care reform; climate change reform; banking and financial services reform; campaign finance reform; extension of unemployment benefits; consumer affairs reform; a partial ban on deep-sea drilling; and immigration reform, among other legislative initiatives. Moreover, they have not even bothered to offer any constructive or reasonable alternatives whatsoever. It's just like they dusted off and put on their old Nancy Reagan JUST SAY NO buttons.

Instead of offering creative alternatives, Boehner and McConnell slavishly recite—as does the Republican Congressional Chorus—the same repetitive thirty-second sound bites for the evening television news, day in and day out. They could just as well put a parrot before the mike. Apparently their handlers and pollsters—with fresh research from a focus group of fifteen folks in Hammond, Indiana—have told them that the mantra of "lower taxes, less government" is the winning slogan that will play in Peoria. What's really scary is that this mindless strategy might even win.

If it does work, and the Republican Party—shoved and shouted further to the right of George W. Bush by the Tea Party—gets back in power by having won either the House or Senate in 2010 or the White House in 2012, we'll be in far bigger trouble than we were during the Bush era. We'll have to contend with a more extreme version of Bush's ruinous policies. The Republican leadership—who for eight years partnered with Bush in taking us to the economic abyss—are now doubling down their political bets because of pressure from their right-wing base and the Tea Party, and their belief that voters have short memories.

In July of 2010, thirty-eight Republican members of the House, including two in critical leadership positions, formed a Tea Party Caucus. They are playing with fire, as the angry populism and simplistic rhetoric they are promoting are not a substitute for coherent and comprehensive public policies. For want of creative and serious ideas and policies, the GOP is practicing the art of superficial posturing and caving in to what is called "crackpot realism." The consequences of this kind of cynical pandering—if they win—will be government by provisional catastrophe, which could well lead to man-on-the-white-horse authoritarianism. Just thinking about this possibility reminds me of the words of Robert Frost: "I have seen the future, and I don't advocate it."

If this sounds gloomy, unless you hadn't noticed, we're going through bleak times. But it need not be that way. We have been through bad times before. First, we have to confront the reality that there is no easy or simple solution to the problems we face as a nation. For too long we put our faith in incompetent pitchmen posing as leaders (Ronald Reagan and Bush II), who, with bad ideas and worse policies, have frittered away our natural resources, human capital, and financial security. The deficits and debt that have piled up over the past thirty years are not only economic—they are also moral and social.

Another reality we have to face is that Obama is a political leader; he is not a wizard. He cannot wave a magic wand to change reality and make our problems disappear, just as Washington, Lincoln, or Roosevelt could not during crises of times past. Problems and policies that were thirty years in the making do not go away in two years. What Obama *can* do is to put our problems into perspective and offer reasonable, doable—and sometimes painful—solutions that require patience. Fortunately for us, he is an intelligent, competent, and decent man, and he's displayed qualities of leadership under the most difficult of circumstances. The week of his inauguration the headline in *The Onion* got it right: AMERICA GIVES ITS WORST JOB TO A BLACK MAN. All things considered, he's doing an commendable job without any help from the opposition party and with vicious attacks from the reactionary media.

If Obama had a difficult time getting the Republicans in Congress to cooperate his first two years, the second two will be all but impossible. Having won control of the House and gained several seats in the Senate in the 2010 midterm elections, the GOP will be emboldened to block all legislation proposed by the White House. Their motto will be "No We Can't."

Obama has to accept some blame for this stinging defeat. The two issues uppermost in the minds of voters were the economy/ unemployment and health care. The administration dawdled far too long on health care, talking about a bipartisan approach that was going nowhere. Meanwhile, the Republicans and the Tea Party were spreading false myths about "death panels" and frightening seniors about big cuts in their Medicare. White House strategists also failed to clearly and coherently explain to the American people the long-term benefits of either their health-care reform initiative or their economic stimulus package.

The inability of the White House to communicate effectively on these two issues gave the opposition the opportunity to frame the debate on their own terms; and the mass media had a field day fueling extraneous controversy, especially Tea Party rallies. Facts and truth are no match for angry guys with powdered wigs and tricorn hats. This media diversion and the failure of the White House to provide a coherent message undermined Obama's credibility on other issues and detracted from his solid accomplishments. In politics, perception is often more important than substance. Negative public perceptions—as well as a steady dose of attack ads—made it extremely difficult for Democratic House and Senate candidates to compete in tight races.

Now that the Republicans have a majority in the House, they have absolute power of chairing all committees. They've used these powers in the past to freeze out the Democrats, as they did from 2001 until 2007. The Republican chairs hire staff, decide which issues to consider, set legislative priorities, issue subpoenas,

and determine when to hold investigations, press conferences, and hearings.
During the recent Bush administration,
legislative oversight and accountability of the financial sector
were no more than a wink, a
nod, and a whitewash. That's
how we got into this economic
crisis in the first place and GOP
leadership, having learned nothing from
the past, will try to repeal crucial parts of the financial reform
legislation passed in 2010. Now, more than ever, the Republicans
are beholden to corporate vested interests, who shoveled huge
amounts of money into GOP campaign coffers.

Many pundits are drawing parallels between the 2010 midterm
elections and the 1994 midterm elections, when Republicans cap-
tured both the Senate and House after two years of Bill Clinton's
first term. But there is a huge difference. The economy was in
fairly good shape then. Now, the economy is extremely fragile and
uncertain. If Republicans are hell-bent on destroying the Obama
presidency—as their leadership has said is a priority—they could
very well oppose legislation crucial to putting the nation's economy
back on track. This legislation includes extension of emergency
unemployment benefits; more federal aid to state and local governments to stave off the loss of essential jobs in public safety and
education; and a stimulus package targeted toward creating more
jobs in infrastructure development and green energy projects.
Development of the nation's aging infrastructure—roads, sewer
systems, airports, bridges, mass transit, and the energy grid—is
extremely important if we are to effectively compete in the global
economic market. Republican opposition to these job-creating initiatives could well deepen the Great Recession causing untold pain
to millions of American families now living on the margin.

Not only did the Democratic Party take a big hit in the midterm elections, so did democracy. Secret money was pumped into the campaign in huge amounts, like toxic waste being dumped into reservoirs across the country. This shadow money was provided, in the main, to Republicans by corporations and wealthy individuals—through the Chamber of Commerce and vested interest groups legitimized by the Citizens United decision—who expect dividends in return for their investments. The cash was primarily used for attack ads—targeting Democrats—that flooded our airwaves and mailboxes. At the end of each ad, there should have been a disclaimer: "This message is a dangerous blow to democracy and was made possible by the John Roberts gang-of-five reactionaries on the Supreme Court." Since when is the sanctioning of legalized bribery "judicial restraint" (as the conservatives preach to us) and a "strict construction" of the Constitution? It took a peculiarly contorted form of intellectual and moral jujitsu for the Roberts 5–4 majority to pin that decision on our nation's founders.

If the Tea Partiers have the genuine concern they claim to have for the demise of republicanism in our country, and a decent eleventh grade understanding of American civic history, they'd plant their "Don't Tread on Me" flags around the Supreme Court, the U.S. Chamber of Commerce, the Republican National Committee headquarters, and Fox News. Patrick Henry could then stop turning over in his grave. The stakes are very high, as the flood of undisclosed and unregulated money into our electoral system not only contaminates our politics and undermines our republican values but it threatens the integrity of American democracy.

What allowed American presidents in the past to lead us out of adversity was their ability to focus the American people on the challenges our country faced, in an open and honest way. But it was up to the American people to bear the burden—to pull together to persevere and succeed. What made a big difference in the past was our ability, as a people, to confront reality. Though the problems may be different today, the means of solving them are the same. It is up to us, individually and collectively, to become part of the solution rather than being part of the problem. What do I mean?

We have to put aside irrelevant distractions, mindless entertainment, and false assumptions that somehow everything will work out for the best if we just sit on our rear ends. For example, when we went to war in Iraq, Bush went on television and told the American people to get out in the malls and shop—to spend until they maxed out their credit cards. Guess what? That didn't work, because it was the thumb-sucking material equivalent of binge drinking and denial. No sacrifice, no belt-tightening, no introspection, no questioning, no problemo. That's what people do in television commercials or in sitcoms; not in real life. Can you imagine Washington during the Revolutionary War, or Lincoln during the Civil War, or Roosevelt during Word War II, asking Americans to go out and shop?

Next, Bush told folks—particularly working-class and minorities—to become stakeholders in his "home ownership society." That was going to be the key to solving our social and domestic problems. Just go down to your friendly neighborhood bank and take out an adjustable-interest, sub-prime loan and join the middle class. We know how that turned out.

The Iraq war, shopping at malls, and sub-prime loans; if you meld all these together—a failed foreign policy with a failed domestic policy—what you get is a national economy in the tank and international banking chaos. The Wall Street sharpies call it synergism, but it's spelled *catastrophe*. Only through civic engagement and citizen participation can we turn things around. We only have to look at our recent past to see how our nation was changed, for the better, by homegrown grassroots movements. When our leaders could not or did not act, the people did. The civil rights, antiwar, environmental justice, consumer, antiapartheid, disabilities, gay and lesbian rights, antinuke, and anti-sweatshop movements—among others—are a few examples of how citizen action has had a profound effect on American law, society, and culture.

Let me share a more recent story about what I'm getting at. About three weeks after 9/11, I was listening to NPR. They were doing interviews with New Yorkers about how the tragedy had affected their lives. One of those interviewed was a seventeen-year-old high school student. He told the interviewer, "Before 9/11, when my friends and I went into a music store to get CDs, or to a fast-food place, if we weren't served in two minutes I'd get antsy and irritated. Last week I went down to the Red Cross Center to volunteer to give blood. I had to wait three hours and I never felt better in my life." This story is both real and metaphoric.

The lifeblood of a democracy, in the real world, is volunteering, community service, civic engagement, and citizen participation. And that's what this book is about. It's a win-win-win situation:

It's good for you, vital to those being served, and healthy for your communities and our nation.

There is a postscript to this story that is worth thinking about: My fifteen years of working with volunteers has confirmed what my intuition told me—volunteering for community service could well be the quickest, most rewarding, and least expensive way of gaining self-esteem.

# PART ONE

# UNDER-STANDING COMMUNITY SERVICE

When you volunteer, it helps a lot to understand the economic and social problems that impact the communities where you donate your time. It is also important to become aware of the political decisions and/or the policies that are causing the problems you're trying to deal with through your volunteer work. Often, by necessity, volunteers must become advocates for changing those political decisions or policies.

Volunteers can become advocates as individuals or through public interest groups that lobby for systemic change. If a volunteer does not become an advocate, the problems will keep recurring over and over again. The volunteer will either burn out or succumb to "compassion fatigue." ★

# Volunteering, Public Policy, and Politics

Let's review the economic and social problems facing our people, our communities, and our nation. We are in the midst of a Great Recession that has been thirty years in the making. It is essential that we comprehend the policies and politics of how we got into this colossal mess. Otherwise, as George Santayana observed, "Those who cannot remember the past are condemned to repeat it."

The Census Bureau report of September 2010 on increased poverty in the United States should be a wake-up call. Four million additional Americans found themselves struggling with poverty in 2009, with children comprising the biggest percentage of this population. This brought the total number of people in poverty to 44 million—one in seven Americans—the highest level recorded since 1994.

In addition, the states, individually and collectively, are experiencing their biggest budget deficits since World War II because of the loss of federal aid. The reason for the decline in federal aid is that after four consecutive years of federal surpluses under the Clinton administration, the Bush administration managed to give us eight years of the largest federal budget deficits in our history.

The biggest culprits behind the rising deficit and the soaring national debts were the two Bush tax cuts. The sad truth is that what Washington giveth in tax cuts, the states taketh back in regressive tax increases and service cuts. But there's one critical difference: The state tax increases caused by federal tax cuts were mainly shouldered by the middle class and the poor. The state cuts in education, health care, nutrition, and job training especially hurt 44 million poor Americans and another 55 million who are near-poor. Local cuts in environmental protection, public safety, libraries, the arts, and mass transit hurt everyone. These are not abstract statistics, but the fate of millions of human beings living in real communities. And this happened at a time when over 46 million Americans did not have health insurance. It's not a pretty picture, and the painful consequences will be felt for decades, even though the Bush administration is gone. The future of our children and grandchildren was mortgaged without a serious national debate.

The Bush tax cuts may have been popular, but like snake oil, they sold but they didn't cure. Lost in all the superficial coverage of the tax cuts is the reality that someone making $1 million annually got a break of $92,000, while an average working family got $256.

Just like in the *The Wizard of Oz,* when we finally got to see who was operating the smoke-puffing machine, we found a consummate pitchman. In Bush's case, the man behind the screen was a flag-waving, antiterrorist fearmonger who labeled his opponents antipatriotic. Early in his administration, following the tragedy of 9/11, Bush and his party cooked up the ultimate recipe for keeping political power. A nation in a constant state of anxiety—over the threat of terrorism, or a potential war—is a nation off balance. The Bush administration exploited that insecurity and used it as a cover to divert public attention from the country's serious domestic economic and social problems and the administration's political agenda.

The "Bush doctrine" opened the door to a series of preemptive wars against "evil" regimes, ostensibly to protect the United States and bring security, stability, safety, and democracy to the citizens of Baghdad and Kabul. Meanwhile, the administration showed little or no concern for the security, stability, and safety of the citizens of New York, Los Angeles, Detroit, Cleveland, or thousands of other cities and small towns across America, who were facing enormous economic and social difficulties.

Bush did a clever job of manipulating the mass media, but in reality his smooth imagery and charming personality were steadily and subtly undermining America's values. While he composed hymns to individualism, Sunday piety, trickle-down economics, and family values, he tried to gut most of the programs that provide for social, economic, and environmental justice. America's families needed less pious rhetoric and more policies geared toward a healthy economy, secure jobs, decent health care, affordable housing, quality public education, renewable energy, and a sustainable environment. Bush seemed unable—or unwilling—to grasp that the government has an important leadership role in this. In fact, the only policy that Bush seemed energized by was one of tax giveaways for the rich and for corporate America.

Bush did not seem to understand that, while it is not a sin to be born into privilege, it is a sin to spend your life defending it. John F. Kennedy and Franklin D. Roosevelt understood that. They knew the narrowness that privilege can breed. Bush's policies amounted to a war against the poor and the middle class. The tax and budget cuts were not made, as he claimed, to jump-start the economy or balance the budget. They were simply massive cash transfers. Social programs were slashed to pay for tax giveaways for the wealthy and new defense contracts for arms makers, pharmas, insurance companies, and war contractors (think Halliburton and Blackwater) who just happened to be big campaign contributors.

Bush's economic policies hammered the middle and working classes. An economic research study done for the Rockefeller Foundation measured the percentage of Americans who experienced a decrease in their income of 25 percent or more in a given year, without having the resources to make up for the loss. During the Bush years, the percentage of insecure Americans, relative to the given level of unemployment, rose steadily. In 2008 alone, more than 20 percent of Americans experienced a 25 percent or greater loss of household income over the prior year—the biggest income decline for the most Americans in twenty-five years.

In the eight Bush years overall, our nation experienced the weakest post-recession job creation cycle since the Great Depression, along with record deficits and household debt, a record bankruptcy rate, and a substantial increase in poverty. If that's not enough, we shifted from being a nation with substantial federal surpluses to one with major deficits. The United States is now the world's biggest borrower; we export far less than we import; we produce far less than we consume; and foreign investors own more of American assets than Americans own of foreign assets. That's the Bush economic record.

As bad as the Bush years were, many of the economic and social problems we have been experiencing began before Bush, and can be directly traced back to the 1980s and the Reagan era. It was Reagan's administration that foisted "supply-side economics"— also known as "trickle-down" or Reaganomics—on the nation. To justify their plan to kill the safety net of federal support programs established under President Lyndon Johnson, Reagan's economists claimed that Reaganomics would eradicate poverty. Yet the best research indicates the opposite. Growth in the private economy has had a declining role in reducing poverty, and virtually all of the reduction in poverty since the mid-1960s has been brought about by the expansion of federal social insurance and income transfer programs of the kind attacked by the Reagan and Bush administrations. In point of fact, eighteen months after Reagan took office and trickle-down economics became a reality, 5 million Americans were driven into poverty (a 17 percent increase)—85 percent of whom were women and children.

In addition to the massive cuts, the Reagan administration's strategy was to privatize or turn over to the states specific social, education, housing, and health-care programs, historically the responsibility of the federal government.

In the 1960s, thanks to President Lyndon Johnson's Great Society programs, there was hope. Upward Bound provided basic academic prep support for low-income high school students who wanted to go to college. The Neighborhood Youth Corps provided summer jobs for "at-risk," low-income teenagers, and the Job Corps provided basic technical skills training and education for disadvantaged sixteen- to twenty-four-year-olds. Youngsters who had never before had a chance believed that their dreams could become reality. By the early '80s, however, slashed budgets dashed hope, replacing it with despair, as the youth turned to drugs, crime, and violence.

In a deliberate effort to destroy the credibility of these programs, conservative politicians began manipulating symbols in order to stigmatize them. During the Nixon era, they cleverly and cynically began to refer to them as "minority" and "welfare" programs, rather than as "opportunity" programs, which they were. That switched the message from positive to negative. This kind of deceit and distortion was not an accident; it was designed to exploit fear and racial divisiveness.

These appeals to bigotry worked. They allowed Republicans to defeat moderate Democrats across the South and pick up a substantial number of seats in Congress. This "Southern strategy" of Nixon—part of a deal he cut with arch-segregationist Senator Strom Thurmond of South Carolina in order to secure the Republican presidential nomination—ultimately provided the political cover, and congressional votes, for Reagan and Bush II to enact their reactionary economic and social agendas.

The Nixon administration also tried, illegally (like so much else they were doing), to kill the War on Poverty. Fortunately, a federal judge prevented them from abolishing the antipoverty efforts. Nixon resigned in disgrace shortly thereafter, faced with an impeachment trial over Watergate.

Once the United States reached the Reagan era of the '80s, we had entered a period that at the highest levels of government officially condoned and even encouraged negative attitudes, code words, and symbols directed against the poor in particular and toward basic human and social service programs in general. Conservative politicians were adept at moralizing endlessly over the problems: the unemployed and underemployed, the homeless and hungry, alcoholism, drug abuse, mental illness, infant mortality, child and spousal abuse, and disrupted families. But they had neither the heart nor the will for the rigorous thought and work of finding cures, or even just relieving some of the suffering and symptoms.

Let me give an example. During the course of the 1980 presidential campaign, then-candidate Reagan would entertain crowds with the line, "Do you know how much it costs to keep a kid in the Job Corps—(pause)—and how much it costs to send a kid to Harvard? Well, I'll tell you: $13,000 for the Job Corps and only $12,500 for Harvard." This usually elicited gales of smug laughter. But it was a false comparison. The alternative to the Job Corps was not Harvard; it was despair. There were substantial costs to eliminating the Job Corps. At the time Reagan compared the Job Corps to Harvard, it cost $20,000 a year to keep a youth in prison, and $26,000 to keep a youth in an alcohol and drug abuse program or a halfway house. At $13,500, the Job Corps was a far less expensive investment for taxpayers, and the youth were learning self-respect and job skills so they could become productive, tax-paying members of society.

The real issues, then and now are: What are the values of society, and where do we want to spend our money? Drastic cuts in basic social and human service programs exact social and human costs, and they also appear as direct financial costs to taxpayers at future times, in different ledgers.

Reagan's cuts to human and social services did not promote better family life; they destabilized it. The reduction in services did not reduce alcoholism, but increased it. The cuts did not increase respect for the law; they weakened it.

Politics in the eighties under Reagan reached a level of abstractness removed from the circumstances of ordinary Americans. When a typical family runs into tough financial times, two things happen: The one thing that they *do* is to ensure that those members of the family (or society) who are least able to fend for themselves are given the protection and bare minimum necessary for survival. The one thing that they do *not* do is allow those who have more than enough and are enjoying luxuries to continue to hoard. There are certain natural principles of behavior, of caring and decency, that have prior claim over untested game plans of economic theorists or politicians on the make. And it wasn't only politicians on the make. It was a time when Wall Street hucksters could appear on campuses and tell budding MBAs that greed is good.

As the Reagan era came to a close, pundits of type text and tube gushed over Reagan's ability, as the Great Communicator, to manipulate the American public, and the pundits themselves. At that time, I came across a poem by a seventeen-year-old in the Job Corps. The youngster, from Appalachia, got it right. Perhaps a bit awkwardly, but with keen insight, he wrote:

> Ronald Reagan took an ax,
> to make inflation bygone.
> He gave the budget forty whacks,

and sent the guns to Tehran.
While militarism and space go on apace,
each funded in entirety,
matters of poverty and race
are of the chopped variety.
For each man kills the things
he knows not of.
Farewell, oh Great Society.

The economic policies of Reagan and Bush I during the '80s were failures—a fool's paradise built on the sands of borrowed time and borrowed money. The consequences were staggering debt, industrial decline, shrinking wages, two painful recessions, increased poverty, and structural unemployment. Their reckless spending and borrowing—combined with deindustrialization, deregulation, and privatization—brought us to the brink of economic deprivation and social depression.

In 1992, the nation elected Bill Clinton. The Clinton administration presided over the longest peacetime economic expansion in our history. The national debt was reduced dramatically, the industrial sector boomed, wages increased, and more Americans found jobs. Clinton helped the middle class and working poor by increasing the benefit levels and eligibility for the Earned Income Tax Credit. He restored tax progressivity and fairness, with higher rates on the wealthiest taxpayers. And he fought to increase the minimum wage, to get family-leave legislation, and to protect the environment. Clinton served two terms, but he was on the defensive for six of those years, because Republicans gained control of Congress. After the eight prosperous Clinton years, the nation elected George W. Bush and returned to the trickle-down economic and social policies of Reagan.

Thomas Jefferson warned us that we could be free or ignorant, but not both. We have not taken that warning to heart. We did not have a serious national debate about the Bush administration's economic and social policies. And, thanks to the Tea Party and the mass media, we are not having a serious debate over Obama's policies now.

Obama's critics—in the media, the Republican Party, and to some extent, the American public—are behaving like we live in the unreal world of television commercials, where a problem gets resolved in thirty seconds. You buy a new car and mysteriously, the guy or gal of your dreams suddenly appears. You switch stock-brokerage firms, and you suddenly make a bundle of money. You take a pill, and all your sexual problems are resolved. All of this happens with the snap of a finger. In the real world, especially politics, nothing works that way.

As a frame of reference, we should remind ourselves that the American public had the patience and wisdom to give Franklin Delano Roosevelt four terms in office, and thirteen years to get out of the Depression that Herbert Hoover and the Republicans had created for the country in the late 1920s and early '30s. I am not suggesting that it will take us that long, or that we should let Obama off the hook. What I am suggesting is that we exercise some reason, patience, and wisdom. The economic and social problems that we confront as a nation are like cancer of the body politic. There are no quick or painless fixes. I am reminded of an admonition from the Old Testament prophet Isaiah: "Judge us not by the heights we have achieved but by the depths from which we have come." Considering the absolutely dire circumstances of the economy and the total opposition of the Republicans, Obama has done an exceptional job.

The GOP congressional leadership wants to return to the same failed policies of Reagan and Bush. What Obama understands— and what the Republican congressional leadership does not—is that although the economic difficulties facing our nation are complex, they cannot be used as an excuse for reneging on our national social and moral commitments. National issues—such as health care, consumer affairs, the banking system, the environment,

Medicare, home foreclosures, civil rights, and Social Security—require national policy, oversight, and programs. They should not be ignored, or turned over to the states or the private sector. The issue is not public versus private or federal versus state; rather, it is the diminution or avoidance of any national standards of responsibility and accountability. To deflect, suspend, or fragment responsibility and accountability suggests that we are either renouncing or failing to assert our moral purpose as a nation. Worse, the Republican leadership, then and now, seems to be denying that this moral purpose exists.

The Reagan and Bush administrations' attempts to turn over to the states more program responsibility with less money would end up destroying existing national support systems that were effective and had a proven capacity to deliver services using local implementation capabilities. These systems were replaced with an inequitable structure run by the states, which historically have a poor track record. State-run systems are typically restrictively financed, more bureaucratic, and less accountable, and they are subject to intense local, political, and financial pressures.

The last point is extremely important: Effective and efficient use of limited federal funds was being sacrificed to conflicting political interests in each state. Instead of the more efficient government that Reagan and Bush promised, we have instead fifty bureaucratic and anachronistic messes: government by special interest lobbyists. And the Republican Party is trying to do the same thing with Obama's health-care reform.

The ideological implications behind thirty years of Reagan's and Bush's economic policies and those of GOP leadership today are disturbing. They depart from the genuine conservative leadership that has played such an important role in American history. Historically, conservatives have not promised lower taxes and economic privatism. Traditionally, conservative leaders have focused primarily on the underlying problems of the human community—issues of leadership, equality of opportunity, continuity and order, the obligations of the strong to the weak, and the safeguards needed to keep the privileged from abusing their power.

I am well aware that it is quite unfashionable in these days of Tea Party revolts and antigovernment slogans to speak of more qualitative initiatives from government. Yet, if government is to do its job, we must do ours. A good part of that job is confronting the reality that our nation is facing a brutal political struggle for control over the levers of power.

Not only does Obama face the political challenge of repairing our struggling economy and strengthening our social structure, but he must also overcome the hostile attacks and raw power of an unholy alliance—the Republican Party, the Tea Party, the editorial page of the *Wall Street Journal*, Fox News, the brothers Koch, Rush Limbaugh, Bill O'Reilly, and Glenn Beck. This juggernaut has unlimited amounts of private corporate cash to oppose Obama's, and the Democrats', policies, thanks to the Roberts-led reactionary 5–4 Supreme Court decision in the *Citizens United* case. And they are determined to bust Obama. The stakes are very high in this struggle, as it gets to the core issue of the very role of government in a democracy. The right-wing Axis of Greed cannot be allowed to destroy the safety net that protects the economic security of 95 percent of Americans. This safety net prevents our nation from being turned into a "banana republic," where a plutocracy pulls all the strings. And the rising plutocracy has been adept at pulling the strings.

Wealthy conservatives reacted with a vengeance to the activism of the 1960s and '70s, and to resulting federal legislation providing for economic, environmental, and social justice. Here's a thumbnail sketch of how the Orwellian process works. The rich conservatives plow money into scores of Washington think tanks like the Heritage Foundation and the American Enterprise Institute. The think tanks employ academic and scholarly guns-for-hire who produce ideologically driven position papers with an intellectual aura, usually attacking social programs, public interest and accountability, government, taxes, and the "liberal" media—conforming to the prescribed positions of their wealthy benefactors. These papers then work their way into the mass media as objective analysis and get headlined by Fox News.

Next in the process are the public relations hacks for the Republican Party, who boil down these position papers into simple talking points for GOP leaders and spokespersons, who then mouth this pablum for the evening news and the 24/7 cable networks. And that's how processed propaganda becomes acceptable and eventually turns into widely cited clichés and slogans. It's misinformation run amok.

The practice continues right up to the present. An example is the Americans for Prosperity Foundation, bankrolled by billionaires Charles and David Koch of Koch Industries. Americans for Prosperity provides organizational and training support for the Tea Party. All those noisy and hostile attacks on Democrats in 2009 at local town hall meetings, over their support for healthcare legislation, were not as spontaneous and grassroots-y as they appeared on the TV news. Those attacks were systematically organized and choreographed performances.

This is a short version of how conservative ideas and money-laundering scams work. For a more comprehensive version, I highly recommend reading Jane Mayer's exceptional and enlightening article, "Covert Operations," in the August 30, 2010, issue of *The New Yorker.*

By no coincidence, the Tea Party is most vocal in opposing, and supporting, the very same issues as do the Kochs—like abolishing the departments of Education, Commerce, and Energy, as well as phasing out Medicare, Medicaid, and the income tax and replacing it with a 23 percent sales tax, which is about the most regressive tax there is.

There is almost a Zen perfection to the wrongheadedness of Tea Party activists. They do not seem to understand that the central issue is not "small government" versus "big government," but rather "good government" versus "bad government." No Republican president in their lifetime has ever provided less government. Nor do the activists seem to understand that they are being conned by the Kochs, in that they are voting against their own economic and social self-interests by supporting an oppositional agenda that favors billionaires.

Volunteers face a critical choice: You can work with public interest, nonprofit advocacy organizations that represent your concerns as well as the public good. Or you can do nothing and allow well-heeled organizations and institutions that are fronting for powerful vested, special, and moneyed interests pull the strings and run the show.

The naked truth is that the Republican Party is pandering to, colluding with, and exploiting the most regressive and antisocial tendencies in our national character. It is undermining trust in the ability of the one force—government—that has the potential to balance, secure, and protect the freedoms and liberties of *all* our people and to balance public and private interests. A vital and healthy federal government is indispensable to the well-being and sovereignty of a self-governing people. That is, after all, what democracy is all about. Without this protection, whole segments of our society—especially those who can least afford it—will give up hope and become more frustrated and alienated, and this can only serve to further polarize our discourse and undermine the very social fabric of our communities.

Abraham Lincoln was a Republican who advocated the opposite of the contemporary notion of private interest for selfish personal gain being peddled by today's Republican Party. Lincoln reminded us that our primary task as a nation should be to continually teach and re-teach American political and social history. He was deeply concerned lest we forget the pain and struggle that are so much a part of our unique historical experience. For Lincoln, there was no higher calling than that of striving to preserve a public liberty that would promote the common good.

Our political and civic history provides us with a commonsense vision of the American promise—one that the founding fathers and Lincoln understood—that calls for justice, freedom, equality, and opportunity. We may forget or deny our historical legacy, but we cannot change it. The uniqueness of our nation is that the "noble experiment" was a quest to enhance the human condition, enrich democratic values, ensure the general welfare, endure against adversity, and preserve our natural resources.

# American Values, Citizenship, and Civic Engagement[1]

## The Dilemma

As the new decade began, it became clear that a substantial majority of Americans believed our society to be in serious trouble. Most Americans today think their future will be worse, not better, than their past. Most Americans think their children's prospects are worse, not better, than their own.

---

[1] Author's note: This chapter updates, edits, and revises a section of the *Final Report* by the National Advisory Council on Economic Opportunity, Washington, D.C.

Though this new pessimism has many sources, the most prominent cause is certainly anxiety about the economy. Public opinion surveys indicate that economic issues are dominating public consciousness. There is concern about the recession and unemployment, particularly among youth, minorities, and blue-collar workers. There is concern about energy. But above all, there is genuine fear over unchecked deficits, debt, and deflation. They undermine security about the future, create doubt and suspicion of our fellow citizens, and undercut the commitments that make democracy possible.

In these conditions the economic sector becomes a microcosm of the whole society. Doubts and anxieties about our institutions have been fed by global-warming, environmental degradation, and the Iraq and Afghanistan wars, and are deepened by our apparent inability to deal with severe economic difficulties. The "moral malaise" to which President Carter pointed back in 1980 is perhaps more evident in our economic institutions than anywhere else in our public life.

Moreover, in our present state of economic uncertainty, there has been a tendency for public action to degenerate into the narrowest pursuit of private interest. The more affluent seek to ease the strain by redistributing income from the middle class to themselves through their ability to dominate the political system and curry favor with huge campaign contributions on the federal and state levels. Economic stringency and rising rates of unemployment for those below the median income are defended as "acceptable costs" that will, among other things, "improve labor discipline." There are those who would use our present economic troubles to institutionalize a kind of socioeconomic triage.

Meanwhile, 44 million Americans are poor and another 55 million are near-poor, so almost one-third of our citizens are materially deprived. Those least able to defend themselves economically suffer the most from the maldistribution of wealth. The cost is high not only in material deprivation but also in political withdrawal, for poverty is not a condition for effective citizenship.

Historian Sam Bass Warner Jr. wrote that we are on "the eve of the collapse of the national private economy." In the winter of 2008–09 we came close to that collapse. Indeed, much of the private economy survives only because of direct or indirect subsidization (contracts, tariffs, investment, protectionist trade agreements, and tax benefits) by the federal government, that most ironic form of "welfare." It was the federal government that rescued major banks, AIG, and GM, among others.

The economy is a central sector of our social fabric, closely bound up with all of our other institutions. It is not working very well, and it is working less well for some than for others. Thus, we must also ask what kinds of social and political problems the economy gives rise to, and how they can be dealt with.

In addition, we must pose the question: How can America, in the economic arena, enhance democratic citizenship? The best way to begin seeking answers to these crucial problems is to look at our present in the context of our past—to seriously consider the history of our nation, and to seek out what the American democratic tradition has to say about economic institutions and how that tradition can be adapted to our present needs.

## The Economy in a Democracy

In *Democracy in America*, perhaps the wisest book ever written about America, Alexis de Tocqueville argued 180 years ago that although the physical circumstances of our country contribute to our public happiness, the laws contribute more than the physical circumstances, and the social mores more than the laws. We were fortunate indeed to inherit from the founders of our republic a constitutional and legal order that has proven sound and flexible. But the origin, interpretation, and perpetuation of that order are dependent on the mores embedded in society.

A society with different mores would have long since eroded and subverted our constitutional and legal order. De Tocqueville defines "mores" as "habits of the heart," "the sum of moral and intellectual dispositions of men in society." The mores include the opinions and practices that create the moral fabric of a society. They are rooted in our religious tradition, our long experience of political participation, and our economic life. If we are to better understand the appropriate role of economic institutions in the American tradition, then we must consider relationships of economic, political, and religious ideas and practices, as well as the tensions that have developed among them.

Since colonial times, Americans have had a genuine desire to create a decent society for all. That concern was expressed in the idea of a covenant, so important to our Puritan ancestors, and reaffirmed in the Declaration of Independence, with its pledge of "our lives, our fortunes and our sacred honor" for the common good. But we have also shown a vigorous individualism. The individual, with his needs, desires, and interests, particularly economic interests, was seen as almost the only good, and whatever social arrangements were necessary were to be worked out by contracts that maximized the interests of individuals. Our covenant heritage provided the context within which a contract could work, for only with the fundamental trust that the covenant fosters will contracts be honored. The American Constitution was hammered out in major part as an instrument that could balance the various conflicting interests threatening the stability of the nation, and use the energy of those interests to offset and check one another.

The idea was that an approximate equality of economic conditions was essential to the operation of free institutions, because economic equality—and also, economic independence—is necessary for the creation of enlightened citizens. Alexander Hamilton expressed the commonly held view when he said, "In the general course of human nature, a power over man's subsistence amounts to a power over his will." Concentration of economic power, therefore, would create a degree of dependence for many that would be incompatible with their role as free citizens. Hamilton felt pessimistic that such concentrations of wealth could be avoided, and

so predicted the republican institutions in America would survive
but briefly: "As riches increase and
accumulate in few hands; as luxury
prevails in society; virtue will be in a
greater degree considered as only a graceful appendage of wealth, and the tendency
of things will be to depart from the republican
standard."

Thomas Jefferson, characteristically, was
more optimistic about the possible social and
economic basis for American free institutions. For all the differences between them, the
founders of the republic had a fairly clear understanding of the
interaction of economics, politics, and religion in a republic. Great
wealth and extreme poverty alike were to be avoided. They undermined morality and piety, so important for the social climate of
free institutions, and they produced tyrannical attitudes on the one
hand, and subservient ones on the other, that were equally incompatible with active citizenship.

De Tocqueville, writing about America in the 1830s, continued to raise the social and political issues that were of such concern to our founders. He worried lest too great a concern with
economic prosperity undermine our free institutions by drawing
men's attention too exclusively to their private and selfish interests. Like Jefferson, he thought public participation was the best
school of democratic citizenship. Like our founders, he believed
that economic independence and social cooperation could go hand
in hand in America. As de Tocqueville wrote:

> The free institutions of the United States and the political rights
> enjoyed there provide a thousand continual reminders to every citi-
> zen that he lives in society. At first it is of necessity that men attend to
> the public interest, afterwards by choice. What had become calcula-
> tion becomes instinct. By dint of working for the good of his fellow
> citizens, he in the end acquires a habit and taste for serving them.

## Citizen Participation

De Tocqueville, then, in ways consistent with the beliefs of Jefferson and John Adams, argued that the key to American democracy was active civic associations. He observed that only through active involvement in common concerns could the citizen overcome the sense of relative isolation and powerlessness that was a part of the insecurity of life in an increasingly commercial society. Associations, along with decentralized, local administration, were to mediate between the individual and the centralized state, providing forums in which opinion could be publicly and intelligently discussed and the subtle habits of public initiative and responsibility learned and passed on. Associational life, in de Tocqueville's thinking, was the best bulwark against the condition he feared most: the mass society of mutually antagonistic individuals who, once alienated, became prey to despotism.

What de Tocqueville sought, then, was a modern version of classic political democracy. He thought social differentiation inescapable, since the division of labor creates differences among groups in the goals they seek to attain. Democratic politics must seek to coordinate—and adjust—these differentiations in the interest of equity and concern for the liberty of all.

A vital democracy, then, requires a complex effort to achieve a political community through balancing the relationships among the administrative organization of the state, the individual citizen, and the associations that come between individual and state. By association, individuals become citizens and thereby acquire a sense of personal connection and significance that is unavailable to the depoliticized, purely private person. Through mutual deliberation and joint initiative, moral relationships of trust and mutual aid are established and come to embody the meaning of citizenship for the individual.

Politics in the genuinely associational sense is substantially more than the pursuit of self-interest, since it involves sharing responsibility for acts that create a quality of life quite different from the mere sum of individual satisfactions. De Tocqueville hoped that civic participation could make the individual an active, politically aware subject rather than a passive object of state control. For de Tocqueville, lack of participation, no matter what its material effects, was humanly degrading and finally a manifestation of despotism. In this he was restating the traditional, and basic, civic republican notion that human dignity requires the freedom that exists and grows only in a context of active civic community.

## The Individual and the Community

In de Tocqueville's America, as for most Americans throughout the nineteenth century, the basic unit of association and the practical foundation of both individual dignity and participation was the local community. There a civic culture of individual initiative was nurtured through custom and personal ties inculcated by widely shared religious and moral values. Concern for economic betterment was strong, but it operated within the context of a still-functional covenant concern for the welfare of the neighbor. In the town the competitive individualism stirred by commerce was balanced and humanized through the restraining influences of a fundamentally egalitarian ethic of community responsibility. These autonomous small-scale communities were dominated by an active middle class, the traditional citizens of a free republic, whose members shared similar economic and social positions and whose ranks the less-affluent segments of the population aspired to enter, and often succeeded. Most men were self-employed, and many who worked for others were saving capital to launch themselves on enterprises of their own. Westward expansion, as de Tocqueville noted, reproduced this pattern of a decentralized, egalitarian democracy across our continent. American citizenship was anchored in the institutions of the face-to-face community— the neighborliness—of the town. Such communities provided the social basis of the new Republican Party in the 1850s, and Abraham Lincoln was perhaps their noblest representative.

## Undemocratic America

De Tocqueville carefully noted two forms of socioeconomic organization that differed profoundly from this form of civilization—which he considered basic to American democracy—and threatened its continued existence. One was the slave society of the South, which not only treated blacks inhumanly but also, as de Tocqueville in ways quite similar to Jefferson noted, degraded whites as well, reducing them to something considerably less than autonomous, responsible citizens.

The second ominous social form was the industrial factories, evident at first in the Northeast, which concentrated great numbers of poor and dependent workers in the burgeoning mill towns. Here de Tocqueville feared a new form of authoritarianism was arising that made petty despots out of owners and managers and reduced workers to substandard conditions incompatible with full democratic citizenship. Ironically, the traumatic civil war that destroyed slavery enormously furthered the growth of the industrial structures that so profoundly threatened the original American pattern of decentralized democratic communities.

## A National Economy

By the end of the nineteenth century the new economic conditions fatally unbalanced the community pattern of American life. New technologies, particularly in transportation, communications, and manufacturing, pulled the many quasi-autonomous local societies into a vast national market. Problems arising in this increasingly centralized and economically integrated society required the growth of the structures of central government, and steadily sapped the ability of local associations to deal with local problems. Under these conditions the very meaning of the traditional idea of American citizenship was called into question.

This shift in emphasis had a profound effect on the role of the individual in society. One response was to adapt to the new structures of centralized economic power by choosing a career whose

rewards are wealth and power rather than a calling that provided status and meaning within a community of complementary callings. This shift was becoming evident by the mid-nineteenth century but has progressed enormously in the twentieth, and is now dominant. Virtually all Americans depend directly or indirectly for livelihood, information, and, often, ideas and opinions, on great centralized and technologized organizations, and they identify themselves more by professional prestige and privilege than by community ties. The increasing uniformity of national life has developed concomitantly with the rise of a national pattern of social inequality that has replaced the more immediately perceived differentiations of local community.

In modern American experience, constraints and social discipline such as tax paying, company loyalties, and professional commonality have been increasingly justified because they are instrumental to individual security and advancement. Some measure of equality of opportunity seemed the appropriate and "American" way to democratize this new national society, but the focus has been on private, economic betterment, not on the quality of shared, public life.

These tendencies—which bear an all-too-close resemblance to de Tocqueville's fear that an exclusive concern with material betterment would lead America away from free citizenship and toward a form of what he called "soft despotism"—have not gone unopposed. Some forms of opposition, like the efforts of the late-nineteenth-century Populists and, later, the Progressives, to defend the integrity of the local community, have failed, though even in failure they have presented examples of a citizenry that will not passively accept its fate.

## Democracy at Work

Other efforts to control the most exploitative tendencies of the industrial sector, such as the enactment of health and safety laws and the regulation of working hours and minimum wages, have been more successful. The growth of labor unions has brought some sense of citizenship rights into the workplace. The tendencies toward despotism inherent in profit-oriented bureaucratic corporations have been muted at the bargaining table where wages, hours, and working conditions, as well as grievance procedures, have all become subject to quasi-political negotiation. This has not, with minor exceptions, given the worker a say in the direction of the corporation that employs him, but it has given him some sense of active participation in the conditions of his employment, and some protection against any tendency of his employers to disregard his needs.

In our recent history, significant social movements such as the civil rights movement or the movement to oppose the Vietnam War have continued to have an impact on public policy. Such movements have mobilized large coalitions of people, motivated by a combination of self-interest and a great deal of disinterested civic concern, to a degree of participation in the political process not common in day-to-day political life. That such movements can still make a difference in our society, even though not as quickly or as completely as some would desire, is evidence that the civic republican spirit is still present among us.

## Diluted Principles

Although the spirit of republican citizenship and the social conditions that support it are by no means gone from American life, alarming danger signals are visible. The belief in the individual as a self-interested "economic animal" is certainly not new in our history, but it is less and less tempered by the covenant values based in local communities and religious mores. Now, shorn of many of the nurturant values of traditional civic association, the ethos of self-advancement as an exclusive strategy has been able to run rampant with fewer constraints. The result has been a definition of personal worth almost exclusively in terms of competitive success, measured by status and advancement in large organizations. The ideals of loyalty and service based on personal trust and commitment have faltered in this atmosphere.

Even when the national economy was rapidly expanding and the hope of significant self-advancement was realistic, the social consequences were often what we have recently heard described as "moral malaise." Inability to commit oneself to or believe in anything that transcends one's private interests leads to a less positive commitment to family and community and a negative self-absorption and greed. These very same traits put the nation at the edge of financial bankruptcy in 2008–2009.

Unfortunately, the difficulties arising from too exclusive a concern with self-betterment have of late been enormously compounded by the gradually dawning knowledge that the cup of plenty is not inexhaustible. Material blessings were never shared equitably in America, but while the economy was growing everyone could look forward to more. However, if wealth is not going to grow, or is going to grow much more slowly, and our values have become focused on self-interest, then we are on the verge of the war of all against all, as each interest group strives to get to the well first before it dries up.

## The Role of Government

We have for a long time turned, not unwisely, to government to regulate the quest for economic aggrandizement. The ideology of radical individualism, with its notion that the pursuit of self-interest is the best incentive for a free society, has always required a mediator who will guarantee at least minimal conditions of fairness in the race for material goods. Government has been that mediator and has become increasingly active in that role in recent decades. While privileged individuals and groups have often viewed the role of government as intrusive and even destructive, less-privileged groups have found in government a protector against the worst consequences of being crushed by the inequities of our competitive economy. Social programs, with all their inadequacies, and affirmative action have brought a measure of justice to people (women and minorities) who have been deprived and/or handicapped by poverty and prejudice. Perhaps it is a sign of the times that such minimal and basic human programs are viewed by the privileged as programs designed to victimize *them*.

Our present danger does not come from government as such, or from self-seeking individuals either, for that matter. The danger to our democratic institutions comes rather from the declining effectiveness of the intervening structures—the variety of civic associations—that serve to mediate between individual and state. It is those intermediate structures that encourage citizenship and provide the best defense against despotism, soft or hard. Without them, the government, even when acting benevolently, may encourage a dependence and a lack of civic concern that play into the hands of authoritarianism. The danger increases when the economic pie is shrinking or growing slowly and erratically, when the privileged are talking about "social discipline" while the deprived feel existent inequalities more keenly.

In the meantime, public cynicism about the modern American notion of pursuit of economic self-interest in the context of free enterprise, tempered by a degree of expert bureaucratic fine-tuning by the federal government, is growing. The failures of conventional economics (particularly in the past decade) to meet certain problems—unemployment, underemployment, slow economic growth, and national concern about the energy crisis—have engendered widespread public disillusionment in government and business corporations alike. One form of this disillusionment is a growing cynicism and a tendency to "look out for number one," together with a deepening fear of one's fellow citizens. Such sentiments as these, republican theorists warn, are the preconditions of despotism.

## Volunteerism and Civic Engagement

But another response to the failures of the recent pattern of American political and economic life is to look to the possibility of the revival of our democratic civic culture and social structures, and above all, the intermediate local and neighborhood associations that nurture them. There are many who view the present necessity—to rethink the notion that quantitative, undifferentiated economic development is the answer to all our problems—as a genuine opportunity to recover aspects of our public life that could never be fully absorbed into that pattern. They view the present challenge not with dismay but rather as a stimulus to become our true selves as a democratic society.

On both the right and left of the political spectrum there is much talk of intermediate structures. Some use the language of participatory public life simply as a means to attack the growth of "big government" without a reasonable assessment of the social benefits government confers—one that *no other structure* in our society can presently provide. For such critics the ideal intermediate structure is the business corporation, which they believe should be freed from "government interference." (This seems to be the role of the Tea Party, which has been co-opted by corporate America to blame government for our problems.)

Others who talk about intermediate structures view business corporations as massive structures of bureaucratic power, largely unresponsive to citizen needs, and certainly not forums for civic participation and democratic debate. Or else they see business corporations as needing drastic reform before they can function as truly representative intermediate structures. At any rate, however important it may be to nurture religious, ethnic, neighborhood, and other forms of civic association, it is the economic institutions that are the key to present difficulties, and it is a new way of linking our economic life with our democratic values that is the key to their solution.

Let us consider the relevance of the early American pattern to our present situation. The founders saw occupation and economic condition as closely linked to the religious, social, and political bases of a free society. They feared excessive wealth, excessive poverty, and lack of independence in one's occupation. They thought self-employment the best guarantee of good citizenship, which would then lead to civic cooperation in the local community, particularly when nurtured by the religious and moral ideal of the covenant.

Our present circumstances—massive economic interdependence, employment mostly in large organizations, and the near disappearance of the self-employed farmer, merchant, and artisan—would seem so far from the vision of the founders as to have no connection with it. But if we consider the intentions and purposes of the founders, and not the economic conditions they found close at hand, then we might understand how their vision and wisdom could apply to our present situation.

If the intention of the founders was to create independent citizens who could then cooperate together in civic associations so as to produce a democratic society conducive to the dignity of all, we must consider how we might attain the same ends under conditions of our present political economy. A renewed citizenship must build upon our still-living traditions of volunteerism, civic engagement, and cooperation wherever they may be found, but it cannot take the older forms and resources for granted. Contemporary citizenship requires a moral commitment as well as an institutional basis appropriate to our interdependent, occupationally segmented national society. And because professionalism and occupational identification have become so crucial to contemporary society and personal identity, a renewed civic identity must be institutionalized in the workplace as well as the community at large if we want to avoid the classic war of "all against all."

## Private/Public Enterprise

If we would recover again the social and personal commitment to free institutions that is the lifeblood of a democratic society, then we must bring the public democratic ethos into the sphere of economic life. To view economic institutions as "private" made sense when most Americans spent their lives on family farms or in family firms. But today, when most American men, and a rapidly increasing proportion of American women, spend much of their lives in large economic structures that are for most purposes "public" except that the profits they make go to institutional and individual "private" stockholders, it becomes imperative to bring the forms of citizenship and of civic association more centrally into the economic sphere. There is no simple formula for achieving that end; it certainly does not require "nationalization," which, by bringing vast economic bureaucracies under the domination of the federal government, would make the democratization of economic life even more difficult. What we need is a series of experiments with new forms of autonomous or semiautonomous "public enterprise" as well as reformed versions of "private enterprise" as we pursue, with circumspection, our aim of a healthy economy that is responsive to democratic values.

If the profit imperative creates problems even under "normal" conditions of economic growth, its consequences become severe under conditions of economic stringency. The experimentation and free-wheeling nature of a period of growth begins to close down because everything must be justified in terms of the bottom line. Social purposes and human needs—perhaps even the survival of some individuals—that cannot be translated into a short-term prospect of profitability are necessarily ignored. This is especially true if we analyze the impact of past inflations on wage-earners in the basic necessities: health, energy, housing, and food. It is under these conditions that a new, more public and more civic purpose must be injected into the economy, and the language of "economic democracy" comes into play.

## The Dynamics of Bureaucracy

The profit imperative and the bureaucratic form of social organization often combine in an unfortunate way. The profit imperative itself can become a kind of tyrannical command that limits the options even of top management. Concerns for the humanization of the work process or more vigorous corporate social responsibility may have to be shelved under pressure to show profitability. Unfortunately, it is not true that all good things are "good business." If they were, our economy and our society would not be suffering their present difficulties. In any case, it seems clear that a broadening of the purposes of economic organization to include a greater range of social responsibilities rather than the obligation to show a profit goes hand in hand with a concern to make the internal operation of economic organization more genuinely responsive to human needs.

## Nonprofit Corporations and Cooperatives

This is not the place to more than hint at the possibilities for transforming our economy into a more democratic and socially responsible one. Clearly we have only begun to realize the values of consumer, publicly owned, or cooperative forms of economic nonprofit enterprise. Where there is expert assistance and capital available, a variety of small-scale economic nonprofit enterprises can be organized as self-help development efforts. Such ventures make excellent sense in economically depressed areas; they provide multiple opportunities for those otherwise excluded from employment. In addition to fostering the self-respect that comes from steady employment, the owners of a cooperative enterprise receive an education in the democratic process when they choose their board of directors and participate in a variety of functions in running their own business. Further, the cooperative is not tempted to drain the profits away from its own community as a branch of a large firm would do. Profits are plowed back into local expansion, the proliferation of other cooperatives, and, often, some forms of local social services, such as day-care centers, health clinics, and credit unions.

The nonprofit corporation has already proved its usefulness in the form of Community Development Corporations (CDCs). By combining profitable or at least viable economic undertakings with a variety of community services, the nonprofit corporation has many of the advantages of the cooperative on a larger scale. Undoubtedly, we have only begun to realize the potential in a variety of forms public enterprise can take. The Tennessee Valley Authority, for all the opposition it has generated, stands as a reasonably successful venture in public enterprise. As economic difficulties beset some of our largest corporations, experiments with mixed public/private enterprise might be contemplated.

Of course, all these forms of experimentation are dependent on a climate of financial and governmental support. There should be ways to make tax savings available to corporations that can show a consistent record of public responsibility at the cost of their own reduced profitability. A program of government grants might be made available to support innovative efforts to create energy-efficient businesses, to democratize the workplace, to humanize work, or to heighten community responsibility. Particularly in a situation of little or no economic growth, the emphasis must shift from quantitative expansion to qualitative improvement.

Even though the past failure of public courage may be discouraging, there are still some aspects of our present situation that could lead to a reinvigoration of our mores and a new sense of

the importance of the covenant model. The greatest opportunity exists in the growing realization that endless—and mindless—economic growth is not the answer to all of our problems, even if it were possible. And we are only beginning to comprehend some of the inherent brutalities of an overly technologized society. If the rise of industrial capitalism, for all the material benefits it has conferred, also lies at the root of many of our problems, then the faltering of the economy that has become evident since the 1970s, and that shows no early sign of change, may provide an occasion for some profound reflections about the direction of America in the decades ahead. If serious Americans in large numbers realize that the cause of our difficulties is not "big government" but, rather, a way of life that worships wealth and power, that makes economic profit the arbiter of all human values and that delivers us into the tyranny of the bottom line, then it may be possible to reexamine our present institutions and the values they embody.

A democratization of our economic institutions, by whatever name, is a key to the revitalization of our mores and our public life. Clearly the fusion of economic and governmental bureaucracies into a kind of superbureaucracy is not the answer, but would only compound the causes of our difficulty. The crisis in confidence that has overtaken our present system of bureaucratic capitalism can lead to a new shared public interest in our economic life.

We must develop the conditions for a new, shared public interest through a movement for the reform of economic life. The process needs to invite the enclaves of neighborly cooperation out from their present defensive position on the peripheries of our public life to join in a larger effort to transform mainstream institutions into vehicles for and expressions of citizen concern and positive values. This necessitates a process of moral education at the same time it attempts to restructure institutions. The effects of such a positive movement, already beginning in many areas, would be to revitalize the principle of civic association, to strengthen the intermediate structures that make it possible for individual citizens to maintain their independence and to make their voices heard, and, thus, to reinforce the vitality of our free institutions generally. Moving into a world of little or no economic growth, without such a process of democratic character and values, would only precipitate no-win Hobbesian struggles among groups wanting to profit at one another's expense—a struggle already too evident in our present politics of special interests.

But a healthy shift in the organization of our economic life, with all it would entail in our society, cannot be expected as a result of mere technocratic or organizational manipulation. So great a change—overcoming not only entrenched power, but entrenched ways of thinking—could be brought about only by a change in social or moral consciousness. We are, like it or not, going to face a world of increasing scarcity and simplicity, voluntary or involuntary. We can enter that world with bitterness and antagonism, with a concern to protect ourselves and our families, no matter the consequences to others—or we can enter with the keen sense of freedom, justice, opportunity, and community bequeathed to us by our founding fathers.

To come to terms with what has happened to us in the last century in a way that allows us to regain the moral meaning and the public participation that characterized our formative period— that seems the only way to create a livable society in the decades ahead. There are no easy formulas as to how to attain this goal. A great deal of creative experimentation and a variety of types of organization that will explore different possibilities are surely needed. But only the presence of a new sense of moral commitment and human sensibility can provide the time and space for such experimentation.

## Summary

It would seem clear that although the rise of corporate capitalism has brought Americans many good things, it has also disrupted our traditional social system while creating enormous economic problems that it cannot seem to solve. The national private economy has not only created problems but has, through its enormous political influence, involved government and massive government spending in ways that have been self-serving and thus compounded those problems.

Ever since World War II, high-technology and service industries have boomed in the "Sun Belt," with the help of massive military orders and huge federal underwriting for infrastructure. During the same years the industrial cities of the Northeast and Midwest have been allowed to deteriorate. The housing bust is yet another example. Profits have been enormous, but the human costs have been very high. It has been suggested that this unbalanced pattern of growth and stagnation will exact enormous sums in taxpayers' money in the decades ahead. Just reflect on the Wall Street and banking bailouts; these could have been avoided if the public interest had been given greater consideration in the planning of a healthy and balanced national economy, along with providing appropriate regulatory oversight and accountability.

Another example of the disastrous consequences of economic decisions made solely on the basis of profitability is the proliferation of energy-consuming, pollution-creating automobile and truck transportation at the expense of rapid transit and railroad systems, especially since World War II. Due to the power of automobile and oil lobbies, billions have been spent on federal highway programs, while railroad and mass-transit supports have been attacked as "wasteful." Dependence on initially cheap foreign oil, which was part of this transportation package, has proved to be not only an economic time bomb but also an international political disaster that has made our national interest highly vulnerable.

Stephen A. Marglin, professor of economics at Harvard University, recently wrote:

> The real issue of the next decade is not planning, but what kind of planning. If planning is to be democratic in process and end product, the entire structure of the capitalist economy must be overhauled to become significantly more participatory, from the shop floor to the corporate board room.
>
> Either our dominant economic institution, the corporation, will come to reflect democratic ideals, or the polity will come increasingly to incorporate the notion of the divine right of capital.
>
> My own position is clear. Authoritarian capitalism is no longer a vehicle of human progress, but an obstacle. By contrast, democracy, extended to our economic institutions, has a rich and glorious future.

Professor Marglin, as our historical review has shown, sets the issue in terms thoroughly consonant with our American democratic tradition.

In dealing with our economic problems, then, we must not be oriented to technical efficiency alone; that could produce an authoritarian solution. The economy is part—a central part—of our entire social system. This means that the criterion of success cannot be cost-accounting alone. The human implications of various forms of organization must always be considered. Above all, the economy must reinforce, not undermine, that structure of intermediate voluntary associations upon which the vitality of our democracy rests. Only an economy that can provide security, dignity, equality of opportunity, and participation to all our citizens will be a democratic economy.

We have in America the human and natural resources as well as the cultural and spiritual values to surmount the present challenges, to reinvigorate our democratic life, and to revitalize our communities. That is the challenge of this decade.

# The Value of Service

Nearly fifty years ago, when President John F. Kennedy launched the Peace Corps, he articulated a memorable and oft-quoted challenge: "Ask not what your country can do for you; ask what you can do for your country." This quote signaled a new, and hopeful, direction in American political and cultural life. The country was in transition, moving away from a difficult and trying period: the pain of the Great Depression; World War II; the Korean War; the threat of mutual nuclear destruction during the height of the Cold War; and the repression and cynicism of the McCarthy period.

And Americans, young and old, responded to the call by joining the Peace Corps, Volunteers in Service to America (VISTA), the Teacher Corps, and, soon after, the War on Poverty. It was a time of idealism, hope, and promise. More recently, Americans responded with the same spirit and enthusiasm to other crises, such as 9/11, Hurricane Katrina, the earthquake in Haiti, and the BP oil spill in the Gulf of Mexico.

Indeed, volunteerism has a long and honored tradition in the history of our nation. The traditions of community service and citizen participation have been at the heart of American civic culture since the nation was founded. Whether through town hall meetings, the local school board, a political party, a hospital auxiliary, or one of our innumerable other national and local organizations, Americans have felt and acted on the need to give something back to their communities. Since the events of September 11, 2001, and in the midst of our nation's severe economic decline, this need has become more urgent as Americans have become more introspective and more patriotic, and more anxious. Patriotism and anxiety have taken many different forms, but one thing is clear: Our concern for our country, our communities, our families, and our neighbors has become more acute, and our need to contribute more urgent.

The response to 9/11 was probably the most vivid example, with firefighters, police officers, and rescue teams leading the way. After September 11, many thousands of ordinary citizens—ironworkers, teachers, public health clinicians, professionals, businesspeople, and schoolchildren—volunteered to go to Ground Zero, or offered their support from a distance. Everything from blankets to blood, peanut butter to poetry arrived in New York City by the bale, the gallon, the barrel, and the ream. Americans didn't wait until New Year's Day to make resolutions; in mid-September, many resolved to be more caring and giving.

Once again, our nation is in a crisis of major proportions. The Great Recession has hit our country like a steamroller, and some economists are predicting that the present level of unemployment could continue for several years. In cities and towns across the nation, and particularly in America's industrial heartland, factories are closing and Main Street stores are being boarded up. Families are experiencing loss of homes, health insurance, and unemployment benefits, as well as increases in bankruptcies, divorce, and substance abuse problems. Most of all, fear and anxiety are undermining family stability.

How we respond to these crises as individuals, as families, as communities, and as a nation is absolutely critical. One of the main purposes of this book is to help harness the compassion, energy, and concern of those who want to serve their communities in creative, constructive, and useful ways. So, if volunteering is one of those things you've been meaning to do all along but just haven't gotten around to, or if you're just curious about what's out there, this book can help you take the next step. It is designed to help you realize that you can make a contribution to the well-being of your community. It will help to answer the why, the how, the what, and the when. Why is community service important? How can you get in touch with a group that promotes the values and goals that you believe in? What specific volunteer activities match up with your skills and experiences? When is a good time to volunteer?

Each of the organizations profiled in this book has been selected because of its commitment to educational, social, economic, environmental, and community development goals. Some have been in existence for many decades; others are fairly new. Most are national organizations, and some are local prototypes, but all have a solid track record of delivering services that are useful and meaningful. Before you select an organization to volunteer for, ask yourself a few questions:

- How much time do you want to serve?
- What kind of service fits your personality?
- What neighborhood and community do you want to work in?
- Which target population do you want to work with?

- What skills do you have to offer?
- What would you like to gain from the experience?

Historically, our greatest strength as a nation has been our willingness to be there for one another. Citizen participation is part of our birthright. As Thomas Paine put it, "The highest calling of every individual in a democratic society is that of citizen!" Accidents of nature and abstract notions of improvement do not make our communities better or healthier places in which to live and work. They get better because people like you decide that they want to make a difference.

Volunteering is not a conservative or liberal, Democratic or Republican issue; caring and compassion simply help to define us as being human. Volunteering not only helps communities, but it also helps individual volunteers to integrate their own idealism and realism in a healthy way. An idealist without a healthy dose of realism tends to become a naive romantic. A realist without ideals tends to become a cynic. Community service helps you put your ideals to work in a comprehensive approach to complex problems. I've seen it happen time and again with my students, and with VISTA and AmeriCorps volunteers.

Volunteering is very much a two-way street. It is about giving *and* receiving, and the receiving can be nourishing for the heart and mind. The very act of serving taps into a wellspring of empathy and generosity that is both personally gratifying and energizing. Again and again, former volunteers describe their experiences with words like these: *adventure, growth, human connection, exciting, spiritual, maturing, learning,* and *enjoyable.*

I have seen this in action firsthand for the past ten years, since I decided to give the students in each of my classes, mostly university seniors, the choice between a mid-semester exam or sixteen hours of community service. The students unanimously chose service, though most of them didn't know what was in store for them. They had a choice of over eighty different activities organized by the Public Service Center at the University of California, Berkeley.

Here's what one student wrote about this experience:

Before I started volunteering, I had very different expectations about the [afterschool] program. I thought it would be very sports-oriented with little academic emphasis. Luckily, my expectations proved false. The program—for fourth- and fifth-graders at the Thousand Oaks/Franklin Elementary School—has a set schedule for each grade. The students rotate between free play, sports, library study time, circle time, and arts and crafts.

It was in the library that I saw how truly behind these children are in mathematics, reading, and grammar. In addition, I never expected to see the immense poverty that these children experience, or to be so emotionally affected by it. Last week I learned that one of my favorite children is homeless. It seems so silly to be reprimanding him for not doing his homework and not putting in the effort at school. This seems so trivial compared to the real-life horrors that he must experience. Although I had my expectations, never did I anticipate the emotional attachment that I now share with these children. I find myself yearning to become a teacher, which was a career I never thought about before this program. I know that as these children grow, they will probably forget about me; but I know I will never forget them. I have truly changed and matured as a result of working with them.

A second student wrote:

Before I started tutoring I was really scared, because I didn't know what tutors did in junior high schools. I was afraid of not being able to explain things so that kids could understand. I thought I might lose patience quickly with kids who were slower in understanding, and for whom I would have to repeatedly state the same thing. I was concerned that the kids would resent me or not respect me because I wasn't the teacher and was closer to their age. And finally, I thought they wouldn't like me; the first day I even had trouble introducing myself because of this initial uncertainty.

Contrary to these preliminary fears, however, tutoring at Willard *has been a life-changing experience for me*. I've found that I have more patience working with kids than I've ever had in any other area of my life. I work hard to come up with lots of examples when the kids I'm working with don't understand. We relate well to one another because they know that I'm there to help them. It's been the joy of my semester to work with these students, who I really appreciate.

These comments were typical of the experiences of nearly all the students. Their testimony is consistent with the more formal academic research and evaluations, which tell us that service-learning clearly enriches and enhances the individual volunteer in multiple ways.

At the university level we know that service-learning contributes to a student's critical thinking skills, creative imagination, and moral intelligence. And for the past fifteen years there has also been a substantial body of research with respect to the impact of service-learning in K–12 schools—primarily in the tenth and eleventh grades.

What better way for students to understand early on the connection between ideas and behavior, between the values and ideals that people hold and the ethical consequences of those beliefs, than integrating civics, American history, and social studies with quality service-learning.

Recent studies in K–12 schools across the country have demonstrated that:

- Service-learning has a positive effect on the personal development of young people.
- Students who participate in service-learning are less likely to engage in "risk" behaviors.

- Service-learning helps develop students' sense of civic and social responsibility and their citizenship skills.
- Service-learning helps students acquire academic skills and knowledge.
- Students who participate in service-learning are more engaged in their studies and more motivated to learn.
- Service-learning helps students to become more knowledgeable and realistic about careers.
- Service-learning results in greater mutual respect between teachers and students, as well as improving the overall school climate.

It's interesting to observe that students today are responding the way I did during my own community service forty-five years ago, when I taught in Harlem during the early years of the War on Poverty and VISTA.

Just as I experienced, my students now confront the complexities of the everyday worlds of individuals and communities quite different from their own. They are forced to deal with difficult social and economic realities. It's an eye-opener to learn about the inequities and injustices of our society, to see firsthand the painful struggles of children who do not have the educational, social, or economic opportunities that we take for granted. This experience is humbling. It broke down my insularity, for which I'm truly grateful. Margaret Mead called this "heart-learning."

Community service also taught me an important lesson about our society: Ethical values and healthy communities are not inherited; they are either re-created through action by each generation, or they are not. That is what makes AmeriCorps, VISTA, and other forms of community service unique and valuable. They help us to regenerate our best values and principles as individuals and as a society. From Plato to the present, civic virtue has been at the core of civilized behavior. My experience as a teacher and with service-learning has taught me that moral and ethical values cannot survive from one generation to the next if the only preservatives are academic texts or research studies. Real-life experience is the crucible for shaping values. Out of it develops an intuition and a living memory that are the seeds of a humane and just society.

The task of passing along to the young our best civic traditions has been made more difficult in the past thirty years by the steady shift of emphasis away from qualitative values (civility, cooperation, and the public interest) to quantitative ones (competition, making it, and privatism), as well as the demoralizing pursuit of mindless consumerism and trivia force-fed to us by the mass media. Just about every parent and teacher I know has, in one way or another, expressed the concern that they cannot compete with the marketing techniques of the mass media, particularly television. They are worried about the potential consequences of the growing acquisitiveness, indulgence, and self-centeredness of children. I hear this from conservatives, liberals, and moderates. Small wonder. The average eighteen-year-old in the United States has seen more than 380,000 television commercials. We haven't begun to comprehend the inherent brutality of this media saturation on our children's psyches.

Materialism and assumptions of entitlement breed boredom, cynicism, drug abuse, and crime for kicks. Passivity, isolation, and depression come with television and online addiction. Ignorance, fear, and prejudice come from insularity and exclusivity. A national and local effort to promote community service by young people is the best antidote to these social ills. It's also important for parents to volunteer, because in the same way children develop good reading habits, they learn from the examples set forth by adults.

I have devoted a good deal of space to why it's important for young people, as well as their parents, to volunteer and participate in the civic life of their communities. Now I'd like to focus on the role of the not-so-young: seniors, boomers, and pre-boomers who are retired, semiretired, or thinking of retiring. I'll do so by sharing a story told to me by the late senator Jack Gordon, an old friend and former president pro-tem of the Florida Senate. Jack was an outstanding legislator and had an inquiring mind. He thought that there was a meaningful interrelationship between the health and well-being of seniors—an important constituency—and their active participation in the life of their community. So, one day he decided to launch a pilot project to test this hypothesis, helping to raise the money needed for this unique undertaking.

Miami Beach was part of his district, and he knew that many of the retirees who resided there were musicians. They were "snow-birds," like many other residents, who came from northern climates to vacation in the winter and eventually decided to live there permanently. He put a call out, and they responded—cellists, oboists, cymbalists, pianists, trumpeters, drummers, flutists, and what have you—from the symphonies, philharmonics, orchestras, and ensembles of Boston, Buffalo, Chicago, Cleveland, Detroit, Philadelphia, and beyond. They practiced and practiced and then performed at free public concerts. There was one caveat, however; each individual had to do a before and after—to record the number of times they visited their doctors, and how much medication they took before they participated, and then keep a weekly record after they began rehearsing and performing. The results bore out Gordon's hunch. Astoundingly, the number of doctor visits was reduced by 70 percent, and the amount of medication was reduced by 64 percent. A word to the wise is sufficient. My advice to all retirees is simple: Keep active, and do so with the kind of rewarding efforts that make you feel needed and useful.

You don't have to volunteer more than a few hours a week. If you're an architect, work with Habitat for Humanity; an accountant, help low-income people with their income taxes; a teacher, work with disadvantaged kids in a reading program or a literacy program for immigrants; a dentist, doctor, nurse, or psychologist, volunteer at a community health center. (When my own dentist announced his retirement, he also told me that he was going to volunteer two days a week at a clinic for migrant workers.) You can figure out what makes sense for you; there are plenty of opportunities listed in the book. Keep in mind that it will be good for your health and vitality. Stay young at heart!

In summary, the goals of service are inclusive and nourishing; they seek to honor diversity, protect the environment, and enrich our nation's educational, social, and economic policies so that they enhance human dignity. On a personal level, volunteering— the very act of caring and doing—makes a substantial difference in our individual lives because it nourishes the moral intelligence required for critical judgment and mature behavior.

Dr. Seuss reminded us in *The Lorax* that nothing is going to get better unless someone like you cares enough to pitch in and make it happen.

As you may recall, the main characters in this tale are the Once-ler, a faceless character who makes garments from beautiful Trufulla trees, and the wise Lorax, who warns the Once-ler that

the forest and its fantastical inhabitants are being harmed by his business.

Still, the Once-ler continues to chop down the forest's trees and starts a factory to increase volume. The trees quickly disappear and the factory's operations pollute the air and water, hurting the forest's animals. Soon enough, everything is bare. The Lorax disappears, leaving behind a pile of rocks bearing the word "unless." The story concludes with the Once-ler handing a Trufulla Tree seed to a young boy, who now has the potential to re-grow the forest.

Throughout our history we have responded to crises with introspection, generosity, and caring. Now is not the time to push the snooze button and be complacent. Just as we mobilized our capacities to confront hardship in the past, we must take action and confront our present economic and social problems. In the real world, we know that taking ordinary initiatives can make a difference. It is within our power to move beyond this economic crisis and to create new opportunities. What it comes down to is assuming personal responsibility. If we decide to become involved in voluntary efforts, we can restore idealism, realism, responsiveness, and vitality to our institutions and communities.

# Volunteer Stories

Community service has an enormous impact on peoples' lives—both the volunteer and the recipient. As I said at the beginning of this book, I've never seen anything like the power of public service to bring an extraordinary sense of self-esteem to a person. ★

## A CHANGE IN WORLDVIEW

My parents volunteered. After a great tornado devastated parts of Lubbock, Texas, my hometown, my father, a dryland wheat farmer, went to the bank and took out $500. Then he went alone to the poorest section of town hit by the storm, helped each family dig out, left $20 for groceries, and moved on to the next house. Even as a teenager, I admired my mother's involvements, which included serving on the library board and the board of Faith City Mission, while supporting international initiatives such as Frank Laubach's literacy program, Each One Teach One. One parent responded in a hands-on way to immediate needs; the other addressed systemic change. In my involvements since, I have tried to keep an eye on both.

One weekend early in my college days at the University of Texas, I went on a service trip to Monterrey, Mexico, where we built a basketball court for a church camp. Later, during my senior year, a group of us traveled only a few blocks away to East Austin, where we spent Friday and Saturday nights in the basement of an African American church, doing carpentry during the day to help an elderly woman get her house back up to code after a fire. The Friday night before we got to work, an economics professor led a discussion in the basement of that church. He asked if we knew why poor people sometimes drove big cars, and then explained that cars can be easily repossessed, while loans for home repairs cannot. With that simple insight, my worldview shifted on its axis.

From these two experiences I realized that one doesn't have to go very far or stay very long for a life to be changed. Later, while a professor at Vanderbilt University, I helped interested students organize an alternative spring break program that became a template for similar programs at universities all over the country, and led to many service-learning courses at Vanderbilt.

A year after I graduated from college, I had to choose between going to Mississippi for Freedom Summer, or learning German and French to prepare for a PhD program. My head eventually followed my heart, and I chose the academy. Over the years, however, I have found plenty of opportunities for activism: helping to create a women's studies program; organizing a faculty march against apartheid in South Africa; supporting a major lawsuit that sought gender equity at my university. For a scholarly article, I spent a summer researching the history of civil disobedience. Much later I chose to practice it with two hundred other members of Soulforce in protest against the anti-gay policies of a mainline church. That led to a day in the Cleveland city jail in good company that included Reverend James Lawson and Arun Gandhi, grandson of Mahatma Gandhi.

I do what I do out of gratitude and responsibility—grateful for those who brought us this far, responsible for those yet to come.

**—Susan Ford Wiltshire**

Wiltshire is the former chair of the classics department at Vanderbilt University. She was appointed to the board of the National Endowment for the Humanities by President Bill Clinton.

---------------------------------- ★ ----------------------------------

## VISTA TO POLITICS

When I left New York City in 1966 to serve as a Volunteer in Service to America (VISTA) in Eagle Pass, Texas, I had no idea that I would wind up staying in Texas, pursuing graduate degrees in both social work and law at the University of Texas, and, ultimately, serving as a long-standing member of the Texas House of Representatives. As I look back at my career, I realize that everything I've done is directly related to the community organizing skills I developed as a "front-line warrior" in Lyndon B. Johnson's War on Poverty.

Working at the grassroots level as a VISTA volunteer, trying to implement the policy of "eliminating the paradox of poverty in the midst of plenty in this nation," was always a challenge. We started preschool programs and teen clubs, laid the groundwork for a legal aid program, tried to get water and sewers to a barrio called Seco Mines, and organized neighborhood councils to advocate on behalf of low-income families.

While we didn't eliminate poverty, we did succeed in developing local leadership and maximizing the involvement of poor people in decision-making processes that directly affected their lives. Through community action programs, we gave people opportunities in education, job training, and economic development. We helped them learn to negotiate the system. It was an exciting era in the history of this country, and it put me on a path toward public service, as well as advocacy for the needs of low-income and vulnerable populations.

After graduate school, I ran a legislative internship program as staff counsel for a state senator who'd been one of my supervisors in VISTA. I developed legislation that enhanced protective services for elderly people and abused children. I drafted an anti-hazing bill. I helped the senator become a champion for dropout prevention. I used my training in social work and the law to address, at the state level, many of the same issues we'd focused on during the War on Poverty.

In 1990, I was approached by a group of people who thought I should run for a seat in the Texas House of Representatives, against a three-term incumbent who'd never lost. I told them that as a native New Yorker and ex–VISTA volunteer, I wouldn't have a chance. They convinced me that if I used my organizing skills to put together an effective campaign, I might win.

The incumbent had the money, but I had dedicated volunteers and a strong organization. We won, and I took the oath of office in January 1991 and have been reelected nine times. My focus in the House has always been on health, human services, housing, domestic violence, discrimination, and social justice. I work on issues that affect the elderly, people with disabilities, children, minorities, women, and all vulnerable populations. I take pride in what I do, face new challenges every day, and sleep well knowing that I'm working on behalf of people who occasionally need assistance from their government or laws passed that will protect and enhance their rights and dignity.

**—Elliott Naishtat**

Naishtat was a VISTA volunteer in Eagle Pass, Texas. He is a lawyer with a degree in social work and is serving his tenth term in the Texas House of Representatives in Austin.

---------------------------------- ★ ------------------------------------

## NURTURING INTERESTS

When I was eight years old, I volunteered for the Weinberg Nature Center and Kerr Riding Stables in Scarsdale, New York. I would like to think that I was precocious in my social consciousness, but in fact I was just looking for a way to access my greatest loves: nature, small creatures, and horses. At both the nature center and the barn I had the lowliest of jobs: I cleaned the tanks and the stalls. But this meant that I got to handle the animals. I studied the snakes, salamanders, and toads. I picked the horses' hooves, removed the burrs from their tails, and saddled them for lessons and pony rides. After some time at the stables, I was allowed to exercise the ponies. And at the nature center, I soon was allowed to lead nature walks and talks.

I entered Dartmouth College at sixteen years old, and majored in English. After graduation, I found a job in New York City writing advertising copy for *Redbook* magazine, and, after earning a master's degree in business from Columbia University, I worked my way up the corporate ladder to become a managing director for an investment bank. In my late twenties, after a cancer scare that required a bone transplant, I left my corporate job to focus on starting a family. Once my daughters were in school, I joined a small group of other motivated parents who ran the school fair, auction, and other fund-raising events. That wasn't very inspiring, so then I volunteered to train the horses and officers for the mounted park rangers who protected the New York City parklands, and discovered a hidden world of nature in the Big Apple.

I chose my volunteer jobs because I loved what I got to do. I had chosen my business career because I was good at it and could make money, but not because it was how I wanted to spend my life. Work was interesting enough, and I kept getting promoted. But it took the threat of my illness to force me to consider how my values were important enough to make them my life's work.

So I turned my volunteering into a career. I became the director of the park rangers, accepting a salary that was a fraction of my corporate pay. But as a public servant, my rewards far exceeded anything I had received before. I started free public canoe and camping programs, opened nature centers and challenge courses, created The Natural Classroom programs that bring inner-city schoolchildren into the parks, and even reintroduced the bald eagle to Manhattan. I also volunteered as a board member of the city's animal shelters.

Today, as the executive director of the Horticultural Society of New York, I run social service programs in prisons, supportive housing, and public schools that teach the benefits of gardening and fresh vegetables. I build community gardens and urban farms. And I just volunteered to help start New York City's first Farm School. My older daughter is in AmeriCorps working for the volunteer organization New York Cares, and my younger daughter just started volunteering at a small museum. Their values are guiding them, and volunteering is their pathway. I guess it runs in the family.

**—Sara Hobel**

Hobel was an investment banker in New York City before volunteering with the city's park rangers. She became director of the park rangers and is now executive director of the Horticultural Society of New York.

------------------------------------ ★ ------------------------------------

## THE TOUGHEST JOB YOU'LL EVER LOVE

Growing up on my family ranch near Mokelumne Hill, a small community in California's Mother Lode country, I quickly learned about community service from my parents. They were constantly involved in the PTA, Boy Scouts, and local community clubs. Having only five kids in my eighth-grade class and three rooms in the school that my great-grandfather helped build in the 1890s made it clear that if something was to get done, we all had to help. On my way to becoming an Eagle Scout, we had the annual duty of cleaning two historic gold rush cemeteries. Service often meant hard work.

But the real lesson in service was taught to me in 1965 by my girlfriend at the University of California, Berkeley (CAL), where I had some success as a football player. In our senior year, I asked her to marry me. She replied, "I would love to marry you, but you're heading for the NFL, and I am going into the Peace Corps." She became committed to the cause following President John F. Kennedy's commencement speech at Memorial Stadium at CAL. She heard his call to service and decided then and there to join the Peace Corps. I joined her.

September of 1966, nine months into our marriage, we arrived in Metu, a village in southwestern Ethiopia. Thirty kilometers from the grass airstrip and an endless muddy road, we found our new home: tin roof, dirt floor, wattle walls, outhouse out back, and unlimited opportunity to serve. Teaching seventh- and eighth-grade students and women's family health education, digging wells, offering smallpox vaccinations, building remote schools, setting up coffee co-ops—every day was filled with helping the community, building friendships, and setting the pace for a life of service. As the Peace Corps motto goes, "It's the toughest job you'll ever love."

We witnessed good people needlessly suffer and die in Ethiopia. Returning to America, we experienced culture shock at Harvard Business School. Upon graduation, Patti and I returned to California with a sense of purpose. We decided that a career in public service, committed to policies that open doors and lift people out of poverty, would be a much more fulfilling life than being a banker.

Patti followed her heart and set out to fulfill JFK's call to service. She returned to Ethiopia in 1996 as the associate director of the Peace Corps, restarting the long-dormant program in that country to give a new generation the chance to serve.

We decided to go to Africa forty-five years ago. After serving as an Assembly member, state senator, California insurance commissioner, deputy secretary of the U.S. Interior Department, California lieutenant governor, and now, as a member of Congress, we are not about to slow down. It has been a marvelous journey, and it's not over yet.

**—John Garamendi**

Garamendi and his wife, Patti, were Peace Corps volunteers in Ethiopia. He holds an MBA from Harvard, was elected insurance commissioner and lieutenant governor of the State of California, and is now a U.S. Congressman.

---------------------------------- ★ ----------------------------------

## A PROFOUND IMPACT

I was born and raised in Seattle, and I received my bachelor's degree in community, environment, and planning from the University of Washington. My first experience volunteering was at the Washington Park Arboretum when I was sixteen. I spent my Saturday mornings at their greenhouse, organizing plants for weekend sales, gathering soil, repotting trees, and getting dirty. Ten years later I found myself living in a rural West African village as a Peace Corps volunteer in Ghana.

The two years I spent living in the village of Apimsu were some of the most remarkable years of my life so far. Like many other twentysomethings with a bachelor's degree, I was trying to find my place in the working world. Joining the Peace Corps seemed like a great way to gain more international experience and expand upon my life skills while doing something that would make a difference. Soon after my arrival in Ghana, I realized that not only was I contributing to the local community, but it was also having a profound impact on me.

As the only American within a ten-mile radius, I lived in a village of about 300 people and worked with a local farmers' organization to improve sustainable farming practices. I made friends in the community, learned how to wash my clothes by hand, eat local foods, and live a completely different lifestyle than the one I had known at home. I quickly overcame the challenges I had initially anticipated, and the new cultural norms I had adopted became second nature. Through these experiences I gained a strong sense of self-assurance and independence. I felt that if I could do *this*, I could do anything.

I finished my Peace Corps service nearly two years ago, but the impact it had on me still resonates. My experiences working with local communities in Ghana have honed my desire to work toward bettering communities here in my own country. I have returned to school, pursuing a master's degree in City Planning, where I will be working on urban issues related to housing, community, and economic development. While I have yet to determine my future career, my desire to learn about foreign lands and different cultures and my interest in helping underserved populations will always be compelling forces in my life.

**—Casey Rogers**

Rogers is a native of Seattle who volunteered for the Peace Corps and served in a rural West African village in Ghana. He is now pursuing a master's degree in planning, focusing on community and economic development.

---------------------------------- ★ ----------------------------------

## HEALING AND SERVING

Fortunately, my parents honored community service and taught by example. My first volunteer experience was in the Charity Hospital Record Room in New Orleans during a summer when I was fifteen years old. The year was 1973! It was an eye-opening experience. It introduced me to the reality of long-standing racial discrimination. I initially was allowed to eat lunch in an air-conditioned dining room with the full-time workers, until they realized that

I was a person of color. I was mistaken for a Native American because of my skin hue and almost-black braids. After that realization, I was relegated to eating in a dusty corner of the record room with other African Americans. This experience strengthened my resolve and desire to want to leave the South and pursue a meaningful profession that I had some passion for, and to persevere. This incident brought to light the painful reality of the pervasive inequalities that existed throughout the fabric of American life, even after the Civil Rights Acts of the 1960s.

Next, I volunteered at a mental health institution when I was nineteen years old—as an undergraduate majoring in anthropology—during summer break at Yale. This opportunity gave me the chance to learn more about mental illness. After medical school at the University of Pennsylvania, I learned that health care is a business, and that providing high-quality and safe care can be a challenge even when the financial resources are abundant.

I am sure that all my experiences have shaped my life in ways that cannot really be explained or measured. I have worked with homeless populations in Chicago during my internship, and with HIV-infected patients in San Francisco when physicians and the medical community did not know very much about the disease and were just speculating about risk factors and its etiology. I have also worked closely with developmentally challenged populations, including people with spina bifida.

I found my place in society and my passion by being a physician . . . a healer. Despite the difficulties those in my profession are experiencing today, there is something quite remarkable about being a physician. Now I work with an underserved population because I realize that this provides a real opportunity to change some of the many health inequalities that are still present in American society. And I feel an incredible encompassing sensitivity for those marginalized in our society: the developmentally challenged, the mentally ill, the homeless, and persons of color from all walks of life. Healing and serving the community go hand in hand, and I am grateful to be doing both.

**—Julie Claire Morial, MD, MPH**

Dr. Morial is from New Orleans, where her family engaged in public service as a tradition. She is an internist who served in the National Health Service Corps in Chicago and now practices in Baton Rouge.

★

## AN AGENT FOR CHANGE

I grew up going to a Presbyterian church in Tucson, Arizona, that was led by a minister who was a great believer in the church's role in seeking "social justice," especially for those who were in poverty and discriminated against. My mother was a great believer in the "Golden Rule," and it was the dominant principle of ethical behavior during my childhood. The church youth group (early teen years) sponsored an activity in which we went outside of town to some of the surrounding farms to work/play with the children of the migrant farm workers (almost all of Mexican descent), whose parents were in the fields, and who lived in substandard housing (run-down shacks). Few spoke any English, but we were able to have a lot of fun with them, and of course, we suburban, middle-class white kids got a lot more out of it than they did. This was probably the first time I ever realized how well-off I was, and how many opportunities I had that others did not.

When I was still in high school in Tucson, John F. Kennedy was elected president, and my dad took me to hear one of the first Peace Corps Volunteers (PCVs) speak to a Rotary Club meeting. I was fascinated by their world. I then went to Occidental College in Los Angeles and studied political science and international relations, while increasing my understanding of the world "out there." President Kennedy's assassination, which occurred while I was at college, made a huge impression on me. I decided to join the Peace Corps after obtaining an MA in international relations at Johns Hopkins.

I learned a lot more during two years in Bolivia than I had during two years in graduate school. I worked with impoverished Aymara Indians on the Altiplano of Bolivia (in the Andes) in a "community development" program, which was intended to help the *campesinos* organize in their communities and mobilize to access resources. Their most pressing needs related to getting/ keeping their kids in school and earning a bit more income for their families. I was able to initiate several projects with the local teachers to improve the local primary school, and to develop several income-earning projects (sheep-shearing to "commercialize" wool, and chicken-raising for egg/meat production). While it was sometimes difficult to adjust one's expectations about "saving the world" to a level that reflected the realities these *campesinos* faced daily, it was gratifying to feel that at least you were having a positive impact on the lives of a few families, one day at a time.

The Peace Corps experience reflected the fundamental values I had acquired earlier in my life. While one individual may only be able to make a modest difference in the lives of others, if you can find a way to make your difference strategically, it can create the "ripple" that Bobby Kennedy spoke about.

The experience of two years on the Bolivia Altiplano clearly guided the direction of my professional career. I returned to the U.S. determined to become an agent for change, and became involved in legal assistance work. Then, after working for a law firm in Washington, D.C., I realized that corporate legal work was not what I wanted to do with my career, and left the firm. I found an opportunity to return to work in international development, and accepted a position as a foreign service officer in the U.S. Agency for International Development. I knew that I had finally found the right place to serve, and a place where I could make a major contribution toward addressing the needs of people affected by poverty and social exclusion. I worked in Haiti, Morocco, Nepal, Guatemala, and South Africa over a period of almost twenty-four years.

In August of 2009 I was appointed by the White House to be the new chief of staff at the Peace Corps, a wonderful way to complete the circle of my career. I feel very much at home doing the community development work that has been consistent with my values from an early age.

**—William Stacy Rhodes**

Rhodes is a lawyer who served in the Peace Corps in Bolivia, worked for the U.S. Agency for International Development, and was appointed by President Obama to be chief of staff of the Peace Corps in Washington, D.C.

------------------------------------- ★ -------------------------------------

## TREATING CHILDREN WITH DIGNITY

In 1972 I was working for the New York State Council on the Arts when my first baby arrived, and I decided I would be a temporary stay-at-home mom. Soon after, I received a call from a family friend who was the board chairman at the Northside Center of Child Development. He wanted to tell me about the work of the organization.

When we got together he told me about doctors Mamie and Kenneth Clark. Kenneth was an influential and pioneering civil rights leader, and both were preeminent psychologists. He told me about how Mamie had developed the "doll study," which was when a child chose the favored white doll over the black doll. In 1954 the Supreme Court cited the doll study when they decided the *Brown v. Board of Education* ruling, declaring segregation in public schools to be unequal and unconstitutional. The Clarks founded the Northside Center for Children in 1946, located in Central and East Harlem. It was a very difficult time, with a great deal of poverty, violence, drugs, failing schools, and substandard housing.

A few weeks later I met with Mamie. She was soft-spoken and very convincing. She was in the midst of moving the Center to Fifth Avenue at 110th Street. We spoke about what would be happening in the new space, and she invited me to visit when it opened, about a month later. I was awed when I arrived. They had done a great job: The halls were painted bright colors, and the walls were covered with wonderful paintings, some by children and some by important painters, that the children could enjoy. She said that she and Kenneth were very excited about all of the new programs: the therapy, the outpatient clinic, the remedial program, six school classes for children who could not learn in large classes, and a library, filled with books from floor to ceiling! (I knew very well that no other mental health center at that time had a library, and even today, there are few.)

Beyond all the programs, what was perhaps most important to the Clarks was being certain that all of their children would be treated with dignity, and that they would develop self-esteem. I left Northside awestruck by the work they were doing, and how much it would help the children and their families. A few weeks later I was asked if I would join the board. I was stunned, but replied that I would be honored. I was the youngest member and initially quite shy at board meetings. The other members were people I admired, and they were all kind and helpful to me.

I spent a lot of time at Northside, working with the staff, being with the children, planning events, meeting with foundations, finding new members for the board, reaching out to others, and inviting people to the center. I have been on the board now for thirty-eight years, eighteen of which I have served as chair, and I have loved it all. It has opened my eyes and taught me so many important lessons about education, psychology, race, and class. And it changed my life more than I ever could have imagined.

**—Susan Patricof**

Patricof is from Albany, New York, and worked for New York State Council on the Arts. She has served as a volunteer for the Northside Center for Children in Harlem (NYC) for thirty-eight years and has been the chair of the board for the past eighteen years.

---------------------------------- ★ ----------------------------------

## BECOMING AN ADVOCATE

When the Peace Corps first started I was working for the Bank of Boston, learning Spanish for an assignment in Buenos Aires. The bank's building there had been under siege with tar bombs, and I was developing a community program to present a more benign image of the bank. However, just as I was set to leave for Argentina, the bank told me that it had solved its problem—with a new solvent that dissolved the tar. This was the jolt that changed my "career." If the bank felt that my job could be replaced with a solvent, my wife, Polly, and I decided that we would join the Peace Corps. We were assigned to Caracas, Venezuela.

While at first I may have worried about what would happen to my "professional" career (my expensive college and business-school education), I soon realized that banking was not for me. I had no further use for my Brooks Brothers suits. In the Peace Corps, the job was to organize the very poor to address issues related to their community infrastructure and gain access to healthy food and clean water. As my focus changed, I began to believe I could change the world, one barrio at a time.

After returning to the U.S. and working in the South for civil rights and the War on Poverty, I worked for George McGovern's presidential campaign, and realized that what I really wanted to do required political power.

While my wife worked for a family planning program, I ran for office to be a Maine state senator as a Democrat—in a district of twenty coastal towns whose voter registration ran twelve to one, Republican. Based on my Peace Corps and McGovern experience, I mounted a door-to-door canvass against an incumbent of twenty-two years, and I won. But getting elected did not change much. I refocused again as an advocate, gathering signatures for three statewide referendums. While I lost two—one to establish a public power agency, and another to elect the public utility commissioners—these campaigns were responsible for the creation of the permanent office of public advocate, and significantly changed the way utility rates were set. And I won one, defeating what the telephone company then called "local measured service." My wife Polly won five terms in the Maine House of Representatives, and sponsored successful legislation, including the state's first seatbelt law.

Later, through all of these victories and losses, we realized that while we didn't change the world the way we first thought we would, we *did* change it. And all the effort was well worth it.

**—Bruce Reeves**

Reeves is a native of Maine who served with his wife, Polly, in the Peace Corps in Caracas, Venezuela. He began his career as a banker. After the Peace Corps, he decided to go into public service and was elected to the Maine State Senate.

-------------------------------- ★ --------------------------------

## THE "LEMON LAW"

Growing up in North Canton, Ohio, I watched my mother devote years to creating new opportunities for young women by volunteering with the League of Women Voters. I also saw my father spending hours after a long day's work, volunteering at the YMCA to train youngsters in gymnastics. I suppose it was in my genes that I would value civic engagement and volunteering, but I never would have predicted how I would end up following in their footsteps.

Years later, after majoring in English at Case Western Reserve University, I was teaching at a university and married to a Navy Judge Advocate General (JAG) officer. During this time, an auto dealer in Lemon Grove, California, kept our car for repairs for three months. After repeatedly claiming it would be ready "tomorrow," he admitted he hadn't ordered all the parts, and threatened that if we complained, he would put bad parts in the car. Desperate for transportation, I started to picket. The dealer tried to have me arrested, but the police refused, and when they would drive by, they gave me the thumbs-up.

Others began to tell me their own auto horror stories. I learned that many people who had bought brand-new cars suffered due to serious—and often life-threatening—defects that kept their vehicles in the repair shop for months, while they had to keep making payments for a car they couldn't drive. I organized protests, generated news coverage, and drafted California's auto "lemon law." Five months later, toward the end of summer, the Admiral of the Sixth Fleet invited us on board his ship. He said he'd heard I was giving a certain dealer a hard time. I feared he would pressure me to stop picketing. Instead he declared, "Those dealers have been ripping off my sailors for years. It harms morale, readiness, and our ability to accomplish our mission. If that dealer hasn't settled with you by the end of September, you get me his coordinates."

Soon afterward, we won, and I founded a nonprofit consumer group. Assemblywoman Sally Tanner agreed to author the "lemon law" bill. We fought the powerful auto lobby for three years. Until then, auto manufacturers had been allowed a "reasonable number" of repair attempts before they had to buy back a lemon. Unfortunately, no definition existed of what would be considered "reasonable." Ford testified that they should be allowed to have thirty tries. The lemon law established a legal presumption that four tries, or a total of thirty days out of service, would be enough to trigger a refund. California's law became the model for similar laws in all fifty states.

Since then, for more than thirty years (the first fourteen as an unpaid volunteer), I've worked to improve protections for consumers and promote auto safety. Auto manufacturers and dealers tend to think of consumers as suckers. The most important lesson I learned is that in a democracy, when we organize for the public good, we can lick them.

**—Rosemary Shahan**

Shahan is a president of Consumers for Auto Reliability and Safety (CARS). She helped develop the California "lemon law" that became the model for similar laws in the other forty-nine states.

------------------------------------ ★ ------------------------------------

## THINK BIG. CREATE A SIMPLE PLAN. GET STARTED.

I tell everyone that I am a selfish person: Every day I try to help others. My joy abounds.

It began at an early age. In the sixth grade, we had a competition to collect food for the poor. This planted the service seed. In 1965, after graduating from Yale, where I majored in American Studies, I had the privilege of working for U.S. senator Robert Kennedy in Bedford-Stuyvesant, revitalizing one of America's poorest communities. A key issue was business ownership for minorities. Imagine—in 1968 in New York City, the banks did not lend even $1 million (in total) to minority businesses.

In 1967, as a volunteer (while also working full-time), I began linking minority businesses to skilled financial professionals. By the end of 1969, we had enlisted over 3,000 volunteers, and the New York banks were lending over $50 million annually to minorities. This was a major pioneering effort. A handful of us across the country changed national lending practices.

Again as a volunteer, in 1972, I founded the Jefferson Awards with Jacqueline Kennedy Onassis and U.S. Senator Robert Taft Jr. For over thirty-five years, working as volunteers, we built the Jefferson Awards into the nation's premier award system for community and public service, and today, we are enlisting over 1 million young Americans into student-led service projects.

These early volunteering efforts led to a full-fledged public service career. Looking back, I'm most proud of the fact that I have had the privilege of dreaming up and running a program for each of the past seven U.S. presidents, from Richard Nixon through George W. Bush.

The greatest National Development Council (NDC) impact was with President Carter. Vision. Think big. Create a simple plan. Get started. In the 1960s and 1970s, although the nation was focusing on Fortune 500 companies, we saw small business as the major job creator—especially in low-income communities. The banks had the money, but they weren't lending in inner cities because government was "bureaucratic." No city employee could read a financial statement. At this time, NDC had a staff of six. We promised President Carter that we would combine the efforts of the above partners and do $1 billion of small-business financing in forty-eight months in sixty-five cities. We surpassed the $1 billion goal in twenty-two months. Our system was generating $1 billion per year. Basically, NDC and a handful of others changed the direction of economic development in our nation.

My message for any young reader: Start with your passion. Volunteer. Think big. Create a simple plan. Get started. You too can create a program for the President of the United States—and possibly craft a joyous and meaningful career along the way.

**—Sam Beard**

Beard is the president of the Jefferson Awards and chairman of the Development Council.

------------------------------------ ★ ------------------------------------

## PROMOTING HUMAN DIGNITY AND SELF-RESPECT

For the past thirty-eight years, I have directed the Federation of Child Care Centers of Alabama, dedicated to high-quality child care and the empowerment of grassroots leaders who work together to sustain the programs in service of families.

From 1968 to 1970, I spent three summers with American Friends Service Committee Community Services Program for youth in Brandon, Vermont; Roxbury, Massachusetts; and Luna Pier, Michigan. I did this as a consequence of a life-changing experience I'd had three years earlier. As a tenth-grader I was among the first African Americans to integrate the all-white high school in Wetumpka, Alabama. Coming from a large, rural, and economically poor family, I thought I knew hardship, but nothing could compare to the firebombing of our family home. It left the ten of us living in a two-room shack for fifteen months. The response of people who placed their lives at risk to help my family led to my very first awareness of the value of service to others.

I spent a summer of service in Luna Pier, a town nestled on the banks of Lake Erie between Toledo and Detroit. Its lush fields of tomatoes, beans, and corn drew migrant workers during the picking season. Our project was to convert an abandoned Catholic school into a health clinic and way station for the migrant Latino families. Recalling my own time in the crowded shack, without personal belongings, without privacy, I was humbled to see the families who had no home for themselves and their children, and had all types of medical conditions that had not been treated. Their resolve to cope with these challenges inspired me in my life's work.

In each of these summer situations, I was one of a handful of youth of color among the group of fifteen predominantly upper-class whites. I had to balance my own discomforts and sense of racial and class issues with keeping our service mission as the primary focus. We all had to learn to live and work together to provide the best service to those we were there to assist. My biases and those of my peers had to be confronted and dealt with for the larger good.

I identified with those we served, and remembered what it was like to be on the receiving end of help. I also realized the importance of the pride that comes from doing for oneself. Promoting human dignity and self-respect became the centerpiece that I took from these experiences, and it's what I carried into my professional life. They remain a passion of mine today. It is not enough to simply give service; what really counts is serving in a way that fosters self-empowerment and independence.

**—Sophia Bracy Harris**

Harris is the director of the Federation of Child Care Centers of Alabama. She is a native of Alabama and was a volunteer with the American Friends Service Committee working with migrant laborers.

--------------------------------- ★ ---------------------------------

## A SENSE OF SOMETHING LARGER

I was nineteen years old and a sophomore at Yale, looking for something to do that was more concrete, useful, and valuable to society than just demonstrating. I reasoned that food, clothing, shelter, and jobs were as basic and concrete as it got, and began to talk with my friends who were working on these issues in adjoining neighborhoods in New Haven. I then found a group of architecture and planning students who were working to create a sweat-equity housing project. Though I knew little about the machinations of housing, I did know how to speak Spanish and I was a friendly guy, so I became the community outreach person for this VISTA project.

There were two other major volunteer experiences that shaped my life. The first was at a bilingual community newspaper. I had been in San Francisco about a year, and had no connections to other Latinos. During that time, there had been a series of arson fires in the barrio near my apartment. Those fires culminated in a horrific hotel fire that I witnessed. I wanted to explain how these fires served a larger negative purpose of pushing poor people out of their barrio. I approached a local community newspaper about writing an analysis of the consequences of the fires. They published my article, and became especially interested in me when they found out I had "basic journalism" experience from high school, including writing, editing, layout, and photography. Within eighteen months, I became editor and business manager of the paper.

My other major experience as a volunteer was becoming a founding member of a pioneering bilingual mental health clinic. I had been working as an organizer and activist in community development for several years. A psychology professor I was working with suggested that I help establish one of the first bilingual and bicultural mental health clinics in California. I developed and implemented political and clinical strategies in order to win funding and then sustain this new institution. The clinic will celebrate its thirty-third anniversary this year.

The newspaper opened the door to a community that embraced me and gave me the sense of something larger than myself—something that I was responsible to and something that would sustain me. And the clinic gave me deep insight into the role of health in a community, and what it takes to build and nurture a community's institutional assets. The work I did as a volunteer at this clinic became the major focus of my career, and the foundation of my efforts to create healthy communities from California to the Deep South, where I now work.

—Juan Cruz

Cruz is the president of Cultural Dynamics. He first volunteered to work with a VISTA project in New Haven, Connecticut. Cruz has worked extensively in the fields of health planning and community development.

---------------------------------- ★ ----------------------------------

## A LIFELONG VOLUNTEER PATH

My first memorable volunteer experience was with my sister, Joan, canvassing neighborhoods for Senator George McGovern's presidential campaign in 1972. She was sixteen and I was twelve, and most people who answered the knock at their doors assumed we were selling Girl Scout cookies. I enjoyed watching the Democratic Conventions on television, and was inspired by the messages of compassion and service. We grew up in Wisconsin, known for its progressive political history, and my father prided himself on pegging Nixon long before Watergate. He also worked with the Peace Corps and Father James Groppi (a peace activist) in Milwaukee. My paternal grandmother helped found a community center and camp for inner-city children. Social activism was a natural family fit.

This early experience carried over into my career choice to become a lawyer, which led me to Washington, D.C., for law school. I was the student director for the Consumer Protection Clinic at George Washington University Law School, a program that helped consumers to mediate solutions to complaints they had against local businesses. Very often we were able to find a resolution acceptable to both parties, with little rancor involved. This was far from the confrontational role for lawyers we read about in class, and it helped us see the possibilities of approaching problems with a goal toward equitable solutions rather than "winning."

While at law school and living in Washington, I realized that politics—in the broadest sense of the word—can impede progress. Direct service, on the other hand, is only limited by time and resources. I volunteered for My Sister's Place, a shelter for battered women and their children, as a way to provide a concrete benefit to the community I lived in. The level of abuse these women suffered was unimaginable. The contribution I made as a volunteer paled in comparison to the sacrifices they made on a daily basis, just to make a better life for themselves and their children.

I'm now a few decades out of law school and have spent my entire career working for nonprofits, mostly with a focus on consumer protection. Sometimes it feels like a lifelong volunteer path, which is exactly how I wanted it to be when I graduated. Social progress is really the story of individuals, together or alone, choosing to act for the public interest.

**—Laura Polacheck**

Polacheck is the advocacy director (for Utah) for the American Association of Retired Persons in Salt Lake City.

---------------------------------- ★ ----------------------------------

## THE VALUE OF ENGAGED PARTICIPATION

I began to do volunteer work in high school. I found that I enjoyed teaching younger kids, and that I could see the effects of my efforts very readily. This was true whether I was teaching swimming in the summer or tutoring math during the school year. As a tutor I found a sense of purpose and satisfaction. The purpose was very clear: Someone had trouble reading, or calculating, or overcoming fear of the water—and the satisfaction came from the tangible results one could see almost immediately.

At Berner High School in Massapequa Park (Long Island, New York), I organized a tutoring service that helped students at the nearby elementary school. I did this through our chapter of the National Honor Society. As I recall, the Honor Society up to that point had had no other function but to recognize the academic achievements of its members, and I developed the tutoring program to connect the group to something useful—to do what we would today call "service." It was great fun, and I think we did some good.

I then worked in a psychiatric ward while a first-year student at Wesleyan University. This was an extraordinarily important experience for me. At the time I thought that mental illness was a myth, and that the patients were only part of an oppressed group waiting to be liberated from the shackles of convention. After working with some people who were suffering greatly, and who were sometimes deeply disturbed, I realized that learning about pathology from books was not enough. My respect for the patients grew as I came to know them, and not just think of them as facets of an ideological apparatus.

Like many volunteers, I learned that "giving back" is immensely satisfying, and that by engaging in the life of a community, one enhances one's own life. I got to know some amazing people—as coworkers and as friends. I also learned a lot about organizations, and about how successful institutions can function in relation to their neighborhoods, regions, and the country as a whole. In a word, I learned more about the value of engaged participation.

I have been an active proponent of community partnerships throughout my professional life. At Scripps College in Claremont, California (where I began my career as a professor), many of my students became active volunteers, especially around women's issues. At the Getty Research Institute, I led a staff deeply committed to working in parts of Los Angeles that were typically underserved by the Getty (and many other cultural organizations). They studied and stimulated participation in the arts in a robust way. As president of California College of the Arts (2000–2007) and at Wesleyan University, I have supported service-learning, community partnerships, and the development of an ethos of engagement as a crucial part of our educational experience. I believe that only an engaged university can be a great university, and that belief was formed through my own efforts as a volunteer.

—**Michael Roth**

Roth is the president of Wesleyan University in Middletown, Connecticut.

---------------------------------- ★ ----------------------------------

## MORE THAN AN EXTRACURRICULAR ACTIVITY

My first experience with public service was on the receiving end, at the age of ten, when our house burned down in the Oakland hills fire. Fortunately for my family, we had a safety net: insurance to help us rebuild what we lost; the kindness of family and friends to house us for those few months when we— along with thousands of others—were without shelter; and services from the Red Cross. This experience inspired me to get involved with community work in high school, working with the Red Cross and running an arts program at a homeless shelter. I also founded the Human Rights Club at my high school. Initially, the club focused on international violations of human rights. With time, our focus expanded to include local issues, recognizing that human rights violations exist in our own backyards as well as abroad.

However, it wasn't until college that I realized public service was more than an extracurricular activity, and that it would strongly influence my studies and career. As an undergraduate at Stanford University, I majored in urban studies, with a focus on community organization. Then, upon graduation, I applied for the AmeriCorps VISTA program. Through VISTA, I worked with Habitat for Humanity in New York City, advocating for policies to increase affordable housing. While my daily work focused on program planning and policy, I was most moved by my interactions with community members. I remember working side by side with family partners on the weekends to help them finish their homes, and proudly witnessing the moment they received the keys to their hard-earned, finished homes.

These experiences shaped my professional career, inspiring me to develop professional skill sets around policy analysis and research. So, I went graduate school to get my master's in community economic development and housing at UCLA's Urban Planning department. I have now come full circle, working again in the nonprofit sector for a leading advocacy organization, the Los Angeles Alliance for a New Economy, where we promote a new economic approach based on good jobs, thriving communities, and a healthy environment. As a research/policy analyst, I work with environmental, community, labor, faith, and community groups, advocating for systemic change, recognizing that policy is most effective when applied and combined with coalition building, strategic communications, and thorough research.

I feel very fortunate to have a career rooted in public service, and my dedication to this field is reinforced by times of growth and victories—from building four new units of affordable housing to major policy wins—and by working with the talented and motivated individuals I've met along the way.

—**Sabrina Bornstein**

Bornstein is a graduate of Stanford University. She volunteered with AmeriCorps VISTA, working with Habitat for Humanity in New York City. After graduate school at UCLA, she now works as an advocate planner for comprehensive community development in Los Angeles.

---------------------------------- ★ ----------------------------------

## MOMENTS OF "RIGHTNESS"

Kindness, connection, giving—to see these elements in motion is to enter a rarefied space. Sincere gestures of interest—be they simple nods of understanding or the running of a soup kitchen—grant us moments of, well, "rightness." In committing to a lifestyle of volunteering, we answer both philosophical riddles of meaning and sociological calls to community change.

I didn't always recognize this. Growing up in St. Joseph, Michigan, I was an egotistic athlete whose primary ambition, like that of many kids, was the cultivation of my own image. My bemused mother, however, was well beyond such concerns. Although raised in suburban wealth, she was never drawn to superficial attention or her own mother's country-club pressures. Her discomfort with self-absorption or pretension of any sort is neither dramatic nor forced. When she began opening our home to the gang kids from across the river in Benton Harbor, I was embarrassed—even ashamed. These were kids who grew up in crack houses; they dressed and spoke with rough edges. To my mother, they were simply human beings with a common need to be someone's priority. She would listen to them, feed them, house them. More often than not, this was all that was needed to change their lives, and hence—one person at a time—the nature of our socially and racially divided towns. Week after week, year after year, she was the odd "white woman" attending the graduations, deliveries, weddings, and funerals of the gang kids from across the bridge. In volunteering to help those in the forgotten parts of a forgotten community, she understood the power of giving, of transcending the self.

Such wisdom comes to us in mysterious ways. What my mother seemed to know intuitively about volunteering, I discovered in stages. My first act of volunteering occurred in college. I had always been interested in military history, and often volunteered to read to the veterans at a hospital that rarely saw visitors. Most recently, I have been volunteering with a group called "Birthday Wishes." We work with a shelter for homeless (and often fatherless) families. Our role is to organize birthday parties for children who otherwise have no access to the cakes, candles, and gifts that all boys and girls deserve. The genuine pleasure I've seen in these children for even the simplest gift or moment of attention humbles me, and I can say without exaggeration that I have received much more from them than anything I have given.

At some point in each of our journeys, we start to feel the value of service, the pleasure of connecting and engaging. Volunteering begins the moment we understand the power of stepping momentarily outside of our own interests to honor another's. What concerns me today, and what prompted my launching of the Emerson Circle, is a visceral sense that the conditions of our times (social, economic, and civic) are sliding away from generosity and connection and tilting more toward self-interest and disconnection. There is, I feel, something uniquely toxic about the modern era and its endemic "me-first-ness." Our new media—its tweets, friend requests, chat rooms, etc.—offer tremendous access to others, but at what expense? At what diluted valuation? We come away from such experiences diverted but internally malnourished—for there is little substance in such empty lands of form. Whether channel-surfing or net-surfing, bonus-seeking or bond-selling, we seem to be falling deeper and faster into ourselves and further from our relations to each other.

Over 500 million of us are social networking, spending 700 billion minutes a month (!) on Facebook alone. Imagine what could be achieved if just 1 percent of this online time was diverted to volunteering? When I consider this faith in technology, I think immediately of St. Exupery's observation that today we are capable of manufacturing 5,000 pianos a day, but incapable of creating a single worthy pianist . . .

I harbor no illusions that anything I do in my acts of volunteering or in my personal connections at the Emerson Circle will, of themselves, reverse the direction of this largely (but not entirely) shallow river. Instead, I put my faith in the example of my mother and her rough-edged gang kids, the books read aloud to forgotten war heroes in veterans' hospitals, or the smiling birthday girl at the shelter in Boston. Stepping away from all the noise and headlines, we can discover a space for ourselves and others where, one person, one smile, one connection, and one kind gesture at a time, we finish each day a little better than it began. That, at least, is what volunteering has confirmed for me.

**—Matthew Piepenburg**

Pipenburg is the founder and director of the Emerson Circle.

---------------------------------- ★ ----------------------------------

## EXPLORING WHAT IT MEANS TO SERVE

I come from a long line of preachers and teachers, so I probably learned about the value of service at a very early age. My first memory of deliberately volunteering to take action was my first year in college at Lewis and Clark, in Portland, Oregon, when I volunteered to be an ESL tutor for homeless Latino men. I was touched by the men's life stories, and within weeks, I started organizing other college students to lobby the city for more services for the homeless and to stop police raids on encampments of people without homes. It was a powerful learning experience that expanded my sense of community, and taught me how important it is to be involved in addressing systemic, structural issues that create inequity. My service with the Latino community inspired me to bring Cesar Chavez to speak on my campus, and my experiences organizing my peers inspired me to start the Community Service Office at Lewis and Clark.

Those experiences ultimately led to my current career. For the past ten years, I have been the director of the Public Service Center at the University of California, Berkeley. Last year, over 6,500 CAL students volunteered to work with 270 local community-based organizations and schools. In addition, we recruited, trained, and placed 170 AmeriCorps volunteers.

It has been an incredible experience to work with others to not only create opportunities for students to learn the value of service, but also to work on creating a culture where everyone is exploring what it means to serve— every day and from every department. I thoroughly enjoy teaching students that meaningful service does not only take place when we go off campus and volunteer for three hours, but that service also means deliberately choosing a research project that may benefit others; being involved in shaping local public policy; and choosing to live our lives in intentional ways that serve the common good.

I love helping others realize that service is not just about the act of serving, although that act alone is very important. It is also about being willing to touch and to be touched, and it is about the experience of belonging. Volunteering is about experiencing genuine connection with others and the world around us, and using our gifts to create a world that is better for all of us.

**—Megan Voorhees**

Voorhees is the director of the Public Service Center at the University of California, Berkeley. She first volunteered to be an ESL tutor working with migrant laborers while in college in Portland, Oregon.

--------------------------------- ★ ---------------------------------

## THE BEST LEARNING OPPORTUNITIES

Volunteer work, over many years, has brought me some of the richest, most rewarding experiences in my life. Also, I have discovered some of the best learning opportunities that have literally opened up the world. It started in grade school in Peoria Heights, Illinois, where Dominican nuns sent me and all of my classmates who would "volunteer" out into the neighborhoods, selling Christmas cards to raise money for the "pagan babies" of the world. I had no clear idea what a "pagan baby" was, but my fourth-grade teacher assured me that "these are very poor children in all remote parts of the world who are far less fortunate than you or me; they don't have enough food or clothing or books for school." I decided right then that one day, I would go to see these pagan children for myself, to see what might be done for them directly.

Next came Troop 28 of the Boy Scouts of America, and food drives for poor folks right in our own community. In college, at Northwestern University, I joined a campus group that traveled by bus two nights a week to tutor school kids in Chicago's South and Southwest neighborhoods. My eyes were opened to harsh poverty and deprivation, but I also met children who were ever so eager to learn, curious youngsters who wanted to be "better at math and reading," but who also wanted to learn about "white college students, like you."

Medical school at Northwestern provided me with an opportunity to do my clinical work in the neighborhood health centers. At that time I discovered an opportunity to develop, on my own, a transitional program for women who were being paroled from the Illinois State Prison for Women at Dwight, Illinois. This program would have its base at St. Leonard's House, a halfway house for (up to that time) men only, who likewise had recently been paroled from the state prison system. I was able to get supervision and support from "volunteer" faculty at my school, and also from the Episcopal Diocese of Chicago. The program became so popular—with its group therapy meetings designed to help the women "process" the transitional experience from prison to the workaday world—that the men demanded a "program like you do for the women, for us!" Recently, I discovered that the program has evolved into a meeting center for "Friends Outside," a national volunteer program that assists incarcerated individuals in finding jobs and support after leaving prison.

After graduating from med school and completing my internship, I turned down a U.S. Navy commission, entered the U.S. Public Health Service, and "volunteered" to serve with the Peace Corps. I became a staff physician in Malawi, where I worked with a fantastic group of volunteers in the Malawi Health Program, treating patients with tuberculosis. We also developed maternal and child health clinics, many of which were still functioning after forty years. Perhaps best known is the Malawi Children's Village, just outside of Mangoche, Malawi. This "village for children" started up as a clinic and evolved into an orphanage, which included a primary school and, later, a secondary school. Eventually, a technical trade school would offer on-the-job learning in agriculture, computer technology, seamstress work, and yes, teaching, and it now features an alumni organization!

Nearly all of my adult life I have been a volunteer of one sort or another. I volunteered to stay on with the Peace Corps and became chief medical officer, participating in the development of programs all over the world. I also founded a migrant health program in Fort Lupton, Colorado. This program continues from its humble beginnings as Plan de Salud del Valle, which has grown into a large, multi-specialty health center for migrant farm workers, with a number of satellite clinics near Denver.

Upon reflection, I realize that I found the "pagan babies" of my childhood wonderment in all parts of the world, as well as right here at home. Three years ago, I was afforded an opportunity to do a tutorial for six resident physicians in psychiatry at The Royal School of Medicine in Phnom Penh, Cambodia. This was the first group of psychiatrists to complete their training in Cambodia, since the restoration of the medical school after the end of the Khmer regime. Six graduating resident physicians in psychiatry raised the national number of psychiatrists in Cambodia (a country of 15 million people) from twelve to eighteen! Two years ago, I went back to Malawi, where I will continue to be involved with the Malawi Children's Village. This past year I have been involved in relief efforts in Haiti, where I have spent three weeks on two trips, developing a health clinic and community education center in Marie Gracier, about fifteen miles from Port au Prince.

It is extremely gratifying to give to and work with others. But I now find this volunteer work to be truly self-serving. Selfishness binds up the body of altruism. Nothing could be better.

—**Dr. Tom Powers**

Dr. Powers first volunteered to tutor youngsters in the South Side neighborhoods of Chicago. He volunteered for the Peace Corps and was a staff physician in Malawi. After that, he volunteered to work as chief medical officer for the Peace Corps and has worked all over the world.

--------------------------------- ★ ---------------------------------

## A FIRE IN THE BELLY

I am a white woman, age sixty-four, retired and disabled; the only thing about me that hasn't aged is the fire in my belly for equality. What stirred it? A summer job teaching ecology took me to Nevada, home of philanthropist and environmentalist Maya Miller. In 1971, Maya introduced me to southern Nevada's emerging champion for the rights of poor people, Ms. Ruby Duncan. Our rapport was instantaneous, and I agreed to volunteer in her fight against the indignities being imposed on poor women and their children by the agencies designated to "help" impoverished Nevada families. Ms. Duncan and the women had to march, sit-in, and go to court before a federal judge ruled that Nevada's welfare director had "run roughshod over the rights of poor people."

As a VISTA volunteer with Clark County Welfare Rights Organization (CCWRO), I worked at every imaginable task: driving families to health screening appointments, publishing a "know your rights" newspaper, running a food bank, and much more. We wrote demand letters, petitions, and legislative testimony, and organized protests by families desperate for food stamps to replace awful USDA farm-subsidy commodity foods, which included moldy cheese, weevil-ridden flour, and rodent-infested peanut butter, all distributed to the poor. The David-and-Goliath nature of CCWRO's struggles impelled me to go to law school.

I returned to CCWRO as a lawyer for the group's newly created community development corporation, Operation Life, which shaped the entirety of my professional career. Topping the list was the realization that "uneducated" people are capable of brilliance. In pursuit of social justice, there is no substitute for local, hands-on experience, wisdom, and integrity. I learned that grassroots leadership holds the key to social change. People find ways to get things done, at times because of book learning, but also, at times, in spite of it.

Schooling gave me the tools to help my community; and we know that education offers a lifeline out of poverty. But anomalies sometimes teach us the most. This past weekend, I attended the ribbon-cutting ceremony in Las Vegas for the

Ruby Duncan Elementary School. In the sweetness of the moment, a huge crowd had assembled to honor this extraordinary woman, mother of seven, herself a high school dropout who overcame illiteracy—she once told me— by reading *The Congressional Record*. She told the audience how she made certain all her children graduated; she exhorted parents to be activists, their children's first teachers. As her strong voice rose, I heard the brilliance, courage, common sense, and compassion that drew me to her cause forty years ago! What want ad could I have possibly answered that would have shown me all this?

Volunteering allowed me to choose the people who would enhance my life. In giving, we often get far more than we give.

**—Martine Makower**

Makower was a VISTA volunteer in Las Vegas, Nevada. After law school, she returned to Las Vegas to work as attorney for Operation Life, a community economic development corporation. ★

## THE MOTIVATION FOR RIGHT ACTION

"White boy can jump!" I heard this through the fence at West Fourth Street, the legendary and tumultuous basketball fishbowl on Sixth Avenue in Greenwich Village. The son of a Holocaust survivor, I was bred to be a warrior. I didn't jump better than others, but I always wanted the ball more than anyone else. I went to Stanford on a tennis scholarship, but for three decades I ate, slept, and dreamt basketball.

The 1970s was breakout time for the women's movement. Every Saturday morning for five years, from nine to noon, I held a free open-gym session for women who wanted to learn how to play basketball. It was my way of combining the deep love of the game with the need to actively participate in the most important social movement of my early adulthood.

For the past ten years, on my own time, I have run a community garden at the college I work for. In the spring and fall I head out there at the end of the workday. In summer I use my break time. It requires building and maintaining sheds, deer fencing, benches, raised beds, soil, compost, walkways. I get help from students, but the heavy lifting often falls on my shoulders. My dad asks me from time to time, "Now tell me again why you volunteer most of your free time to the college you work for when you could be growing a beautiful garden at your own home?"

I don't really believe in "service." I think we are all just going about our business, trying to make the world the way we want it. I like to play. I like being in a world full of flowers and vegetables. I like work. I want other people to like and want and need these things, too. I consider my volunteer efforts invitations to participate in the world with me.

My mom had a knack for making everyone she came into contact with feel as if they were the most special person on the planet. From her I learned that everyone's contribution to the party counts.

For the past thirteen years I've run a program at Bard College called the Trustee Leader Scholars. I give stipends to students who design and run social action programs based on their own compelling interests. Since Katrina, over 600 Bard students have traveled to New Orleans. Many of them are now professional educators in a rebuilt neighborhood there, called Broadmoor. Other students raised the funds for and built a primary school in a small Ghanaian village. One student started a prison education program, and the college, having hired this former student, now grants degrees in New York State prisons. This summer I traveled to the West Bank with twenty students where we built a children's library and ran a summer camp.

Ultimately, I want my students to leave the college informed, humble, capable, and carrying a quiet and potent sense that what they do matters, and the motivation for right action needs to come from within themselves.

**—Paul Marienthal**

Marienthal is the associate dean of student affairs and director of the Trustee Leader Scholar program at Bard College in Annandale-On-Hudson, New York.

★

## THE STRUGGLE FOR EQUAL JUSTICE

In 1966 I was the assistant chaplain at a prep school in New Jersey, and, hoping to capture the attention of the boys at one of the required chapel services, I invited seminary classmates to come from New York to present a folk music program. They did, and in their presentation they talked about their volunteer work the previous summer in a Student Interracial Ministry project in southwest Georgia. After the service, they urged me to go with them the next summer, and I did.

I was born and raised a white person in the segregated South. I attended Washington and Lee, an all-male segregated university that had disaffiliated its student Christian association from the YMCA because of the national organization's integrationist policies. Thanks to the influence of a new young religion professor at that university, however, I did go to Union Theological Seminary in New York, and it was there that Charles Sherrod of the Student Nonviolent Coordinating Committee (SNCC) came for a sabbatical year and to recruit volunteers for his Southwest Georgia Project.

My stay in Baker County, Georgia, was brief. I taught that summer in a Head Start Program, and I worked with black farmers who were trying to get a fair shake on peanut allotments from the U.S. Department of Agriculture. For the first time, I tried to read and interpret federal regulations. I watched lawyer C. B. King and the law student volunteers with him try to bring justice to that land. I thought they were more effective than I was, so, three years later, I enrolled in law school in the South, because that was where I wanted to live and work for civil rights and the poor.

During my first year at Vanderbilt Law School I applied for a summer job with the Law Students' Civil Rights Research Council. When I did not hear from them, I offered to work for free, but still no response. Finally, I gave up and applied for a summer clerk position at the new legal aid office in Nashville. They gave me a job and paid me, and I stayed for thirty-seven years. Friends and colleagues helped build the organization and expand its services over the years. It became, in time, the Legal Aid Society of Middle Tennessee and the Cumberlands.

I recently retired after thirty-one years as executive director. The volunteer experience in southwest Georgia focused my faith and gave me a rewarding vocation. Prior to that summer, I had been mostly a spectator of the struggle for equal justice. With that volunteer experience, I was inspired to try to do more.

**—Ashley Wiltshire**

Wiltshire is the former executive director of the, Legal Aid Society of Middle Tennessee and the Cumberlands. He first volunteered to work with the Student Interracial Ministry project in southwest Georgia, teaching at a Head Start program. After law school, he worked for and became the director of a Legal Aid Society program based in Nashville, Tennessee.

------------------------------------ ★ ------------------------------------

## THE SOCIAL IMPLICATIONS OF DESIGN

I have a vivid memory of being pushed in a stroller by my mother in what I remember to be a Heart Health Awareness walk in my hometown of Moss Point, Mississippi. It was more fun for me than anything, but most importantly, it set the stage for my community involvement. I participated in my first self-initiated volunteer project in the first grade, when I asked my mother to sign me up for the St. Jude Math-a-thon. I didn't have a complete grasp on what cancer or leukemia was at the time. All I knew was that kids like me were very sick, and I could raise money (by doing math problems) to help make them better.

At Howard University while studying architecture, I participated in a program called School Building Week. The program included a student design competition. The students I worked with were in middle school, and they were challenged to design a new school facility that fostered learning and was environmentally friendly and technologically advanced. As a mentor, my primary "job" was to educate them on architectural principles and guide them through the design process. I visited the students a couple of times a week during the spring semester, and helped them prepare for their final presentation.

After the first year I realized that these students needed more than a mere explanation of architectural principles. Most of the students had heard of architecture and engineering, but they didn't think those were careers that black people were able to do. For the next three years, I augmented the program to include conversations about attending college, career opportunities, and becoming activists in their community.

Because of my volunteer service activities, I developed values with a strong community focus. It's a necessary part of my life, as an individual, to be involved in my community in some capacity. As a black female, it is even more important to me to be an example and a source of encouragement for other young people. I understand that I am able to do the things I do because someone helped and encouraged me. Now, it is my obligation to help and encourage others.

I believe it was no accident that I chose the professions of architecture and city planning. These two professions have a tremendous impact on our physical and mental wellness, as well as how we participate in our communities. In architecture school, I was always more interested in the social implications of design and how to bring good design to underrepresented communities that are usually neglected. I'm convinced this will remain my focus in the future.

**—Anna McCorvey**

McCorvey grew up in Mississippi and studied architecture at Howard University, where she volunteered to advise and mentor middle school students.

-------------------------------- ★ -----------------------------------

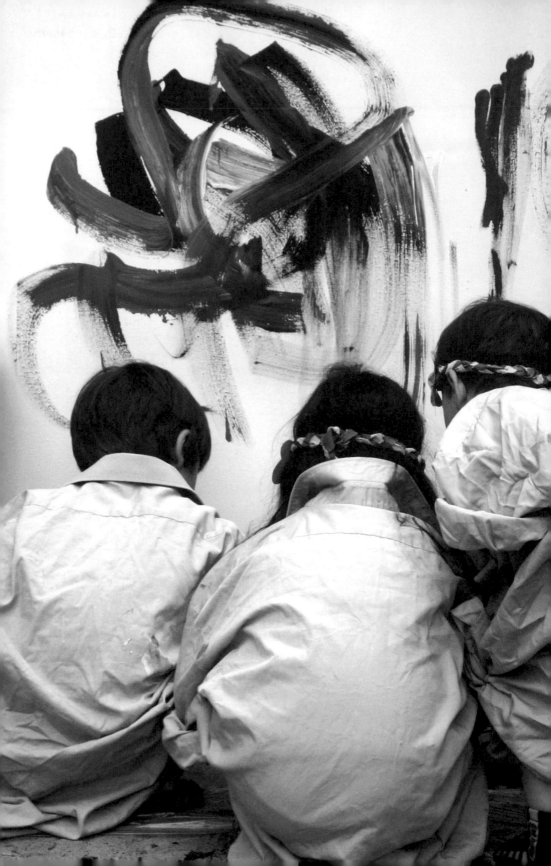

# PART TWO

# MAKE IT HAPPEN: THE LIST

Each of the organizations profiled in this section has been selected because of its commitment to educational, social, economic, environmental, and community development goals. Some have been in existence for many decades; others are fairly new. Most are national organizations, and some are local prototypes, but all have a solid track record of delivering services that are useful and meaningful. ★

# Organizations by Interest

You probably have skills you can share, or interests you can pursue by volunteering. If you're an architect, work with Habitat for Humanity; an accountant, help low-income people with their income taxes; a teacher, work with disadvantaged kids in a reading program or a literacy program for immigrants; a dentist, doctor, nurse, or psychologist, volunteer at a community health center. ★

# CHILDREN

## BIG BROTHERS BIG SISTERS OF AMERICA (BBBSA)

Established in 1904, Big Brothers Big Sisters has operated for more than a hundred years under the belief that inherent in every child is the ability to succeed and thrive in life. Most children served by Big Brothers Big Sisters are in single-parent and low-income families, or households where a parent is incarcerated. As the nation's largest donor and volunteer-supported mentoring network, Big Brothers Big Sisters makes meaningful, monitored matches between adult volunteers ("Bigs") and children ("Littles"). Headquartered in Philadelphia with a network of nearly 400 agencies across the country, Big Brothers Big Sisters serves more than 255,000 children.

### Volunteer Opportunities

Big Brothers Big Sisters provides community-based and school-based mentoring. To become a Big Brother or Big Sister, please contact the Big Brothers Big Sisters agency in your area. While they are affiliated with Big Brothers Big Sisters of America, each is its own agency with its own board of directors, and requirements vary slightly. The simplest way to contact Big Brothers Big Sisters is to visit its website, BigBrothersBigSisters.org, to enter one's zip code. Contact information on a local agency will be provided.

### Contact Information

**Headquarters:** 230 North
  Thirteenth Street
Philadelphia, PA 19107

(215) 567-7000
www.bbbs.org

--------------------------------- ★ ---------------------------------

## CHILDREN NOW

Established in 1988, this national, nonpartisan organization focuses on children's interests, especially in the areas of health care and education, and how the media is influential in both matters. In 2004, Children Now had a notable victory as one of the leaders in a campaign that influenced the Federal Communications Commission (FCC) to protect children from certain forms of advertising and to provide more educational television programming.

## Volunteer Opportunities

Internships are available in Oakland and Sacramento for undergraduate and graduate students. There is a required commitment of a minimum of sixteen hours per week for a period of at least ten weeks. Depending on the policy area, duties can include researching policy and budget proposals, drafting fact sheets, and preparing for meetings and events; researching and summarizing reports and scholarly articles on a range of topics related to key children's issues; updating online data tools and assisting with report releases; and assisting staff with general administrative work, preparing legislative briefing binders, organizing meetings, recording minutes, and attending legislative hearings and policy discussions.

When applying, make sure to include your interest in the following policy areas: education (early learning, K–12, and afterschool), health, and media.

*Desired skills:*

- Interest in and familiarity with policies affecting children and their families, particularly in health, education, and/or media
- Strong analytic, research, and writing skills
- Demonstrated organizational and time-management skills, preferably developed in an office
- Demonstrated ability to work independently and as a member of a team

To apply, submit a résumé, cover letter, and a one- to two-page writing sample (excerpts are fine) in Microsoft Word. The organization asks that applicants include their names in the file name for all documents (e.g., *d.smith–résumé*).

In addition to outlining applicant's qualifications, cover letters should clearly indicate the following:

- Preferred policy area
- Preferred dates
- Hours available per week

The applicant's résumé should include the name, title, and contact information for at least two references.

## Contact Information

**Headquarters:** 1212 Broadway,
  5th Floor
Oakland, CA 94612
(510) 763-2444

E-mail: info@childrennow.org
or jobs@childrennow.org
www.childrennow.org

----------------------------- ★ -----------------------------

CHILDREN

## CHILDREN'S DEFENSE FUND (CDF)

Established in 1973, CDF implements their "Leave No Child Behind" motto by advocating for children nationwide, especially minorities and those living in poverty or with disabilities. Ensuring children have access to quality health care, early education, and faith are several of CDF's priorities. Protection from abuse and neglect is also championed.

### Volunteer Opportunities

CDF asks that people interested in supporting the organization's mission visit its website, www.childrensdefense.org, to sign up to receive e-mail updates about upcoming volunteer opportunities and ways to take action to improve the lives of children.

**Contact Information**
**Headquarters:** 25 E Street, NW
Washington, DC 20001
(800) CDF-1200 (800-233-1200)

E-mail: cdfinfo@childrensdefense.org
www.childrensdefense.org

★

## COURT APPOINTED SPECIAL ADVOCATE ASSOCIATION (CASA)

Established in 1977, the mission of CASA is to provide volunteer advocates for neglected and abused children in court. In an effort to prevent children in foster care from getting lost in the legal maze, CASA educates and prepares regular citizens to study cases, conduct interviews, and write written reports that help children get placed into safe and permanent homes.

### Volunteer Opportunities

CASA offers volunteers thirty hours of training prior to service, followed by twelve additional hours a year midst-service. Volunteers are expected to research the background of assigned cases, represent the best interests of children in the courtroom, and ensure that cases are brought to quick and appropriate conclusions. Most cases last about a year and a half, and the typical time commitment for volunteers is between ten to twenty hours a week. The volunteer stays on each case until it is closed and the child is placed in a safe and permanent home.

**Contact Information**
**Headquarters:** 100 West Harrison
North Tower, Suite 500
Seattle, WA 98119

(800) 628-3233
www.casaforchildren.org

★

## 4-H

4-H (which stands for "head, heart, hands, and health") is the largest outside-of-school youth organization in the country, with the involvement of over 6 million children between the ages of eight and nineteen. The education program offers practical life skills in areas such as nutrition, safety, communication, science, and technology, among others. Youth members can join a 4-H club, attend a camp, or participate in school-based or afterschool programs. Though officially recognized in 1902, the foundation for 4-H began in the late 1800s.

### Volunteer Opportunities

The 4-H community includes over 500,000 volunteers who lead children in a wide array of hands-on activities and help coordinate community clubs. Adult volunteers can also teach a special skill or plan local and national events that help 4-H educate children with their "learn-by-doing" approach. Local 4-H clubs are organized under county extension offices.

### Contact Information

**Headquarters:** 1400 Independence Avenue, SW, Stop 2225 Washington, DC 20250 (202) 401-4114

E-mail: 4hhq@nifa.usda.gov www.4-h.org or national4-hheadquarters.gov

★

## IRIDESCENT

Iridescent is a science-education nonprofit organization that brings cutting-edge science to underserved communities. Iridescent's unique approach is to empower engineers and scientists to communicate their expertise and passion to children through exciting, inquiry-based programs. In addition, Iridescent invites parents to learn alongside their children and participate in Family Science Courses.

Iridescent has been in operation for four years and has trained over 300 engineers to impact almost 4,800 underserved children and parents in three major cities: Los Angeles, San Francisco, and, more recently, New York.

### Volunteer Opportunities

Opportunities are available in New York City, Los Angeles, and San Francisco. Engineers interested in volunteering can attend Engineer Training (Engineers as Teachers), a rigorous sixteen-week training program in NYC and LA that enables participants to serve as role models and provide meaningful science-learning experiences to the public. The engineers develop their public speaking and leadership skills and a deeper understanding of their own field, while communicating complex concepts to large, diverse audiences. Engineers also volunteer significant amounts of time to the Family Science Courses (eighty to hundred hours over the course of four months), and become regular, long-term volunteers. Additionally, volunteer engineers can commit for a short, one-time teaching commitment via Iridescent's four-hour quick trainings (also offered in NYC and LA).

For all other supporting positions—Spanish translation (live and remote), program directors (individuals who evaluate the engineers' teaching), and other opportunities—Iridescent posts these on VolunteerMatch.Org, Idealist.org, and its website. The organization follows up with a volunteer orientation, held the first Saturday of every month from 10:00 AM to 1:00 PM.

**Contact Information**
(310) 309-0766                                          www.iridescentlearning.org
E-mail: info@iridescentlearning.org

---- ★ ----

## KABOOM!
Established in 1996, KaBOOM! is dedicated to the construction of local play-spaces for children while also increasing community engagement. The organization leads community-build projects for playgrounds and also strives to increase public awareness about the benefits of play. One of their objectives is to supply do-it-yourself resources that include an online community, grants, publications, and training for communities that wish to plan a new playspace on their own.

### Volunteer Opportunities
Since many KaBOOM!-led builds are quickly staffed with volunteers, the organization encourages interested parties to check Kaboom.org for other projects occurring in their area. Many of these opportunities are posted on the website by community-based organizations not affiliated with KaBOOM!.

**Contact Information**
4455 Connecticut Avenue, NW, Suite          (202) 659-0215
   B100                                                        www.kaboom.org
Washington, DC 20008

---- ★ ----

## MAKE-A-WISH FOUNDATION

Established in 1980, the Make-A-Wish Foundation allows children with life-threatening illnesses the opportunity to experience one of their wishes coming true. Examples of popular wishes include visiting a theme park, meeting a movie star, or receiving a coveted gift.

### Volunteer Opportunities

With the assistance of nearly 25,000 volunteers, the charity is able to a grant a wish every forty minutes. Opportunities vary by local chapters, but volunteers are strongly needed for wish granting, fund-raising, special events, general administration, language translation, and several other areas.

### Contact Information
**Headquarters:** 4742 N. 24th St., Suite 400
Phoenix, AZ 85016-4862

(602) 279-WISH (9474)
or (800) 722-WISH (9474)
www.wish.org

---- ★ ----

## STANDUP FOR KIDS

Established in 1990, the mission of StandUp For Kids is to help homeless kids, children living on the street, and at-risk youth. Efforts are carried out by volunteers who walk the streets to find and reach out to those without stable homes. StandUp For Kids offers necessities such as food and hygiene products, as well as education programs and job training.

### Volunteer Opportunities

Contact a local chapter to learn about counselor positions. Volunteers can also help with advocacy, development, job-training assistance, tutoring, marketing, grant writing, and graphic design.

### Contact Information
**Headquarters:** 83 Walton Street, Suite 100
Atlanta, GA 30303

(800) 365-4KID
E-mail: staff@standupforkids.org
www.standupforkids.org

---- ★ ----

# CIVIL RIGHTS

## ASIAN AMERICANS FOR COMMUNITY OUTREACH (AACO)

Established in 1994, AACO is a local volunteer-run organization dedicated to bringing together young Asian American professionals and students in order to serve their communities. Its members work to enrich the community at large by participating in social events such as charity fund-raisers. But the organization's purpose is to also promote the awareness of social and political issues relevant to Asian Americans.

### Volunteer Opportunities

AACO offers volunteers the ability to serve at single-day events in the San Francisco Bay area. In the past, volunteers have prepared and served food in a soup kitchen, taken pledge calls at a radio fund-raiser, and performed security at the Northern California Cherry Blossom Festival.

### Contact Information

E-mail: info@aaco-sf.org
www.aaco-sf.org

----------------------------------- ★ -----------------------------------

## DISABILITY RIGHTS EDUCATION AND DEFENSE FUND (DREDF)

Established in 1979, DREDF strives to advance the civil and human rights of people living with disabilities through many means, including legal advocacy, public policy, and legislative development. The fund, which is directed by individuals with disabilities and the parents of children with disabilities, offers training and education to multiple groups of people, and has run a disability rights legal clinic for over fifteen years.

### Volunteer Opportunities

Primary volunteer opportunities are for law students, but DREDF has recently added undergraduate internships in Berkeley.

The Disability Rights Internship for undergraduates is structured to provide interns with an overview of disability rights issues in education, transportation, employment, housing, and physical access. The intern works with the

Children and Family Advocacy, ADA Technical Assistance, and Public Policy Programs, and will leave with legal, practical advocacy skills and knowledge of political and grassroots organizing. Duties assigned after initial training are likely to include:

- Coordination in parent advocacy trainings and workshops with DREDF Parent Advocates
- Assisting with legislative advocacy, including research for potential legislation
- Assisting in grassroots networking and education
- Assisting with social media and Internet advocacy
- Providing research and assistance to policy analysts on disability issues
- Updating DREDF's press and photo archives
- Participating as a member of DREDF staff, including development activities and attending staff meetings, if possible

DREDF also offers field placement internships and possible summer positions for law students. Academic term internships generally involve a commitment of eight to sixteen hours per week. Summer internships generally involve a forty-hour-per-week commitment for at least five weeks, and preferably eight to ten weeks. Individuals with disabilities and, minority women candidates are especially encouraged to apply.

Interns work on a variety of litigation projects under the supervision of DREDF attorneys, including disability rights class-action and individual cases in the areas of employment, access to government programs and activities, architectural access, housing, and educational entitlements of children with disabilities. Projects include researching legal issues, drafting documents for discovery (e.g., interrogatories, requests for admissions, and requests for production of documents), and drafting legal motions and pleadings. Interns will have direct contact with clients, and the opportunity to observe or participate in meetings, depositions, and court proceedings related to litigation on which they are working.

With the close supervision of attorneys, interns may also respond to telephone inquiries about disability discrimination or special education issues that callers with disabilities or parents of children with disabilities are facing, and may provide informal advocacy on clients' behalf. Interns are also invited and encouraged to join DREDF staff in attending disability community events and meetings that occur during their period of internship.

Interested candidates may submit cover letter, résumé, and references to *Attn: Law Student Internships* by mail, e-mail (hmin@dredf.org), or fax.

CIVIL RIGHTS

**Contact Information**
2212 Sixth Street
Berkeley, CA 94710
(800) 348-4232 or (510) 644-2555

E-mail: info@dredf.org
www.dredf.org

★

# INDIAN LAW RESOURCE CENTER

Preserving Indian and other Native nations and tribes is the principal objective of the Indian Law Resource Center. The center works on a range of issues to protect the human rights, lands, culture, and resources of indigenous communities in the United States and throughout the Americas. Legal assistance is offered to help these efforts, and a current project includes providing human rights training to U.S. tribal leaders. This Center was established in 1978 by American Indians who direct the center to this day.

## Volunteer Opportunities

The Indian Law Resource Center does not have a formalized volunteer program, but it does use volunteers sporadically, and mainly in an internship-type arrangement. Its Washington, D.C., office brings in legal interns throughout the year. In the past it has had administrative and communications/translation internships, but these are on an as-needed basis. The center's Montana office also considers applications for legal clerkships throughout the year. The Montana office also coordinates the Center's fellowship program, wherein the Center awards fellowships each year to up to two law students who show particular promise in federal Indian law and/or international indigenous human rights issues.

With the limited number of volunteer opportunities available, the Indian Law Resource Center encourages individuals interested in volunteering to subscribe to its electronic newsletter to stay informed of advocacy activities and educational opportunities.

**Contact Information**
**Headquarters:** 602 North Ewing
  Street
Helena, MT 59601

(406) 449-2006
E-mail: mt@indianlaw.org
www.indianlaw.org

★

## MEXICAN AMERICAN LEGAL DEFENSE AND EDUCATIONAL FUND (MALDEF)

Founded in 1968, MALDEF fights for the legal rights of Latinos in the U.S., and is often referred to as the "law firm of the Latino community." The fund's goal is to implement programs that will improve Latino communities and achieve socioeconomic change. Their approach combines advocacy, educational outreach, and litigation strategies. One of their greatest legal achievements was with the U.S. Supreme Court case, *Plyler v. Doe,* whose conclusion secured free public education for all American children of undocumented immigrant parents.

### Volunteer Opportunities

Each regional office—San Antonio, Chicago, Atlanta, D.C.—utilizes volunteers differently, but help is often needed in administration and for planning events. Interested volunteers should visit the website and submit an e-mail.

### Contact Information

634 S. Spring Street
Los Angeles, CA 90014
(213) 629-2512

E-mail: jobs@maldef.org
www.maldef.org

------------------------------------ ★ ------------------------------------

## NATIONAL ASSOCIATION FOR THE ADVANCEMENT OF COLORED PEOPLE (NAACP)

Founded on February 12, 1909, the NAACP is the nation's oldest, largest, and most widely recognized grassroots-based civil rights organization. More than half a million members and supporters throughout the United States and the world serve as the premier advocates for civil rights in their communities, conducting voter mobilization and monitoring equal opportunity in the public and private sectors. The NAACP's principal objective is to ensure the political, educational, social, and economic equality of minority-group citizens of the United States and to eliminate race prejudice. The NAACP seeks to remove all barriers of racial discrimination through the democratic process.

### Volunteer Opportunities

Opportunities are available at the local level and vary by location. Visit the organization's website to find the contact information for a local office near you.

CIVIL RIGHTS

**Contact Information**
**Headquarters**: 4805 Mt. Hope Drive
Baltimore MD 21215

(877) NAACP-98 or (410) 580-5777
www.naacp.org

---------------------------------- ★ ----------------------------------

## NATIONAL COUNCIL OF LA RAZA (NCLR)
Founded in 1968, NCLR aims to improve opportunities for Hispanic Americans with the help of its formal network of nearly 300 affiliates throughout the country. The organization supports Hispanic community-based organizations, particularly those serving low-income and disadvantaged Hispanics, by offering assistance in management, program operations, and other areas. The affiliates, in turn, are able to reach millions of Hispanics in forty-one states. NCLR also conducts research, policy analysis, and advocacy in areas such as education, employment, immigration, and health.

### Volunteer Opportunities
Volunteers assist with workshops on health, immigration, and the economy that NCLR organizes for its annual conference. NCLR occasionally uses volunteers to help with publicity during its advocacy day.

**Contact Information**
**Headquarters**: Raul Yzaguirre
  Building
1126 16th Street, NW

Washington, DC 20036
(202) 785-1670
www.nclr.org

---------------------------------- ★ ----------------------------------

## NATIONAL URBAN LEAGUE
Established in 1910, the National Urban League has been around for a hundred years, working on their mission to improve the standard of living in underserved African American communities. Efforts to accomplish this include a focus on education (access to scholarships and after-care programs), job training, affordable health care, and the protection of civil rights for African Americans. The league has more than a hundred local affiliates that pursue this objective and provide direct services.

## Volunteer Opportunities

Volunteers are recognized as a fundamental part of the National Urban League, serving in the New York headquarters and in the League's local offices. Opportunities include fund-raising for events, such as the annual Equal Opportunity Day (EOD) Dinner and Annual Conference, mentoring youth, participating in various community projects, and providing support to staff.

## Contact Information

**Headquarters**: 120 Wall Street
New York, NY 10005

(212) 558-5300
www.nul.org

CIVIL RIGHTS

COMMUNITY DEVELOPMENT AND ECONOMIC JUSTICE

# COMMUNITY DEVELOPMENT AND ECONOMIC JUSTICE

## AMERICORPS

Established in 1993, AmeriCorps offers 75,000 opportunities each year for adults of all ages and backgrounds to serve through a network of partnerships with local and national nonprofit groups. AmeriCorps members address critical needs in communities all across America. As an AmeriCorps member, you can:

- Tutor and mentor disadvantaged youth
- Fight illiteracy
- Improve health services
- Build affordable housing
- Teach computer skills
- Clean up parks and streams
- Manage or operate afterschool programs
- Help communities respond to disasters
- Build organizational capacity

Full-time AmeriCorps members who complete their service earn a Segal AmeriCorps Education Award of $4,725 to pay for college, graduate school, or to pay back qualified student loans; members who serve part-time receive a partial Award. Some AmeriCorps members may also receive a modest living allowance during their term of service.

AmeriCorps is made up of three main programs: AmeriCorps State and National, AmeriCorps VISTA, and AmeriCorps NCCC (National Civilian Community Corps).

## Volunteer Opportunities

The largest of AmeriCorps programs, AmeriCorps State and National, provides funds to local and national organizations and agencies committed to using national service to address critical community needs in education, public safety, health, and the environment. Each of these organizations and agencies, in turn, uses their AmeriCorps funding to recruit, place, and supervise AmeriCorps members.

AmeriCorps members serve in AmeriCorps State and National projects in every state, U.S. territories, and on tribal reservations. State and National programs are open to U.S. citizens, nationals, or lawful permanent resident aliens age seventeen and older. Members may serve full- or part-time over a period not to exceed twelve months.

After successful completion of their term of service, AmeriCorps members earn a Segal AmeriCorps Education Award that can be used to pay for college or graduate school at Title IV schools, or to repay qualified student loans. Full-time AmeriCorps members also receive a modest living allowance, health-care benefits, and child-care assistance.

AmeriCorps VISTA is the national service program designed specifically to fight poverty. Founded as Volunteers in Service to America in 1965 and incorporated into the AmeriCorps network of programs in 1993, VISTA has been on the front lines in the fight against poverty in America for more than forty years.

VISTA members commit to serve full-time for a year at a nonprofit organization or local government agency, working to fight illiteracy, improve health services, create businesses, strengthen community groups, and much more.

During your service, you'll also receive a modest living allowance, health care, and other benefits. And, upon completing your service, you can choose to receive either a Segal AmeriCorps Education Award or a post-service stipend.

AmeriCorps NCCC (National Civilian Community Corps) is a full-time, team-based residential program for men and women ages eighteen to twenty-four. Members are assigned to one of five campuses, located in Denver, Colorado; Sacramento, California; Perry Point, Maryland; Vicksburg, Mississippi; and Vinton, Iowa.

The mission of AmeriCorps NCCC is to strengthen communities and develop leaders through direct, team-based national and community service. In partnership with nonprofits—secular and faith-based, local municipalities, state governments, federal government, national or state parks, Indian Tribes, and schools—members complete service projects throughout the region in which they are assigned.

AmeriCorps NCCC requires an intensive, ten-month commitment. Members serve in teams of eight to twelve and are assigned to projects throughout the region served by their campus. They are trained in CPR, first aid, public safety, and other skills before beginning their first service project.

AmeriCorps NCCC serves communities in every state. Members are based at one of five regional campuses and travel to complete service projects throughout those regions. Sponsoring organizations request the assistance of AmeriCorps NCCC teams by submitting a project application to the regional campus that covers that organization's state. The campuses provide assistance in completing the application, developing a work plan, and preparing the project sponsor for the arrival of the AmeriCorps NCCC team.

AmeriCorps NCCC members receive a living allowance of approximately $4,000 for the ten months of service (about $200 every two weeks before taxes), housing, meals, limited medical benefits, up to $400 a month for child care (if necessary), member uniforms, and a Segal AmeriCorps Education Award upon successful completion of the program.

**Contact Information**

1201 New York Avenue, NW
Washington, DC 20525
(202) 606-5000 or

TTY: (202) 606-3472
E-mail: questions@americorps.gov
www.americorps.gov

---

★

## CENTER FOR THIRD WORLD ORGANIZING (CTWO)

CTWO is a training and resource organization that promotes social, economic, and racial justice for people of color, with a focus on the poor. To achieve its objective, CTWO strives to build a network of activists and communities, and provides training for new and experienced organizers. Training sessions include the Movement Activist Apprenticeship Program (MAAP), an eight-week-long intensive program that provides people of color with the opportunity to develop skills and experience in grassroots organizing, and the California Lead Organizer Institute (CLOI), which unites lead organizers who wish to advance their leadership abilities.

### Volunteer Opportunities

Volunteer tasks vary by program, and range from research and fundraising to clerical work. Interested individuals can also apply to the organization's Movement Activist Apprenticeship Program (MAAP). MAAP is an eight-week summer internship program for people of color who want to pursue a career in community organizing. Participants receive training in CTWO's retreat center in Oakland, California, and are then placed in active campaigns where they become full-time community organizers. For details, contact program coordinator Araceli Centeno at araceli@ctwo.org, or by phone at (510) 355-7583 ext. 13.

**Contact Information**

1218 E. 21st Street
Oakland, CA 94606

(510) 533-7583
www.ctwo.org

---

★

## CITY YEAR

Established in 1988, City Year—a member of AmeriCorps—unites young people (ages seventeen to twenty-four) of all backgrounds for a year of full-time service, giving them the skills and opportunities to change the world. As tutors, mentors, and role models, these young leaders help children stay in school and on track, and transform schools and communities across the United States, as well as through international affiliates in Johannesburg, South Africa, and London, England.

### Volunteer Opportunities

There are occasional opportunities during the year for people to join City Year for a day of service, such as painting murals and renovating facilities at a school in which a City Year team is in service year-round.

### Contact Information

287 Columbus Avenue
Boston, MA 02116

(617) 927-2500
www.cityyear.org

★

## COMMUNITY ACTION PARTNERSHIP (CAP)

Established in 1972, CAP represents the interests of more than a thousand community action agencies that work to eliminate poverty. Community action agencies are nonprofit private and public organizations established under the Economic Opportunity Act of 1964 to fight poverty and make America a better place to live. CAP assists these agencies by sponsoring an annual convention, publishing a quarterly magazine, providing training and technical assistance, and releasing a weekly electronic newsletter. Most recently the federal Office of Community Services in the Department of Health and Human Services designated the Partnership as the lead national nonprofit for two working groups: Jobs and Job Creation, and Community Economic Development.

### Volunteer Opportunities

Each individual community action agency handles its own volunteers and sets the criteria for recruiting, training, and utilizing volunteers, so opportunities vary.

### Contact Information

1140 Connecticut Avenue, NW, Suite 121
Washington, DC 20036
(202) 265-7546

E-mail: info@communityactionpartnership.com
www.communityactionpartnership.com

★

COMMUNITY DEVELOPMENT AND ECONOMIC JUSTICE

## FIELD MOBILIZATION DEPARTMENT OF THE AFL-CIO

Established in 1955, the American Federation of Labor and Congress of Industrial Organizations (AFL-CIO) is comprised of fifty-six national and international labor unions. This department within the AFL-CIO mobilizes members at the state and local levels to support organizing and political action. The department also coordinates the AFL-CIO's Community Services program, which provides training, information, and referral services to workers who face economic and other crises.

**Volunteer Opportunities**

Contact the organization for details.

**Contact Information**
**Headquarters:** 815 16th Street, NW | www.aflcio.org
Washington, DC 20006

---- ★ ----

## HABITAT FOR HUMANITY

Established in 1976, Habitat for Humanity is a nonprofit, ecumenical Christian housing ministry that seeks to eliminate poverty housing and homelessness from the world and to make decent shelter a matter of conscience and action. To accomplish these goals, Habitat invites people of all backgrounds, races, and religions to build houses together in partnership with families in need. Through volunteer labor and donations of money and materials, Habitat builds and rehabilitates simple, decent houses alongside its homeowner (partner) families. In addition, the organization monitors public policies related to housing, community, and international development, and advocates policy changes that increase access to decent, affordable housing for people around the world.

**Volunteer Opportunities**

Local opportunities include working in the office, building on-site, or renovating homes. Habitat also offers specific volunteer programs for youth and women. Visit the organization's website to find the nearest Habitat for Humanity in your area and learn of its opportunities.

Volunteers wishing to make a long-term commitment can work at the organization's international headquarters in Americus, Georgia, for two to six months, or participate in the Habitat AmeriCorps/VISTA program. Under the program, individuals ages eighteen and older live and work with local Habitat affiliates while earning living allowances and receiving an education award upon completion of service.

International opportunities are also available. Through the organization's Global Village Program, volunteers build decent, affordable housing around the world on short-term volunteer trips. The International Volunteer Program allows participants to spend six to twelve months working in Habitat offices overseas.

### Contact Information

**Operational Headquarters:** 121 Habitat Street
Americus, GA 31709-3498
(800) 422-4828

**Administrative Headquarters:** 270 Peachtree Street, NW, Suite 1300
Atlanta, GA 30303
(800) 422-4828
www.habitat.org

---

★

---

## NEIGHBOR TO NEIGHBOR (N2N)

Established in 1970, Neighbor to Neighbor (N2N) fosters stable housing and promotes housing opportunity through counseling, education, supportive services, and community partnerships for residents of Colorado.

### Volunteer Opportunities

The organization offers opportunities in northern Colorado for youth, adults, groups, service-learning students, interns, and court-referred volunteers. Online volunteer programs run weekdays during regular business hours, but special weekend and evening projects are also available. Areas in need of volunteers include landscaping, fund-raising, research, and both office and education support. Opportunities vary by location as follows:

*Loveland Office:* Volunteers and interns provide information and referral, greeting clients and answering phones, and providing screening for programs.

*Murphy Center:* Volunteers can help with Spanish translation for housing counseling sessions.

*Fort Collins Office:* Volunteers can assist with data entry, outcomes measurement, and mailings.

N2N also owns and manages affordable apartments in scattered-site communities around Larimer County. Volunteer groups can help with landscaping and property-improvement projects, such as community gardens. Volunteers under the age of sixteen must be accompanied by parent and/or guardian for their volunteer shifts. Interested individuals should contact Tracy Schwartz at (970) 488-2369, or tschwartz@n2n.org.

**Contact Information**

N2N operates in Colorado's Larimer County. The organization's website (www.n2n.org) provides additional contact details.

**Two locations in Fort Collins, CO:**

1550 Blue Spruce Drive
Fort Collins, CO 80524
(970) 484-7498
242 Conifer Street
Fort Collins, CO 80524

(970) 494-9940
**Loveland, CO, location:** 565 North
   Cleveland Avenue
Loveland, CO 80537
(970) 663-4163

------------------------------------ ★ ------------------------------------

# VOLUNTEERS IN SERVICE TO AMERICA (AMERICORPS VISTA)

AmeriCorps VISTA is the national service program designed specifically to fight poverty. Founded as Volunteers in Service to America in 1965 and incorporated into the AmeriCorps network of programs in 1993, VISTA has been on the front lines in the fight against poverty in America for more than forty years.

## Volunteer Opportunities

VISTA members commit to serve full-time for a year at a nonprofit organization or local government agency, working to fight illiteracy, improve health services, create businesses, strengthen community groups, and much more. During service, volunteers receive a modest living allowance, health care, and other benefits. And, upon completing your service, you can choose to receive either a Segal AmeriCorps Education Award or a post-service stipend.

See also "AmeriCorps" under Community Development and Economic Justice (page p. 112).

**Contact Information**

1201 New York Avenue, NW
Washington, DC 20525
(800) 942-2677 or TTY: (800) 833-3722

E-mail: questions@americorps.gov
www.americorps.gov/about/pro-
   grams/vista.asp

------------------------------------ ★ ------------------------------------

# VOLUNTEERS OF AMERICA

With thousands of human service programs, Volunteers of America, established in 1896, helps some of the country's most vulnerable groups and is one of the nation's largest nonprofit providers of quality, affordable housing for low- and moderate-income households. Integrating spirituality into their efforts, Volunteers of America is also an interdenominational church and considered an "auxiliary" to the universal Christian church, with a special mission of service. Volunteers of America provides services to people of all faiths, and works to better the lives of individuals returning from prison, people living with disabilities, the elderly, the homeless, and at-risk youth, among others.

## Volunteer Opportunities

Volunteers of America has thirty-eight offices across the country, offering many opportunities at the local level. Tasks include delivering Meals on Wheels to clients, providing administrative support, offering professional services (legal, public relations, training, motivational speaking), and managing other volunteers. Volunteering inquiries should be sent to tansmith@voa.org or volunteers@voa.org.

## Contact Information
**Headquarters:** 1660 Duke Street
Alexandria, VA 22314

(800) 899-0087 or (703) 341-5000
www.voa.org

★

# CONSUMER AFFAIRS

## AARP

Founded in 1958, AARP is a nonprofit, nonpartisan membership organization that helps people age fifty and over to improve the quality of their lives. AARP has offices in all fifty states, the District of Columbia, Puerto Rico, and the U.S. Virgin Islands. As a social welfare organization, as well as the nation's largest membership organization for people age fifty and over, AARP is leading a revolution in the way people view and live their lives.

### Volunteer Opportunities

Contact the organization for details.

### Contact Information

601 E Street, NW
Washington, DC 20049
(888) OUR-AARP (888-687-2277) or

TTY: (877) 434-7589
E-mail: member@aarp.org
www.aarp.org

---- ★ ----

## CONSUMERS UNION (CU)

Founded in 1936, Consumers Union (CU) is an expert, independent, nonprofit organization whose mission is to work for a fair, just, and safe marketplace for all consumers, and to empower consumers to protect themselves. CU publishes *Consumer Reports*, one of the top-ten-circulation magazines in the country, and ConsumerReports.org, in addition to two newsletters, *Consumer Reports on Health* and *Consumer Reports Money Adviser*. All of CU's work is informed by the more than 1 million readers who respond to its Annual Ballot & Questionnaire. In 2008, CU also launched several initiatives, including ConsumerReportsHealth.org and the Consumer Reports Health Ratings Center, which serve to educate and empower consumers to make more informed health-care decisions and to help change the market.

### Volunteer Opportunities

Contact the organization for details.

### Contact Information

101 Truman Avenue
Yonkers, NY 10703-1057

(914) 378-2000
www.consumersunion.org

---- ★ ----

## U.S. PUBLIC INTEREST RESEARCH GROUP (U.S. PIRG)

U.S. PIRG, the federation of state Public Interest Research Groups (PIRGs), stands up to powerful special interests on behalf of the American public, working to win concrete results for our health and our well-being. With a strong network of researchers, advocates, organizers, and students in state capitols across the country, it takes on special interests on issues such as product safety, political corruption, prescription drugs, and voting rights, where these interests stand in the way of reform and progress.

### Volunteer Opportunities

Each U.S. PIRG internship offers students a structured experience working one-on-one with one of U.S. PIRG's staff of advocates or campaign organizers—the intern's staff mentor. Interns learn basic skills that allow them to analyze issues and articulate solutions to the pressing problems of the day. Interns learn that activism and participation in the democratic process yield results. Though responsibilities vary, most internships include:

- Conducting research into critical public policy problems and preparing investigative reports;
- Coordinating media events, and assisting in the preparation of news releases and opinion pieces;
- Working with coalition partners and PIRG offices to coordinate grassroots campaign activities; and
- Monitoring the progress of legislation in Congress and the actions of federal agencies.

Interns may have the opportunity to attend local, regional, and national program briefings and trainings where they will learn more about public interest issues and gain political skills. Summer interns participate in "brown bag lunch" discussions with leaders within U.S. PIRG and the State PIRGs, as well as with leaders within other organizations.

Types of internships available include campaign, legislative, media, and administrative. For more information, visit www.uspirg.org, or contact Brian Walker, the internship coordinator, at (202) 546-9707 or dcinternships@pirg. org. Although U.S. PIRG internships are unpaid, students may receive academic credit from their college or university.

Internships are also available in the organization's state offices and on college campuses with PIRG student chapters. Other opportunities are listed on the website's Online Action Center, and include contacting local representatives.

### Contact Information

44 Winter Street, 4th Floor
Boston, MA 02108
(617) 747-4370

**Federal Advocacy Office:** 218 D Street, SE, 1st Floor
Washington, DC 20003-1900
(202) 546-9707   www.uspirg.org

★

# EDUCATION

## 826 NATIONAL

Cofounded by writer Dave Eggers, 826 National is a nonprofit tutoring, writing, and publishing organization with locations in eight cities across the country. Its goal is to assist students ages six to eighteen with their writing skills, and to help teachers get their classes excited about writing. The organization's work is based on the understanding that great leaps in learning can happen with one-on-one attention, and that strong writing skills are fundamental to future success.

Through volunteer support, each of the eight 826 National chapters provides drop-in tutoring, class field trips, writing workshops, and in-school programs—all free of charge. The 826 chapters are especially committed to supporting teachers, publishing student work, and offering services for English-language learners.

### Volunteer Opportunities

The 826 National centers use volunteers for running field trips, helping local students learn how to write stories, and assisting student writers during one of the organization's Young Authors' Book Programs.

In addition to support with writing projects, 826 National centers depend on their volunteers to help with more specialized tasks—grant writing, event coordination, outreach, website maintenance, training expertise (provided by credentialed-teacher and university-professor volunteers), computer hardware and software support, written and verbal bilingual translations, help with construction projects, book design and layout, marketing expertise, and a variety of other talent-demanding needs at different chapters.

### Contact Information

826 Valencia Street
San Francisco, CA 94110
(415) 642-5905 x204

www.826national.org
information@826national.org

★

**Name: Abigail Jacobs**

**Location: San Francisco, California**

**Organization: 826 National (Valencia)**

**Can you describe what you do as a volunteer for 826 Valencia?**

I am a drop-in tutor on Sundays; I teach a few different workshops through-out the year (one coming up is College Essay Writing); and I help with the development committee and in a few other ways here and there.

**What inspired you to volunteer?**

I was looking for a way to help out in my community. I love to read and write, and I love kids, so 826 Valencia seemed like a perfect fit. More important is what inspired me to continue volunteering, and that is the constant recognition and thanks that I get for everything I do at 826 Valencia. It's an incredible organization, and they really know how to keep their volunteers engaged.

**Is there a particular memorable moment you can recall as a volunteer at 826 Valencia?**

One of my favorite moments was the great personal statement week-end that 826 Valencia hosted for the first time last year. This was a weekend where any high school student who wanted help with their personal statement (college essay) could come and get one-on-one assistance from a tutor. We took over two computer labs at a local high school for the event, and we must have helped hundreds of students that weekend. Every one of them left with a better essay than when they walked in. It was really incredible to see the rooms full of tutors and students working in tandem

all day long, and the line out the door of students patiently waiting for a tutor's help.

**How has volunteering impacted your life?**

It's had a huge impact. First, and very simply, it has connected me with my community. I've met some incredible people, from the students we work with, to their parents, to the teachers in the classroom, to all the other volunteers and employees of 826 Valencia. It has opened up my eyes to the realities of our public education system and the struggles of teachers, parents, and students at underserved schools. And I've learned a lot about myself—how valuable my skills can be, and what an impact an hour of my time can have in someone else's life.

**What advice would you give to someone who was considering doing volunteer work in their community?**

Do it! Find an organization where your skills will be put to work and appreciated. You won't regret it.

---

★

---

## BEHIND THE BOOK

Behind the Book's mission is to excite children and young adults about reading. Working with low-income students in New York City's K–12 public schools, Behind the Book brings authors and their books into individual classrooms to build literacy skills and nurture a new generation of book readers. The organization was founded in 2003 by a part-time school librarian.

### Volunteer Opportunities

Each of Behind the Book's programs occurs during school hours in a small classroom setting, is taught as part of the class curriculum, incorporates multiple author visits and a writing project, and includes book donations to students and the school library. There are a number of ways you can help as a volunteer:

As a volunteer that helps with author visits in the classroom, you may assist students in crafting stories, writing essays, and/or producing other projects; or, you may take photographs of the classroom in action which will be posted on the Behind the Book and sponsor websites. (Note: No previous experience working or volunteering in classrooms is necessary, as Behind the Book and school staff are present in the classrooms at all times and will be there to help guide you.)

As a volunteer that helps in the office, you may conduct community media outreach and public relations, or, you may extend Behind the Book's community outreach by building classroom/community partnerships, creating relationships with local businesses, and liaising with local political leaders.

If you choose to volunteer in the classroom, please note that each author visit lasts from one and a half to two hours. Typically, volunteers work with the same group of students in the same classroom for three to five author visits, which will be spaced over one to three months. As a volunteer, you will not only experience, but also be integral to, the program from beginning to end.

For volunteer work outside of the classroom, Behind the Book will work with you to establish a schedule of equivalent time.

Interested individuals should contact the organization at volunteer .behindthebook@gmail.com to request a volunteer application. In the body of the e-mail, please identify which volunteer opportunity you are most interested in (classroom or office). You and a member of the Behind the Book team will coordinate an activity that best suits your schedule and abilities.

### Contact Information

145 West 96th Street, Suite 1E
New York, NY 10025

(212) 222-3627
www.behindthebook.org

--------------------------------- ★ ---------------------------------

## EDUCATORS FOR SOCIAL RESPONSIBILITY (ESR)

Established in 1982, the goal of ESR is to improve America's education system by working directly with educators to employ practices that create safe, caring, and equitable schools. ESR provides professional development and training, consultation, and educational resources to adults who teach young people in preschool through high school. The organization's online teacher center offers educators resources on topics ranging from security, conflict resolution, peacemaking, violence prevention, and others.

### Volunteer Opportunities

ESR occasionally uses volunteers for administrative tasks (which is of great benefit to the small organization). Most of its non-staff positions are filled with paid work-study students. ESR is located very close to several universities with schools of education, which allows it to offer students an opportunity

EDUCATION

to work with the organization while in their educational program. Volunteers and work-study students engage in research, provide administrative support, and carry out other duties as needed in our fund-raising, publications, and professional services departments.

Training is available for all of ESR's work-study participants and volunteers in the discrete tasks they're asked to do. Some tasks require a level of prior experience; for example, experience with book-design software would be helpful with assisting the organization with a publishing project.

While there is no official time commitment, ESR asks that volunteers be prepared to remain until a particular project is completed, if possible.

### Contact Information

23 Garden Street
Cambridge, MA 02138
(617) 492-1764 or (800) 370-2515

E-mail: educators@esrnational.org
www.esrnational.org

------------------------------------ ★ ------------------------------------

## FIRST BOOK

First Book provides new books to children in need, addressing one of the most important factors affecting literacy—access to books.

### Volunteer Opportunities

Volunteers can serve on First Book advisory boards. These are committees of volunteers, representing a community or campus, that come together to raise awareness and funds in order to provide new books to local literacy programs serving children from low-income families. There are more than 270 advisory boards nationwide, and you can visit the organization's website to find one in your community. It is also possible to start an advisory board if one does not already exist in your area.

### Contact Information

1319 F Street, NW, Suite 1000
Washington, DC 20004-1155

(202) 393-12222
www.firstbook.org

------------------------------------ ★ ------------------------------------

## PARENTS FOR PUBLIC SCHOOLS (PPS)

Established in 1991, parents for Public Schools (PPS) is a national organization of community-based chapters working with public school parents and other supporters to improve and strengthen local public schools.

## Volunteer Opportunities

PPS has fifteen chapters across the country that work with volunteers. Also, its national office in Mississippi has a statewide program in place for volunteers. Tasks and projects vary by chapter, but may include working in outreach, mentoring programs, arts programs, and in the promotion and marketing of public schools in the community. Individuals not living near a chapter of PPS can contact the organization to learn details about how to form a new chapter.

### Contact Information

200 North Congress Street, Suite 500
Jackson, MS 39216
(800) 880-1222 or (601) 969-6936

E-mail: ppschapter@parents4
  publicschools.org
www.parents4publicschools.com

---

★

---

# PROLITERACY WORLDWIDE, INC.

ProLiteracy was born when two of the leading adult literacy organizations, Literacy Volunteers of America and Laubach Literacy International, merged in August 2002. With the help of their network of organizational and individual members, ProLiteracy is able to promote literacy in all fifty states and the District of Columbia. The organization helps strengthen the programs that are teaching adults to read, write, compute, use technology, and learn English as a new language. ProLiteracy also advocates for public policies and legislation that benefit adult learners and the people and programs that serve them.

## Volunteer Opportunities

Most of ProLiteracy's approximately 1,000 local member organizations are heavily dependent on their volunteers. They recruit volunteers to tutor adults, help organize and staff fund-raisers, become board members, and assist with administrative tasks. Other opportunities are possible and vary by each individual organization's needs. Volunteers who are interested in becoming adult literacy tutors must complete eighteen hours of training and make a commitment to meet with their student for two hours a week for at least one year. ProLiteracy has a search function on its website to help potential volunteers (and students) locate a program in their area.

### Contact Information

**Headquarters:** 1320 Jamesville
  Avenue
Syracuse, NY 13210

(315) 422-9121 or (888) 528-2224
E-mail: info@proliteracy.org
www.proliteracy.org

---

★

---

EDUCATION

## PUBLICOLOR

Officially incorporated in 1996, Publicolor is a New York City–based not-for-profit that engages at-risk students in their education and empowers them to plan and prepare for college and career. Through its gateway program, Paint Club, Publicolor teaches students the skill of commercial painting, with the belief that transforming environments—such as public schools and community centers—with vibrant colors transforms the attitudes and behaviors of the people who use these spaces. In addition, Publicolor provides youth development programs, including weekly career exposure and life skills workshops for middle and high school students, and one-on-one tutoring and mentoring sessions for college students. College scholarships are also offered through the organization.

### Volunteer Opportunities

Publicolor does not take on individual volunteers, but it welcomes volunteers (ages thirteen and up) from corporations, colleges, churches, and established volunteer organizations. Volunteers serve as mentors for students during painting projects, and work every Saturday during the academic school year and Tuesdays through Thursdays during July and August.

### Contact Information

149 Madison Avenue, Suite 1201
New York, NY 10016
(212) 213-6121

E-mail: volunteers@publicolor.org
www.publicolor.org

★

## ROCK 'N' ROLL CAMP FOR GIRLS

The Rock 'n' Roll Camp for Girls builds girls' self-esteem through music creation and performance. Providing workshops and technical training, it creates leadership opportunities, cultivates a supportive community of peers and mentors, and encourages social change and the development of life skills. The organization serves girls ages eight to seventeen.

### Volunteer Opportunities

The Rock 'n' Roll Camp for Girls is almost entirely volunteer-run, with summer and year-round camp opportunities available. Positions include helping with Girls Rock Institute, Summer Camp, and Ladies Rock Camp programs; grant writing/research; supporting shifts with the front desk; administrative assistance; procuring a variety of donations; outreach; data entry; gear and music librarian; and store/record label merchandise manager. The Summer Camp program has full- and part-time positions for female mentor volunteers as college-level intern program coordinators, band coaches, band managers, workshop leaders, and instrument instructors. Male and female volunteer positions are available for roadies/gear management, craft/food service, maintenance/janitor, publicity/outreach, receptionists, and administrative support.

The organization has affiliates in many cities in the U.S. Visit the Girls Rock Camp Alliance web page (www.girlsrockcampalliance.org) for contact information. Volunteer opportunities vary by location.

### Contact Information

P.O. Box 11324
Portland, OR 97211
(503) 445-4991

E-mail: Get_involved@girlsrockcamp
.org
www.girlsrockcamp.org

---- ★ ----

## TEACH FOR AMERICA

Established in 1989, Teach for America aims to eliminate educational inequity by enlisting recent college graduates to teach in low-income public schools through the country in both rural and urban environments. The organization provides training and support to college graduates to help them become leaders in an effort to expand educational opportunity.

### Volunteer Opportunities

Prospective participants must submit an online application (available at www.teachforamerica.org), and if chosen for the program, attend a rigorous five-week summer training session in one of eight locations (New York, Los Angeles, Philadelphia, Chicago, Atlanta, Houston, Phoenix, and Mississippi Delta) before beginning to teach.

### Contact Information

315 West 36th Street, 7th Floor
New York, NY 10018

(212) 279-2080 or (800) 832-1230
www.teachforamerica.org

---- ★ ----

# ENVIRONMENT AND SUSTAINABLE COMMUNITIES

## AMERICAN RIVERS (AR)

American Rivers is a conservation organization that protects and restores America's rivers for the benefit of people, wildlife, and nature. Founded in 1973, American Rivers has more than 65,000 members and supporters, with offices in Washington, D.C., and nationwide.

### Volunteer Opportunities

American Rivers is always looking for volunteer help, which can take many forms. Individuals interested in helping their community can work with American Rivers to clean up a local river. American Rivers will provide trash bags, guidance on organizing the event, and help with promoting the event. This can be done whether the person lives near an AR office or not. People can also volunteer to participate in an already-established event by visiting the organization's website.

Individuals with less time can volunteer to become e-activists. These are people who receive action alerts via e-mail when a particular piece of legislation is being introduced. AR asks these volunteers to write their congressperson or senator in support of the bill.

In the spring, summer, and fall, American Rivers brings on several unpaid interns to learn about the inner workings of an environmental nonprofit, including lobbying, communications, and conservation work. Housing is not provided.

AR welcomes any interested participants to contact the organization to see if their schedule and skills are a good fit for AR's current needs. Potential volunteers are also encouraged to visit AR's website, friend the organization on Facebook, and/or follow it on Twitter. Contact a local office directly to learn more about its opportunities.

### Contact Information

**Headquarters:** 1101 14th Street, NW, Suite 1400
Washington, DC 20005
(202) 347-7550

E-mail: outreach@americanrivers.org
www.americanrivers.org

## CENTER FOR HEALTH, ENVIRONMENT AND JUSTICE (CHEJ)

The Center for Health, Environment and Justice (CHEJ) is a national environmental organization founded and led by Lois Gibbs, the woman responsible for the relocation of 900 families due to a leaking toxic waste dump in Love Canal, New York. CHEJ is committed to helping communities protect themselves from exposure to dangerous environmental chemicals in the air, water, and soil. Since it was founded about thirty years ago, CHEJ has worked with thousands of organizations and groups, providing the research, advice, and leadership skills necessary to keep families and communities safe. The organization also builds nationwide collaborative initiatives and advocates for responsible corporate behavior. It has been instrumental in persuading the McDonald's corporation to move away from using Styrofoam packaging, and Microsoft to move away from utilizing PVC plastic in their products.

### Volunteer Opportunities

Though CHEJ does not have a formal volunteer program in place, it does welcome individuals who wish to support the organization's mission. Volunteers can work in the national office, in CHEJ's regional offices in Albany, New York, and Columbus, Ohio, or remotely in certain cases. Volunteers typically assist with office work and mailings, but web developer help is also needed. Project-based work utilizing the volunteer's specific skills is also a possibility.

### Contact Information

P.O. Box 6806
Falls Church, VA 22040-6806
(703) 237-2249

E-mail: chej@chej.org
www.chej.org

★

## COUNCIL FOR RESPONSIBLE GENETICS (CRG)

Established in 1983, CRG is a nonprofit, nongovernmental organization that works through the media and concerned citizens to distribute information and represent the public interest on emerging issues in biotechnology. The organization fosters public debate about the social, ethical, and environmental implications of genetic technologies, and publishes a bimonthly magazine, *GeneWatch*, on such issues. The publication has covered a broad spectrum of topics, from genetically engineered foods to biological weapons, genetic privacy and discrimination, reproductive technologies, and human cloning.

### Volunteer Opportunities

CRG offers unpaid internship opportunities to qualified undergraduate and graduate students during the summer and the academic year. Interns work with senior staff and board members on individual research, writing, or outreach projects in specific program areas.

ENVIRONMENT AND SUSTAINABLE COMMUNITIES

Internships are available part-time during the school year (September–December, January intersession, and February–May), and part- or full-time during the summer (June–August). Because the position is unpaid, interns' schedules are flexible. Interns are required to meet with their supervisor on a regular basis during the internship period. Interviews are scheduled by phone or in person at the CRG office in Cambridge, Massachusetts.

Requirements include computer literacy (Mac OS, Microsoft Office), organizational skills, familiarity with Internet research, and good academic standing. Interns should be able to work five hours a week at the CRG office in Cambridge, Massachusetts, or in New York City.

## Contact Information

**Massachusetts Office**: 5 Upland Road, Suite 3
Cambridge MA 02140
(617) 868-0870
E-mail: crg@gene-watch.org
www.councilforresponsiblegenetics.org

**New York Office:** 30 Broad Street, 30th Floor
New York, NY 10004
(212) 361-6360
www.councilforresponsiblegenetics.org

★

## EARTH ISLAND INSTITUTE (EII)

Established in 1982, EII acts as an umbrella organization, providing support to individual environmental projects by offering a wide range of professional services, from fiscal administration and program management to office space and equipment. EII also publishes a quarterly magazine, *Earth Island Journal,* that offers how-to on environmental activism, hosts an annual awards ceremony through their New Leaders Initiative that highlights the accomplishments of youth working for sustainability, and funds community-based coastal protection and wetland restoration efforts in Southern California.

### Volunteer Opportunities

Opportunities in the Berkeley office range from event assistance to office assistance. Volunteers working on events perform tasks such as greeting guests, sign-in, setup, breakdown, registration, and ushering. For office assistance, volunteers typically proofread, assist with filing, reception, mailings, and pre-event coordination.

Earth Island is also a fiscal sponsor for many projects worldwide. Each project has its own volunteers who perform numerous tasks. Some of the many current projects under Earth Island sponsorship include the Global Service

Corps, which provides service-learning opportunities for adult volunteer participants to live and work on environmental, health, and social justice projects in developing countries, and Green Café Network, which is dedicated to addressing America's overconsumption by "greening" the coffeehouse industry at the grassroots level.

For more information, contact Claudia West, volunteer manager, at volunteer@earthisland.org.

**Contact Information**
2150 Allston Way, Suite 460
Berkeley, CA 94704-1375

(510) 859-9100
www.earthisland.org

---- ★ ----

## ENVIRONMENT AMERICA

Environment America is a federation of state-based, citizen-funded environmental advocacy organizations. Its professional staff in twenty-nine states and Washington, D.C., combines independent research, practical ideas, and tough-minded advocacy to overcome the opposition of powerful special interests and win real results for the environment. Environment America draws on thirty years of success in tackling environmental problems.

**Volunteer Opportunities**
Contact the organization for details.

**Contact Information**
44 Winter Street, 4th Floor
Boston, MA 02108
(617) 747-4449
**Federal Advocacy Office:** 218 D
  Street, SE

Washington, DC 20003
(202) 683-1250
E-mail: info@environmentamerica
  .org
www.environmentamerica.org

---- ★ ----

## FRIENDS OF THE EARTH (FOE)

With a network of grassroots groups in seventy-seven countries, FOE supports individuals and organizations who are working to ensure a healthy environment in their communities. Established in 1969, its current campaigns focus on clean energy and solutions to global warming; protecting people from toxic and new, potentially harmful technologies; and promoting low-pollution transportation alternatives. FOE's accomplishments through the years include reforming the World Bank to address environmental and human rights concerns, fostering a debate on global warming, stopping more than 150 destructive dams and water projects worldwide, banning international whaling, and winning landmark regulations for strip mines and oil tankers.

## Volunteer Opportunities

Most opportunities for volunteers are not based in an FOE office, but revolve around advocating for environmental causes, sometimes in the comfort of one's own home. FOE provides individuals with the tools to play an active role in shaping public policies that affect the environment. FOE's website offers instruction on how to support national campaigns, such as the Clean Air Act, by organizing letter-writing campaigns, scheduling meeting with members of Congress, and contacting local newspaper editors.

## Contact Information

| | |
|---|---|
| 1100 15th Street, NW, 11th Floor | www.foe.org |
| Washington, DC 20005 | 311 California Street, Suite 510 |
| (202) 783-7400 | San Francisco, CA 94104 |
| | (415) 544-0790 or (877) 843-8687 |

★

# GREENPEACE

Established in 1971, Greenpeace is an independent campaigning organization that uses peaceful direct action and creative communication to expose global environmental problems and to promote solutions that are essential to a green and peaceful future. Topics of interest include sustainable agriculture, nuclear energy, and global warming.

## Volunteer Opportunities

The organization is looking for people to join its National Activist Network, an alliance of volunteer leaders who take bold action to protect the planet in coordination with Greenpeace's highest-priority campaigns. The Network is made up of Lead Activists who build grassroots power on hundreds of campuses and in thousands of communities nationwide to help Greenpeace save the climate, stop deforestation, fight for the whales, and much more. As part of the Network, you can connect with your own team of grassroots organizers to make a difference in your community. Opportunities are available for people ages fourteen and up. Greenpeace asks that interested individuals complete an online contact form, available on their website.

Internships are also available every spring, summer, and fall in a number of cities and in all parts of the Greenpeace organization. Positions range from organization to photography to administration and everything in between. As a Greenpeace intern, you will help promote solutions to the global warming crisis, stop the destruction of the world's last ancient forests, empower consumers and shareholders to hold corporate polluters accountable, and save the whales and other endangered species. Interns receive training in corporate campaigning, nonviolent direct action, media relations, materials production, and grassroots outreach. All internships are unpaid, and interns are responsible for covering their own travel and housing. The organization strongly encourages applications from women, people of color, and other underrepresented communities.

### Contact Information
702 H Street, NW, Suite 300
Washington, DC 20001
(202) 462-1177

E-mail: info@wdc.greenpeace.org
www.greenpeace.org

★

## THE NATURE CONSERVANCY
Established in 1951, The Nature Conservancy is an organization that strives to protect ecologically important lands and waters around the world. By partnering with groups such as indigenous communities, businesses, governments, and other nonprofits, The Nature Conservancy operates more than a hundred marine conservation projects globally and addresses threats to preservation that include climate change, fire, and marine ecosystems.

### Volunteer Opportunities
Indoor opportunities are available on weekdays and consist of administrative assistance in one of The Nature Conservancy's offices. Outdoor projects are scheduled on both weekdays and weekends, and call on volunteers to perform a range of tasks including trail development and monitoring visitor facilities in preserves. Visit www.nature.org to learn about opportunities in your area.

### Contact Information
**Headquarters:** 4245 North Fairfax
Drive, Suite 100

Arlington, VA 22203-1606
(703) 841-5300 or (800) 628-6860

★

## PESTICIDE ACTION NETWORK NORTH AMERICA (PANNA)
Established in 1982, PANNA links local and international consumer, labor, health, environment, and agriculture groups in a global network to fight the proliferation of pesticides. It promotes ecologically sound and socially responsible alternatives to hazardous pesticides, and works to ensure that people—as well as the soil, water, and air—are free from pesticides, and that information and resources regarding the issue are available worldwide.

ENVIRONMENT AND SUSTAINABLE COMMUNITIES

**Volunteer Opportunities**

PANNA is looking for volunteers and interns who share a commitment to environmental and social justice issues and a special interest in pesticide reform. Volunteer opportunities depend entirely on the needs of the organization at any given time, whereas interns typically perform tasks such as research, writing, editing and updating web pages, participating in team meetings and programming, data entry, and event planning.

**Contact Information**

49 Powell Street, Suite 500
San Francisco, CA 94102

(415) 981-1771
www.panna.org

★

## RAINFOREST ACTION NETWORK (RAN)

Established in 1985, RAN seeks to protect rain forests through grassroots organizing, public education, and nonviolent action campaigns. It works with environmental and human rights groups in sixty countries to coordinate the role of the U.S. in the security of rain forests and their inhabitants. RAN supports the efforts of activists in rain forest countries, seeks to transform government and corporate policies, and places public pressure on American organizations that refuse to adopt responsible environmental policies.

**Volunteer Opportunities**

Contact the organization for details.

**Contact Information**

**Headquarters:** 221 Pine Street, 5th
   Floor
San Francisco, CA 94104

(415) 398-4404
E-mail: rainforest@ran.org
www.ran.org

★

## SIERRA CLUB

Established in 1892, the Sierra Club is one of the oldest and largest grassroots environmental organizations in the U.S., and aims to protect communities, wild places, and the Earth. Its current initiatives include increasing sustainable transportation options; limiting greenhouse emissions; decreasing the reliance on coal; strengthening wetlands, forests, and barrier islands; and protecting wildlife habitats from climate change. In addition, Sierra Club's mission includes the educating and enlisting of humanity to protect and restore the quality of the natural and human environment.

## Volunteer Opportunities

Sierra Club is a volunteer-based organization. Every state, plus Puerto Rico, has a Sierra Club chapter which is comprised of local groups. Most major cities have a group, which is often the best first interface for potential volunteers.

Sierra Club engages in policy campaigns, lobbying, and activism, and develops outdoor activities and community service projects. All of these areas provide opportunities for volunteers. While there are more volunteer "leadership" opportunities for members, you do not have to be a member to volunteer.

On the local level, there are various types of opportunities. Most local groups participate in "service outings," which combine an outdoor activity (such as hiking) with a community service (like park maintenance). Sierra Club also has programs to give inner-city youth outdoor experiences, and is always looking for volunteers to help. There are even "volunteer vacations" that allow volunteers to travel around the country or around the world, providing service while on the trip.

A particular local policy campaign could be anything from a fight to protect a local wetland from development, to lobbying for a new public transit system or clean-air laws, to taking on an outdated coal-power plant. These kinds of activities need volunteers at all levels, from walking door to door, to creating materials, to showing up at public hearings and voicing your opinion. These campaigns can last from a few weeks to a few years, and can greatly vary in scale. Large campaigns will have multiple levels of volunteer involvement and will include training for everything from technical environmental policy to organizing tactics and media skills. Sierra Club also participates in local, state, and federal elections, and looks for volunteers to assist with public education and get-out-the-vote efforts.

In addition, there is an array of online volunteer opportunities, which can include sending e-mails to members of Congress, participating in a phone-bank operation from your own home, writing letters to the editor, and much more. Visit the organization's website for more information on their numerous volunteer opportunities.

## Contact Information

**Headquarters:** 85 Second Street,
2nd Floor
San Francisco, CA 94105

(415) 977-5500
E-mail: information@sierraclub.org
www.sieraclub.org

★

ENVIRONMENT AND SUSTAINABLE COMMUNITIES

## TRUST FOR PUBLIC LAND (TPL)

Established in 1972, TPL is a national land conservation organization that preserves natural and historic spaces—such as parks, community gardens, and rural lands—for human enjoyment. TPL's federal affairs team works with government and other conservation groups by providing information and guidance about federal policy and funding resources. The organization also helps community groups by identifying lands to be protected, locating funding for conservation projects, offering education, and negotiating land transactions.

### Volunteer Opportunities

TPL's regional offices occasionally have volunteer opportunities; details for specific positions are routinely listed on their website. Skills they are usually in need of include general administration and coordination, research and report writing, marketing, and fund-raising. All interested individuals are encouraged to send a brief cover letter and résumé to volunteers@tpl.org, in hopes that a unique opportunity can be designed around an office's needs and the volunteer's skill sets.

### Contact Information

**National Office:** 116 New
   Montgomery Street, 4th Floor
San Francisco, CA 94105

(415) 495-4014 or (800) 714-LAND
www.tpl.org

★

## WORLD WIDE OPPORTUNITIES ON ORGANIC FARMS (WWOOF)

Established in 1971 as an international organization, WWOOF operates as an exchange, connecting people who wish to volunteer on organic farms with farmers who are looking for help.

### Volunteer Opportunities

WWOOF provides its members (membership fee is $30 per year) with listings of volunteer opportunities on farms in the U.S. and around the world that grow food without the use of synthetic or chemical amendments. Volunteers help farmers with a variety of tasks, ranging from animal care to gardening for an agreed-upon number of hours per day. Volunteers usually live as part of their host's family and are provided free food and accommodations, as well as knowledge about ecological farming practices.

**Contact Information**
**WWOOF USA:** 430 Forest Avenue
Laguna Beach, CA 92651
(949) 715-9500

E-mail: info@wwoofusa.org
www.wwoofusa.org

-------------------------------------- ★ --------------------------------------

ENVIRONMENT AND SUSTAINABLE COMMUNITIES

# FREE SPEECH AND GOVERNMENT ACCOUNTABILITY

## AMERICAN CIVIL LIBERTIES UNION (ACLU)

The ACLU is the nation's guardian of liberty, working daily in courts, legislatures, and communities to defend and preserve the individual rights and liberties that the Constitution and laws of the United States guarantee everyone in this country. These rights include the First Amendment, equal protection under the law, due process, and privacy. The ACLU also works to extend rights to segments of the population that have traditionally been denied their rights, including people of color; women; lesbians, gay men, bisexuals, and transgender people; prisoners; and people with disabilities.

### Volunteer Opportunities

Interested individuals can check out the ACLU Action Center on the organization's website for downloadable material, action alerts, and for information and suggestions for activists.

### Contact Information

125 Broad Street, 18th Floor
New York, NY 10004

(212) 549-2500
www.aclu.org

★

## COMMON CAUSE

Established in 1970, Common Cause operates as a vehicle for citizens to make their voices heard in the political process, and to hold their elected leaders accountable to the public interest. The organization remains committed to honest, open, and accountable government and serves as a watchdog against corruption and abuse of power. Along with its sister organization, the Common Cause Education Fund, Common Cause employs grassroots organizing, coalition building, research, policy development, public education, lobbying, and litigation to win reform at all levels of government.

### Volunteer Opportunities

Common Cause welcomes volunteers to join its "Washington Connection" program at the organization's national headquarters in downtown D.C. Volunteers work with Common Cause activists across the country to build grassroots pressure on elected officials on critical issues. Opportunities are also available for individuals who would like to help with administrative tasks in Common Cause's human resources, accounting, or membership services departments. Many volunteers work a shift between 10:00 AM and 4:00 PM on Tuesdays or Wednesdays, but Common Cause also has opportunities after 5:00 PM at certain points during the year. Many of its state offices also welcome volunteers, so interested individuals are encouraged to contact their state office directly (information is available on their website), or to contact Betty Brossy at (202) 833-1200.

**Contact Information**
**Headquarters:** 1133 19th Street, NW, 9th Floor
Washington, DC 20036

(202) 833-1200
www.commoncause.org

## NATIONAL COALITION AGAINST CENSORSHIP (NCAC)
Established in 1974, NCAC opposes the suppression of information and strives to facilitate the creation of a more hospitable environment for free speech and artist freedom. An alliance of fifty literary, artistic, religious, educational, professional, labor, and civil liberties groups, NCAC provides resources and advocacy support to individuals and organizations responding to censorship.

### Volunteer Opportunities
NCAC seeks volunteers and interns with computer skills who are interested in its mission to protect freedom of speech. Most volunteers work out of the organization's New York City office, but location, as well as tasks and time commitment, is discussed with the program's supervisor. Interested individuals are encouraged to e-mail a cover letter and résumé to ncac@ncac.org.

**Contact Information**
275 7th Avenue, #1504
New York, NY 10001

(212) 807-6222
E-mail: ncac@ncac.org
www.ncac.org

## PEOPLE FOR THE AMERICAN WAY (PFAW) AND PFAW FOUNDATION
Established in 1980, People for the American Way is dedicated to preserving constitutional rights, opposing bigotry, and encouraging civic and political participation. Areas of interest include defending public education, religion, and reproductive freedom while challenging censorship and discrimination of all kinds.

**Volunteer Opportunities**

Interested individuals can join PFAW's e-mail list through its website, to receive updates on ways to get involved.

**Contact Information**

2000 M Street, NW, Suite 400　|　(202) 467-4999
Washington, DC 20036　　　　　|　www.pfaw.org

---　★　---

# PROJECT VOTE

Project Vote is a nonpartisan organization that works to increase voting participation among low-income, minority, youth, and other underrepresented groups. Since 1982, Project Vote has helped to register more than 5.6 million Americans in low-income and minority communities through programs such as Get Out the Vote. The organization also applies research, legal services, and advocacy to ensure that marginalized groups are not prevented from registering and voting.

**Volunteer Opportunities**

Contact the organization for details.

**Contact Information**

737 1/2 8th Street, SE　|　(202) 546-4173 or (800) 546-8683
Washington, DC, 20003　|　www.projectvote.org

---　★　---

# PUBLIC CITIZEN

Founded by Ralph Nader in 1971, Public Citizen represents the consumer public against special interest and corporate lobbyists. Public Citizen describes itself as the "countervailing force to corporate power," and has challenged abusive practices by the pharmaceutical, nuclear, and automobile industries. It currently has five policy groups in place: the Congress Watch division, the Energy Program, the Global Trade Watch division, the Health Research Group, and the Litigation Group.

**Volunteer Opportunities**

Public Citizen has multiple opportunities available, usually for organized events such as bank protests, or for contacting members of Congress. Interested individuals should sign up at www.citizen.org to receive news on upcoming events.

**Contact Information**

Main Office: 1600 20th Street, NW
Washington, DC 20009

(202) 588-1000
www.citizen.org

★

## THE RUCKUS SOCIETY

Established in 1995, The Ruckus Society provides resources to environmental, and human rights, and social justice activists and organizations. Through its own training camps or via personalized sessions requested by communities, The Ruckus Society helps people learn the skills they need to practice nonviolent direct action. Material covered includes action planning, media outreach, building leadership and political analysis, and nonviolent philosophy and practice.

**Volunteer Opportunities**

Contact the organization for details.

**Contact Information**

P.O. Box 28741
Oakland, CA 94604
(510) 931-6339

E-mail: ruckus@ruckus.org
www.ruckus.org

★

# GAY AND LESBIAN RIGHTS

## GAY, LESBIAN AND STRAIGHT EDUCATION NETWORK (GLSEN)

Established in 1993, GLSEN works with educators, policymakers, community leaders, and students to combat homophobia in the education system. The network strives to protect students from harassment, to empower principals to make their schools safer, and to build the skills of educators to teach respect for all people. Among its campaigns, the organization sponsors National Day of Silence, an event that addresses anti-LGBT name-calling and bullying in schools, and the annual No Name-Calling Week, which consists of educational activities that provide schools with the tools to eliminate bullying in their communities.

### Volunteer Opportunities

Contact the organization for details.

### Contact Information

**National Headquarters:** 90 Broad Street, 2nd Floor New York, NY 10004

(212) 727-0135
E-mail: glsen@glsen.org
www.glsen.org

## INTERNATIONAL GAY AND LESBIAN HUMAN RIGHTS COMMISSION (IGLHRC)

Established in 1991, IGLHRC advocates for human rights on behalf of people who experience discrimination or abuse on the basis of their sexual orientation, gender identity, or expression. IGLHRC works with local activists and partners by monitoring and responding to human rights violations against lesbians, gay men, bisexuals, transgender and intersex people, and others whose identities do not fit the LGBTI paradigm. The commission's goals are to advocate for the elimination of discriminatory laws and practices, and to support the implementation of antidiscrimination policies. IGLHRC also strives to reduce family-, community-, and state-sanctioned violence, and to promote economic, social, and cultural rights.

### Volunteer Opportunities

Internships are available for undergraduate and graduate students in IGLHRC's New York office, as well as in its offices in Cape Town, South Africa, and Buenos Aires, Argentina. Interns in the New York office mostly perform research and writing tasks (responsibilities are commonly based on an individual's skills), and are required to commit at least two full days per week. The international offices do not have structured programs but are willing to discuss possibilities with potential interns.

**Contact Information**

80 Maiden Lane, Suite 1505
New York, NY 10038
(212) 430-6054

E-mail: iglhrc@iglhrc.org
www.iglhrc.org

★

## NATIONAL GAY AND LESBIAN TASK FORCE (NGLTF)

NGLTF works to build the grassroots power of the lesbian, gay, bisexual, and transgender (LGBT) community by providing training and support to activists and state and local organizations seeking to advance pro-LGBT politics. NGLTF's Action Fund lobbies to defeat anti-LGBT ballot initiatives and legislation and to pass pro-LGBT legislation and other measures. It also analyzes and reports on the positions of candidates for public office on issues of importance to the LGBT community. Established in 1973, the Task Force is the oldest national LGBT organization.

### Volunteer Opportunities

There are myriad volunteer opportunities at the Task Force, and each of its six offices (D.C., New York City, Cambridge, Miami, Minneapolis, and LA) utilizes volunteers. Its development team works with volunteers on special events, such as the Winter Party Festival, the Miami Recognition Dinner, and the D.C. Recognition Dinner. The Academy for Leadership and Action collaborates with volunteers to train local grassroots activists to work on phone banks, campaigns, and fund-raising efforts. Volunteers help with NGLTF's public policy and government affairs team on phone banks to call legislators and voters to support efforts to attain LGBT equality. Volunteers are also an important component of the National Conference on LGBT Equality: Creating Change and NGLTF's faith work department, which has training throughout the U.S. and an annual conference of pro-LGBT people of faith. Time commitment is flexible, with opportunities available during business hours as well as nights and weekends. Volunteers mostly do work around the foundation, but occasionally contribute to the Action Fund when it's related to policy or advocacy.

### Contact Information

1325 Massachusetts Avenue, NW,
    Suite 600
Washington, DC 20005

(202) 393-2241
E-mail: info@thetaskforce.org
www.thetaskforce.org

★

GAY AND LESBIAN RIGHTS

# HEALTH CARE, HUNGER, AND HOMELESSNESS

## BREAD FOR THE WORLD

Established in 1972, Bread for the World strives to end hunger in the United States and abroad with its network of individual members, churches, and Christian denominations. The organization mobilizes individuals to raise awareness about hunger and poverty, and provides tools for advocacy, including tips on media outreach and event organizing. Members write to and meet with members of Congress in an effort to change policies and programs. Its partner organization, Bread for the World Institute, provides education and research, and publishes an annual report on hunger.

### Volunteer Opportunities

The organization encourages those interested in eradicating hunger to write to Congress and to engage their local church in supporting Bread for the World's mission. Resources for advocacy and education are provided at www.bread.org.

### Contact Information

50 F Street, NW, Suite 500
Washington, DC 20001
(202) 639-9400 or (800) 822-7323

www.bread.org
bread@bread.org

★

## BRIGHT PINK

Bright Pink is a national nonprofit organization that provides education and support to young women who are at high risk for breast and ovarian cancer. It arms young women with knowledge and options, and offers companionship and empathy during their journey.

### Volunteer Opportunities

Bright Pink depends on its volunteers to help further its mission, so there are many ways to get involved. Interested individuals can visit Bright Pink's website to join its network and sign up to volunteer. A volunteer coordinator will be in contact with details about a local active chapter or about beginning a new chapter in your area.

In Bright Pink's Chicago headquarters, there are monthly volunteer orientations at 6:00 PM on the first Wednesday of each month for new volunteers. For those interested in volunteering in Chicago, attending one of these meetings is mandatory. E-mail emily@bebrightpink.org for more information on upcoming orientations and to get involved in the Chicago chapter.

**Contact Information**

400 N. State Street, Suite 230
Chicago, IL 60654

E-mail: welcome@bebrightpink.org
www.bebrightpink.org

★

## DAILY BREAD

Established in 1983, the Daily Bread project is an entirely volunteer-run, grassroots organization in California that picks up nutritious surplus food from local restaurants, bakeries, caterers, and markets and brings the food to local free-food kitchens, pantries, and shelters.

### Volunteer Opportunities

Daily Bread offers volunteer opportunities for people who can transport food to recipient organizations. Daytime, evening, weekday, and weekend opportunities are available throughout Berkeley, Oakland, and Richmond, California.

**Contact Information**

(510) 526-3123

www.facebook.com/
pages/Daily-Bread-
Berkeley/123947177634828

★

## ELIZABETH GLASER PEDIATRIC AIDS FOUNDATION

Established in 1988, the Pediatric AIDS Foundation was renamed in 1994 after Elizabeth Glaser, a pioneer in advocating for the rights of children living with HIV. With a focus on research, the foundation strives to eliminate pediatric AIDS, and provides HIV prevention, care, and treatment services to women, children, and families in seventeen countries.

### Volunteer Opportunities

Opportunities mostly consist of helping with events, such as university-run dance marathons.

**Contact Information**

1140 Connecticut Avenue, NW, Suite
  200
Washington, DC 20036
(202) 296-9165
E-mail: info@pedaids.org

www.pedaids.org
11150 Santa Monica Boulevard,
  Suite 1050
Los Angeles, CA 90025
(310) 314-1459

★

## FEEDING AMERICA

Established in 1979, America's Second Harvest was renamed Feeding America in September 2008. The hunger-relief charity provides food to more than 37 million low-income individuals through its nationwide network of member food banks.

### Volunteer Opportunities

Feeding America has a handful of opportunities at its national office, but stresses that more opportunities for volunteering are available at its network of local food banks.

### Contact Information

National Office: 35 East Wacker
   Drive, Suite 2000
Chicago, IL 60601

(800) 771-2303
www.feedingamerica.org

★

## FOOD FIRST

Food First—also known as the Institute for Food and Development Policy—works to eliminate the injustices that cause hunger and poverty. Established in 1975, it carries out research, analysis, training, advocacy, and education for citizen engagement, believing that everyone has a right to healthy food produced through ecologically sound and sustainable methods. The organization also collaborates with community colleagues, and is known for its many publications about hunger and the global food crisis.

### Volunteer Opportunities

Volunteers typically assist with non-research-related tasks, such as gardening and envelope stuffing. Food First also has a need for interns who can work at least fifteen hours a week for a minimum of twelve weeks. Interns help with research, analysis, and writing.

### Contact Information

398 60th Street
Oakland, CA 94618
(510) 654-4400

E-mail: foodfirst@foodfirst.org
www.foodfirst.org

★

**Name: Catherine Sullivan**
**Location: New York City**
**Organization: Housing Works**

**Can you describe what you do as a volunteer at Housing Works Bookstore Café?**

I take responsibility for the children's book section of the store. I sort donated books, stock shelves, and assist customers. I train other volunteers to work in the section and do whatever special tasks I'm given by the manager.

**What inspired you to volunteer?**

Housing Works' mission was very important to me. I lost several friends to AIDS and wanted to do something more than donate money to help deal with the crisis. Providing housing and services for homeless people with AIDS and raising the money to do that by operating thrift stores and a bookstore seemed like a brilliant concept. I have some expertise in children's books, and I thought I would make a useful contribution by volunteering at the bookstore.

**Why do you feel it is important to volunteer?**

I think there is a tension between individual and community and, in recent times, an unwillingness to acknowledge how interdependent we have become. I think volunteering in some enterprise that strengthens the community is something every citizen should do.

I believe the organization makes a real difference in people's lives; this includes everybody working at Housing Works, from Charles King (President and CEO of Housing Works) to the custodian who cleans the bathrooms. It is a diverse group of people with very different talents, working hard, cooperating, and supporting each other's efforts to achieve a common objective. I feel proud to be a part of it.

HEALTH CARE, HUNGER, AND HOMELESSNESS

## HOUSING WORKS

Housing Works is the largest community-based AIDS service organization in the United States, as well as the nation's largest minority-controlled AIDS service organization. Since its founding in 1990, it has provided lifesaving services, such as housing, medical and mental health care, meals, job training, drug treatment, HIV prevention education, and social support to more than 20,000 homeless and low-income New Yorkers living with HIV and AIDS. Housing Works operates more than fifty facilities in the five boroughs of New York City, at the state capital in Albany, New York, and in the nation's capital, Washington, D.C.

Housing Works also runs social enterprise businesses that raise millions of dollars every year to help pay for the services that it provides; to spread awareness of its mission; and to provide jobs to graduates of its Job Training Program. The organization's best-known businesses are Housing Works Thrift Shops, a chain of upscale thrift shops located throughout New York City, and the Housing Works Bookstore Café, a used-book store, literary hub, and concert venue located in downtown Manhattan.

### Volunteer Opportunities

The organization considers volunteers to be its backbone. They run the bookstore café and thrift shops, help with annual events, tutor Housing Works' clients, work in outreach and art therapy programs, provide administrative support, and much more.

### Contact Information
**Headquarters:** 57 Willoughby Street, 2nd Floor
Brooklyn, NY 11201
(347) 473-7400 or

TTY: (212) 925-9560
www.housingworks.org
volunteer@housingworks.org

★

## MEN'S HEALTH NETWORK (MHN)

Men's Health Network (MHN) is a national nonprofit organization whose mission is to reach men and their families where they live, work, play, and pray with health prevention messages and tools, screening programs, educational materials, advocacy opportunities, and patient navigation.

MHN was founded in 1992 by a group of health professionals and others interested in improving the health and well-being of men, boys, and families. Today, MHN has a board of advisors totaling over 800 physicians and key thought leaders.

## Volunteer Opportunities

Volunteers can participate in local health fairs and screening events, serve on MHN's speakers' bureau, help with administrative duties in the organization's home office, or serve as advocates for men's health at a local, state, and national level.

MHN hosts many community outreach programs throughout the year, and volunteers serve by registering people for health screenings, passing out health education materials, and—for those volunteers with certain health training—speaking with individuals about their health. The organization also does several mailers every year that volunteers assist with.

Internships include working in legislative advocacy, health outreach, and research. Applications are available for download or to complete online at www.menshealthnetwork.org.

## Contact Information

P.O. Box 75972
Washington, DC 20013
(202) 543-MHN-1 (6461)

E-mail: info@menshealthnetwork.org
www.menshealthnetwork.org

★

# MENTAL HEALTH AMERICA (MHA)

Established in 1909 as the National Mental Health Association, MHA is an advocacy organization addressing mental and substance-abuse conditions and their effects nationwide. The nonprofit works to inform, advocate, and enable access to quality behavioral health services for all Americans. With over 300 affiliates across the country, MHA practices national and grassroots actions that promote its mission, with an emphasis on recovery from mental and substance-abuse conditions.

## Volunteer Opportunities

The organization's national office is comprised of five basic departments: Affiliate and Consumer Services, Public Policy, Development, Public Education, and Administration. Through these departments, the organization develops and provides support to its 300-plus affiliates and chapters. Mental Health America's affiliates typically use volunteers to a great extent in multiple areas of service and outreach. Tasks include event planning, serving on agency programming committees, and providing office staff support on either a special task or a regular basis.

Mental Health America has internships for one or two semesters for undergrad or graduate students with one of the organization's primary departments at its national office. It also has occasional volunteer support for a specific event or temporary replacement for a staff member.

Volunteer time commitment can run from one hour per month up to twenty hours per week, depending on the circumstances.

## Contact Information

**Headquarters:** 2000 N. Beauregard Street, 6th Floor
Alexandria, VA 22311
(703) 684-7722 or (800) 969-6642

E-mail: infoctr@mentalhealthamerica.net
www.mentalhealthamerica.net

★

## NATIONAL COALITION FOR THE HOMELESS (NCH)

Established in 1984, NCH is a national network for advocates, community-based, and faith-based service providers, people who have personal experience with homelessness, and others committed to ending homelessness. NCH engages in public education, policy advocacy, and grassroots organizing to carry out its mission. Examples of the coalition's sponsored projects include the "You Don't Need a Home to Vote" voting rights campaign, and the Homeless Challenge Project, an event that asks economically privileged individuals to spend time on the streets as homeless people for up to forty-eight hours.

### Volunteer Opportunities

NCH encourages interested people to seek volunteer opportunities at shelters and direct service agencies in their own communities. A partial listing of service providers can be found on the NCH website of local homeless service organizations. The website also provides suggestions for volunteer activities, such as providing professional skills (e.g., catering, plumbing, legal services, writing) to a direct service provider, planning a game night, or serving food at a shelter.

### Contact Information

2201 P Street, NW
Washington, DC 20037
(202) 462-4822

E-mail: info@nationalhomeless.org
www.nationalhomeless.org

★

## OPERATION ACCESS (OA)

Operation Access was founded in 1993 by two surgeons and a former hospital executive with the goal of providing health care to the uninsured. The OA network includes community clinics, medical professionals, and medical centers throughout the California Bay Area. OA also supports other communities interested in utilizing its program model or integrating medical volunteerism to improve access to health care in the United States.

### Volunteer Opportunities

Operation Access is a volunteer-driven organization that offers many opportunities. Always in demand are surgeons and specialists who can donate their time and expertise. Other medical departments that rely on volunteers include anesthesia, gastroenterology, operating room, and sterile processing. Positions are also available for anesthesia providers, nurses, technicians, translators (present desired languages are Spanish, Portuguese, Mandarin, and Cantonese), photographers, and people interested in working on administrative tasks such as fund-raising, event planning, communications, and improving the website.

### Contact Information

115 Sansome Street, Suite 1205
San Francisco, CA 94104

(415) 733-0052
www.operationaccess.org

## PLANNED PARENTHOOD FEDERATION OF AMERICA, INC. (PPFA)

Established in 1916, Planned Parenthood delivers reproductive health care, sex education, and information to millions of people worldwide. Planned Parenthood also advocates for policies that promote women's health and allow individuals to prevent unintended pregnancies through access to affordable contraception. The organization's eighty-eight locally governed affiliates nationwide operate more than 840 health centers, which reflect the diverse needs of their communities.

### Volunteer Opportunities

Volunteer opportunities and internships vary by location but can include positions in health center patient services, advocacy and public policy, community outreach and education, administrative projects and support, fund-raising, social networking, and health center administrative office support. Visit www.plannedparenthood.org to utilize the organization's search engine to explore volunteer opportunities.

HEALTH CARE, HUNGER, AND HOMELESSNESS

**Contact Information**

New York: 434 West 33rd Street
New York, NY 10001
(212) 541-7800
Washington, D.C.: 1110 Vermont
  Avenue, NW, Suite 300

Washington, DC 20005
(202) 973-4800
www.plannedparenthood.org

★

## SHARE OUR STRENGTH (SOS)

Established in 1985, Share Our Strength brings together community groups, activists, and food programs to combat childhood hunger in America. Through its No Kid Hungry campaign—a national effort to end childhood hunger in America by 2015—Share Our Strength ensures that children have access to federal nutrition programs, invests in community organizations fighting hunger, teaches families how to cook healthy meals on a budget, and develops public-private partnerships to end hunger.

**Volunteer Opportunities**

Volunteers are needed to assist SOS staff for specific events. Visit its website for current opportunities. SOS also features resources on its website for individuals interested in hosting fund-raising bake sales.

**Contact Information**

1730 M Street, NW, Suite 700
Washington, DC 20036
(202) 393-2925 or (800) 969-4767

E-mail: info@strength.org
www.strength.org

★

## WORLD HUNGER YEAR (WHY)

Founded in 1975 by radio talk-show host Bill Ayres and the late singer-songwriter Harry Chapin, WHY is a leader in the fight against hunger and poverty in the United States and around the world. WHY is convinced that solutions to hunger and poverty can be found at the grassroots level. It advances long-term solutions to hunger and poverty by supporting community-based organizations that empower individuals and build self-reliance, i.e., offering job training, education, and afterschool programs; increasing access to housing and health care; providing microcredit and entrepreneurial opportunities; teaching people to grow their own food; and assisting small farmers. WHY connects these organizations to funders, media, and legislators.

## Volunteer Opportunities

WHY often needs people to perform various tasks at its events and in its New York City–based offices. Visit www.whyhunger.org to complete a volunteer form.

## Contact Information

505 Eighth Avenue, Suite 2100
New York, NY 10018

(800) 5-HUNGRY
www.whyhunger.org

★

# HUMAN RIGHTS

## BRENNAN CENTER FOR JUSTICE

The Brennan Center for Justice at New York University School of Law is a nonpartisan public policy and law institute that focuses on the fundamental issues of democracy and justice. Its work ranges from voting rights to campaign finance reform, from racial justice in criminal law to presidential power in the fight against terrorism. A singular institution—part think tank, part public interest law firm, part advocacy group—the Brennan Center combines scholarship, legislative and legal advocacy, and communications to win meaningful, measurable change in the public sector.

### Volunteer Opportunities

The Brennan Center offers many opportunities for volunteer lawyers to work with its staff on litigation, policy research, and public advocacy efforts. Although the Center is based in New York, it performs work across the country and is often looking for local counsel in other states and localities.

Inquiries from law students, attorneys, and other persons who would like to participate in the work of the Brennan Center are welcome. The organization encourages individuals to learn from its website about the activities of its Democracy and Justice programs, and to approach the Center with ideas for becoming involved. Potential participants can submit a résumé and cover letter to brennancenterjobs@nyu.edu.

The Center also offers semester-term and summer-term internships and externships for undergraduate, graduate, and law students, as well as particular opportunities for NYU School of Law students.

### Contact Information

161 Sixth Avenue, 12th Floor
New York, NY 10013
(646) 292-8310
E-mail: brennancenter@nyu.edu

1730 M Street, NW, Suite 413
Washington, DC, 20036
(202) 785-4747
www.brennancenter.org

## CENTER FOR VICTIMS OF TORTURE (CVT)

Established in 1985, CVT's mission is to heal the wounds of torture on individuals, their families, and their communities and to stop torture worldwide.

The organization fulfills its mission by providing services directly to torture survivors; by training and providing capacity-building support to professionals and organizations who work with torture survivors and refugees; by conducting research on the effects of torture and on effective treatment methods; and by advocating for public policy initiatives worldwide that put an end to the practice of torture.

## Volunteer Opportunities

Examples of opportunities include serving as an English-language tutor, providing donation and moving assistance, driving clients to appointments, working as a bus guide, offering graphic and web design support, educating the public, and gardening for CVT's Garden of Healing.

Medical and mental health professionals can volunteer for the Minnesota Asylum Network, a joint project of The Advocates for Human Rights, CVT, and Physicians for Human Rights. Volunteers provide expert assessments and testimony in support of asylum seekers. Training is provided for volunteers by The Advocates for Human Rights.

## Contact Information

717 E. River Parkway
Minneapolis, MN 55455
(612) 436-4800

E-mail: cvt@cvt.org
www.cvt.org

★

## GLOBAL EXCHANGE

Established in 1988, Global Exchange protects international human rights and works to advance social, environmental, and economic justice. Acting in alliance with partner organizations, Global Exchange works on a variety of issues. Current campaigns focus on promoting fair trade, opposing sweatshops and labor exploitation, helping stop oil wars, and curbing global warming. Global Exchange also offers a Reality Tour program, an intensive travel seminar that links travelers with activists and organizations from around the world who are working toward positive change.

## Volunteer Opportunities

Volunteers work in the San Francisco office in a variety of capacities. Programs/departments that utilize volunteers include media, IT, fund-raising and development/membership, administration, Reality Tours, online fair trade store, and the Cuba campaign. Global Exchange posts specialized opportunities on its website. Time commitments are flexible.

**Contact Information**

2017 Mission Street, 2nd Floor
San Francisco, CA 94110
(415) 255-7296

E-mail: volunteers@globalexchange
.org
www.globalexchange.org

★

# HUMAN RIGHTS WATCH (HRW)

Established in 1978, HRW exposes human rights violations and holds offenders accountable for their actions. In its mission to prevent discrimination and uphold political freedom, HRW offers objective investigations and advocacy, and puts international pressure on abusive governments and others who hold power to end abusive practices.

**Volunteer Opportunities**

HRW offers academic internships at both the undergraduate and graduate level in its regional and thematic divisions, as well as its organizational support departments.

Undergraduate internships are primarily administrative and clerical in nature, but other projects can be assigned as they arise and match the student's interests and abilities, including research, drafting documents, translating, and helping researchers prepare for missions.

Graduate-level interns monitor human rights developments in various countries, draft reports on human rights conditions, and engage in advocacy efforts aimed at curtailing human rights violations. Internships are unpaid, except for certain funded graduate internships that are associated with specific universities.

While internships are generally unpaid, work-study funds are often available depending on the location of placement. Students are often able to arrange academic credit, as HRW internships frequently offer direct exposure to the workings of an international human rights organization, close supervision by the HRW staff, interaction with other U.S. and international organizations and foreign and domestic government officials, and opportunities to attend lectures, trainings, and special events relating to human rights. Students should check with their individual academic institutions for requirements.

Applicants should be well-organized, self-motivated, and reliable, with a strong interest in international human rights. Relevant coursework is highly desirable, and knowledge of foreign languages is a plus. Computer skills (i.e., Microsoft Office, Internet applications) are required.

Internships are posted on the organization's website. Individuals can apply immediately by sending a letter of interest, résumé, names or letters of reference, and a brief, unedited writing sample to the advertised e-mail address included in the listing, with the name of the desired internship in the subject line. Only complete applications will be reviewed.

**Contact Information**

Headquarters: 350 Fifth Avenue,
  34th Floor
New York, NY 10118-3299

(212) 290-4700
www.hrw.org

★

## SOUTHERN CENTER FOR HUMAN RIGHTS (SCHR)

Established in 1976, SCHR advocates for individuals affected by the criminal justice system in the South. The Center provides legal representation to prisoners facing the death penalty, works to end the use of the death penalty, challenges human rights violations in prisons and jails, seeks to improve legal representation for poor people accused of crimes, and fights for criminal justice system reforms. SCHR also publishes reports on such issues, including developing more humane solutions to crime.

**Volunteer Opportunities**

SCHR asks volunteers to commit to at least two hours of service a week for eight weeks. Positions are available in the following areas: impact (civil) litigation, capital litigation, fund-raising, and administrative support. Activities range from assisting attorneys with the assembly of case notebooks to updating resource lists to data entry. To learn more, potential volunteers are asked to contact Renée Myers at rmyers@schr.org. Interested law students can apply to SCHR's internship program.

**Contact Information**

83 Poplar Street, NW
Atlanta, GA 30303
(404) 688-1202

E-mail: info@schr.org
www.schr.org

★

# PEOPLE WITH DISABILITIES

## THE ARC OF THE UNITED STATES

Established in 1950, The Arc is an advocacy organization that protects and fights for the human rights of people with intellectual and developmental disabilities.

### Volunteer Opportunities

Contact the organization for details.

### Contact Information

**Main Office:** 1660 L Street, NW, Suite 301
Washington, DC 20036

(202) 534-3700 or (800) 433-5255
E-mail: info@thearc.org
www.thearc.org

---

## BEST BUDDIES (BB)

Established in 1989, Best Buddies is a volunteer-run international organization that provides one-on-one friendships, integrated employment, and leadership development for people with intellectual and developmental disabilities (IDD).

### Volunteer Opportunities

Volunteers offer the gift of friendship to youth and adults with IDD. The "Best Buddies" commit to seeing each other twice a month, for one year. Best Buddies asks individuals to contact a BB office located in their state for information on the volunteer opportunities offered in that area. To find the office near you, visit www.bestbuddies.org, or e-mail info@bestbuddies.org.

### Contact Information

**Global Headquarters:** 100 Southeast Second Street, Suite 2200
Miami, FL 33131

(305) 374-2233 or (800) 89 BUDDY (28339)
www.bestbuddies.org

---

## BREAD & ROSES

Established in 1974, Bread & Roses strives to boost spirits and support healing by offering live music performances to isolated individuals, such as children undergoing chemotherapy and families in homeless shelters, in the San Francisco Bay area.

## Volunteer Opportunities

Volunteers are needed throughout the year for daily shows, public benefit events, and to support Bread & Roses staff. Event volunteers assist with catering, photography, and a variety of other duties. Hosts emcee shows while musicians perform forty-five-minute sets of upbeat music. Office volunteers help Bread & Roses staff with archiving, data entry, research, and in other capacities in the organization's Corte Madera office. Applications and requirement details for each position are available on the website. All questions should be directed to Lisa Starbird at (415) 945-7120.

## Contact Information

233 Tamalpais Drive, Suite 100
Corte Madera, CA 94925-1415
(415) 945-7120

E-mail: info@breadandroses.org
www.breadandroses.org

★

## LIGHTHOUSE FOR THE BLIND AND VISUALLY IMPAIRED

The mission of the LightHouse, established in 1902, is to help blind and visually impaired people in Northern California live independent and active lives. The LightHouse provides educational, recreational, rehabilitative, and social services to youth, adults, and seniors experiencing varying degrees of vision loss.

## Volunteer Opportunities

There are many opportunities for individuals to get involved, some from the comfort of one's own home. Volunteers can provide personal services (assisting a blind or visually impaired person in their home with reading, writing, and errands); record materials such as articles and manuals onto a cassette recorder; assist with the adult education and recreation program; provide tutoring or organize a class in an area of expertise; serve as a summer camp counselor or a youth program assistant; or help with clerical responsibilities. All volunteers must undergo vision loss awareness training and commit to working with the LightHouse for at least six months. Applications can be downloaded on the organization's website and questions can be directed to Don M. Franklin, dmfranklin@lighthouse-sf.org.

## Contact Information

**Headquarters:** 214 Van Ness
   Avenue
San Francisco, CA 94102
(415) 431-1481 or (888) 400-8933

E-mail: info@lighthouse-sf.org
www.lighthouse-sf.org

★

PEOPLE WITH DISABILITIES

## NATIONAL ALLIANCE ON MENTAL ILLNESS (NAMI)

Established in 1979, NAMI has a national organization as well as state organizations and local affiliates that work to improve the lives of individuals and families affected by mental illness. NAMI offers resources and information about mental disorders through its National Information HelpLine, NAMI Connection (a free recovery support program for adults living with mental illness), and its website. The alliance also advocates for treatment and research, as well as state and federal policies that ensure an end to discrimination and the promotion of effective mental health services.

### Volunteer Opportunities

NAMI is mainly a volunteer organization, so opportunities are plentiful at the national and local levels. The primary volunteer opportunity in NAMI's national headquarters office in Arlington, Virginia, is serving as an information specialist for its National Information HelpLine. Volunteers answer calls, take down voice-mail messages, return calls, respond to letters and e-mails, and perform some data entry. Law students or attorneys can volunteer their time by offering callers general legal information and providing referrals to local attorneys. Volunteers are asked to work at least one four-hour shift a week during HelpLine hours (weekdays from 10:00 AM to 6:00 PM) for at least six months, but college student interns often work more shifts per week for a shorter time period, such as a semester. NAMI seeks applicants who have a good working knowledge of mental illness and recovery, and solid oral and written communication skills. Training is provided.

Local and state volunteer opportunities are available with NAMI affiliates. Options vary according to an affiliate's size, activity level, staffing, support and education programs, and whether there's a designated volunteer coordinator. Tasks may range from stuffing envelopes or answering phones to writing for the newsletter, helping promote events, or organizing an education meeting, to leading support groups or serving on the affiliate's board of directors.

### Contact Information

**Headquarters:** 3803 N. Fairfax Drive, Suite 100 Arlington, VA 22203

(703) 524-7600 or 800-950-6264
E-mail: info@nami.org
www.nami.org

★

## NATIONAL CENTER FOR LEARNING DISABILITIES (NCLD)

Established in 1977, NCLD works to ensure that the nation's 15 million children, adolescents, and adults with learning disabilities have every opportunity to succeed in school, work, and life. It provides essential information to parents, professionals, and individuals with learning disabilities, promotes research and programs to foster effective learning, and advocates for policies to protect and strengthen educational rights and opportunities.

## Volunteer Opportunities

NCLD has various clerical and administrative opportunities year-round in its office. However, volunteers are most needed at the beginning of each year to help with the organization's scholarship review and selection process for its Anne Ford and Allegra Ford Scholarship.

NCLD also invites individuals with learning disabilities, or those with experience teaching children with LD or with raising a child with LD to write for its blog, *LD Insights.*

## Contact Information

381 Park Avenue South, Suite 1401
New York, NY 10016
(212) 545-7510 or (888) 575-7373

E-mail: ncld@ncld.org
www.ncld.org

---

★

---

## SPECIAL OLYMPICS

Special Olympics is a global nonprofit organization established in 1963 that targets individuals with intellectual disabilities. With a presence in over 200 countries, Special Olympics provides year-round sports training and competition for children and adults with intellectual disabilities.

## Volunteer Opportunities

Each one of Special Olympics' programs has different needs for volunteers, but across the board they are always looking for coaches, "Fans in the Stands," and help at games and tournaments. Those in the health-care industry can also contribute their efforts to the Healthy Athletes program, which provides health screenings free of charge at Special Olympics competitions. Visit www.specialolympics.org to locate a Special Olympics near you and learn details of its specific volunteer opportunities.

## Contact Information

**Headquarters:** 1133 19th Street, NW
Washington, DC 20036-3604
(202) 628-3630 or (800) 700-8585

E-mail: info@specialolympics.org
www.specialolympics.org

---

★

---

# SENIORS

## ALZHEIMER'S ASSOCIATION
Established in 1980, the Alzheimer's Association is a voluntary health organization with goals to eliminate Alzheimer's disease with advanced research, reduce the risk of dementia, and provide care and support for sufferers. The association serves individuals through its helpline, local chapters, message boards, emergency response service (MedicAlert + Alzheimer's Association Safe Return), online resources, published journal, and the Alzheimer's Association Green-Field Library, which is the nation's largest library dedicated to the disease. In addition, Alzheimer's Association hosts an annual international conference that unites scientists from around the world to discuss ideas and research.

### Volunteer Opportunities
The Alzheimer's Association encourages volunteers to contact their local chapters to learn about opportunities. Volunteers can usually help organize and work the day of special events (such as the Alzheimer's Association Memory Walk), participate in public education and awareness programs, provide office or helpline assistance, or assist with advocacy.

### Contact Information
**Headquarters:** 225 N. Michigan Avenue, Floor 17
Chicago, IL 60601-7633

(312) 335-8700
E-mail: info@alz.org
www.alz.org

## EXPERIENCE CORPS
Established in 1995, Experience Corps is a national program that connects older adults (typically age fifty-five and older) with elementary school students to serve as tutors and mentors. Members also assist teachers in the classroom and lead afterschool enrichment activities.

### Volunteer Opportunities
Experience Corps operates in twenty-two states, with different time commitments and opportunities available at each local chapter. Depending on the state, volunteers can provide individualized tutoring, conduct small reading groups, and develop parent and family outreach efforts.

**Contact Information**
**Headquarters:** 2120 L Street, NW, Suite 610
Washington, DC 20037

(202) 478-6190
E-mail: info@experiencecorps.org
www.experiencecorps.org

★

## LITTLE BROTHERS—FRIENDS OF THE ELDERLY (LBFE)

Established in 1946, LBFE is a national network of nonprofit, volunteer-based organizations committed to relieving isolation and loneliness among the elderly.

### Volunteer Opportunities

LBFE welcomes volunteers to help elders through a variety of activities, ranging from packing gift baskets and preparing food during the holidays to driving an elder to a special event or spending an hour visiting. Chapters are based in Boston, Philadelphia, Cincinnati, Chicago, Upper Peninsula of Michigan, Minneapolis/St. Paul, Omaha, and San Francisco.

### Contact Information

There is no national office for LBFE. Visit www.littlebrothers.org to find your local chapter.

## MEALS ON WHEELS ASSOCIATION OF AMERICA (MOWAA)

Established in 1954, MOWAA is a national umbrella organization representing local, community-based senior nutrition programs with a goal to end senior hunger by 2020. These programs provide meals to seniors at their homes or at congregate locations like senior centers.

### Volunteer Opportunities

Volunteers can hold a variety of positions with their local Meals On Wheels program. Most help with actual deliveries, but many programs also need help with food preparation and office work.

Since all Meals On Wheels programs are independently run and operated, it's up to each one to require how much training is necessary before someone can fill a role.

Most programs don't have any time requirements, but regarding meal deliveries, ask that the volunteers complete at least one route during their volunteering session, which can sometimes take as little as an hour or less.

### Contact Information

**Headquarters:** 203 S. Union Street
Alexandria, VA 22314
(703) 548-5558

E-mail: Mowaa@mowaa.org
www.mowaa.org

★

## NATIONAL GRAY PANTHERS

Established in 1970, the National Gray Panthers is an intergenerational organization that believes in civic participation and responsibility as a fundamental means to achieving social and economic justice and peace. Some of the many issues the advocacy group focuses on are health care (reproductive choice, medical marijuana, stem cell research); family security (social security benefits and cap, welfare reform, Older Americans Act); peace (rebuilding Iraq, relations with Cuba, Middle East peace); education (access to education, the No Child Left Behind Act); jobs and workers' rights (living wage, right to organize, global trade); and the environment (sustainability, preservation, pollution).

### Volunteer Opportunities

Contact the organization for details.

### Contact Information

**Headquarters:** 1612 K Street, NW, Suite 300
Washington, DC 20006

(202) 737-6637 or (800) 280-5362
E-mail: info@graypanthers.org
www.graypanthers.org

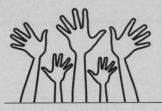

# SOCIAL WELFARE AND EMERGENCY RELIEF

## AMERICAN RED CROSS

Established in 1881, the American Red Cross is an emergency response organization providing care to the victims of war and natural disasters, and services to the needy and military members and their families. With nearly 700 locally supported chapters, the American Red Cross helps people prepare for and respond to emergencies with its health and safety education programs. The organization also works to offer international relief and development programs. Due in part to its magnitude of blood donors, the Red Cross is the largest supplier of blood and blood products in the United States.

### Volunteer Opportunities

The American Red Cross relies on its many volunteers to teach classes in first aid, CPR, and swimming, as well as assist with blood drives, deliver messages to members of the military, connect families displaced by disasters, and work in communities during emergency situations. Opportunities are arranged by local affiliates.

### Contact Information

**Headquarters:** 2025 E Street, NW
Washington, DC 20006

(202) 303-5000
www.redcross.org

---

**Name: Edward Hunkele**

**Location: Elmira, New York**

**Organization: Red Cross**

**Can you describe what you do as a volunteer for the blood drives at the Red Cross?**

There are two jobs I perform at different times. One has to do with registering donors. I greet them, check their names against the appointment schedule, hand them reading materials, and ensure that they are assigned to technicians in the proper order.

The other position is in the canteen. In addition to serving refreshments and handing out T-shirts, I also preregister them for the next blood drive and ensure that they are feeling well. If someone is feeling faint, I call a technician for assistance and assist with their recovery.

**What inspired you to volunteer?**

Blood supply is always at a critical stage. The drives we perform are important, especially in times of disaster. Although my role is on the periphery of the actual drawing of blood, it is important that volunteers perform their roles to ensure that the process flows smoothly. If these jobs were not handled by volunteers, the cost of the drives would increase due to the need for paid personnel. So, I take solace in the fact that it is a responsibility that I can do to help defray the overall cost of such an important endeavor.

From a personal standpoint, I personally benefited from a blood drive in 1986. I was hospitalized after losing a considerable amount of blood due to a bleeding ulcer. The plant where I worked dedicated the next blood drive to cover the blood I was given. Consequently, I tried to donate blood whenever I could and subsequently became a volunteer.

**How has volunteering impacted your life?**

I have always tried to set an example for my family with regard to stressing the importance of sharing the blessings we have with others that may be less fortunate. At Christmas, we deliver food baskets to low-income individuals through the church and distribute toys to underprivileged children. Volunteering sets an example to your children and their children on the basis that your time can be as important as monetary gifts.

I believe that my presence at the blood drives also serves as an example to others in the community, since I am somewhat younger than most of the other volunteers. Hopefully this shows the people donating blood that they too can be a part of the process, regardless of their age. I also reinforce the importance of their donations by thanking them and encouraging them to sign up for future blood drives.

## CATHOLIC CHARITIES USA

Established in 1910, Catholic Charities USA is the national office for local Catholic Charities agencies and institutions nationwide that work to reduce poverty, support families, and empower communities. Its members provide help to people of all faiths.

### Volunteer Opportunities

Contact the organization for details.

### Contact Information

Sixty-Six Canal Center Plaza, Suite 600
Alexandria, VA 22314

(703) 549-1390
www.catholiccharitiesusa.org

★

## SALVATION ARMY

The Salvation Army is a faith-based charity established in 1878 that helps people with all kinds of social needs. Among its services, the Christian organization provides relief efforts to communities impacted by both natural and man-made disasters.

### Volunteer Opportunities

Volunteers carry out numerous activities, including assisting with after-school programs, visiting nursing homes and hospitals, serving meals to the needy, providing instruction (such as piano lessons) to less-fortunate children, and bell-ringing at Christmas. Many units of the Salvation Army list their volunteer opportunities on VolunteerMatch.org. The organization also encourages individuals to contact their local Salvation Army for more information.

**Contact Information**
**National Headquarters:** 615 Slaters Lane
P.O. Box 269

Alexandria, VA 22313
www.salvationarmyusa.org

★

## U.S. COMMITTEE FOR REFUGEES AND IMMIGRANTS (USCRI)

USCRI addresses the needs and rights of persons in forced or voluntary migration worldwide by advancing fair and humane public policy, facilitating and providing direct professional services, and promoting the full participation of migrants in community life.

**Volunteer Opportunities**

Opportunities abound at the local level in USCRI's field offices in Albany, New York; Detroit, Michigan; Colchester, Vermont; Erie, Pennsylvania; Raleigh, North Carolina; or through the organization's nationwide network of partner agencies. Volunteers can teach English as a Second Language (ESL) courses; provide translation and/or interpretation services; accompany refugees to appointments; conduct career, financial literacy, and similar workshops; welcome newly arrived refugees at the airport; and otherwise help refugees become acclimated to life in the United States.

Internships are also available and school credit can be arranged, with a minimum commitment of eight hours per week for at least three months.

**Contact Information**
2231 Crystal Drive, Suite 350
Arlington, VA 22202-3711
(703) 310-1130

E-mail: uscri@uscridc.org
www.refugees.org

★

SOCIAL WELFARE AND EMERGENCY RELIEF

**Name: Deborah G. Taylor**

**Location: East Greenbush, New York**

**Organization: U.S.Committee for Refugees and Immigrants**
**(Albany)**

**Can you describe what kind of work you do as a volunteer for USCRI?**

On a regular basis I see three different families and review their mail, help with job applications or social services forms, make doctor appointments, etc. I don't do this alone; my husband, Kevin Taylor, is also a USCRI volunteer who goes with me to assist. He loves the work as much as I do, and helps the children with homework, drives them to the playground, and helps with the mail. In nice weather we try to bring the children (as many as we can fit in our cars) to the playground or get them out of the house, as there are not many areas for them to play in their neighborhood.

**What inspired you to do volunteer work?**

For some time I had been meaning to volunteer. My children were grown and out of the house, and it was always one of my New Year's resolutions. I didn't want to just write a check, but to make a difference. I was inspired to work with USCRI after reading an article in a local newspaper about the work they do to resettle refugees. I felt compelled to help welcome some of the neediest people to this country from some of the most deplorable conditions. So I contacted USCRI and attended a volunteer orientation. I work full-time and was somewhat intimidated with volunteering to act as a mentor with a family, but I also realized that this is where I could do the most good. Even though I live on the outskirts of Albany, I had no idea there were so many refugees in our area, nor did I know where they came from.

**Is there a particular experience you have had as a volunteer that has left a lasting impression?**

The most profound experience I had was in December of 2009, when I was in the delivery room for the birth of a baby in the family I was assigned to help. I had taken the mother to doctor appointments and ultrasounds and the other children to the doctor. They have named the baby Debbie Meh, after me. They are all so appreciative, so gentle and kind, and to be a friend to them is really very simple.

But there are many rewarding experiences. Last summer I spent many nights driving several carloads of children and adults over to my home to swim in our pool. At first they were afraid of the water because they did not have the opportunity to swim due to the lack of clean water in their countries. Now all of the children can swim to some degree, and they tell me it is their favorite thing about America.

**What advice would you give to someone interested in doing volunteer work in their community?**

Make a commitment to make a difference. Both my husband and I spend several nights a week volunteering and get more from the experience than we give. Any type of commitment is worthwhile. I believe that learning about another culture is so rewarding for everyone. These people, all younger than me, have been through so much in their lives. They have lost everything, yet they are optimistic, and want the same things for their children that we want for ours. We all have so much and the opportunity to share is so rewarding.

## YMCA (YOUNG MEN'S CHRISTIAN ASSOCIATION) OF THE USA

Established in 1851, the YMCA has more than 2,600 local affiliates that serve communities across the country with health programs and activities. The organization strives to help children and youth deepen their positive values and motivation to learn, to help families build stronger bonds, and to help individuals improve their overall well-being.

### Volunteer Opportunities

Each YMCA in the U.S. is run by volunteers, so a variety of opportunities exist, including programming (contributing as an exercise class instructor or a basketball coach), support (working at the front desk, office locker room, or on the grounds), fund-raising, policy (serving on the Y's board of directors), and managerial (act as a pro bono accountant or PR specialist). Needs vary by location, so volunteers should consult with their local YMCA to confirm opportunities and learn details.

### Contact Information

**Headquarters:** 101 North Wacker Drive
Chicago, IL 60606

(800) 872-9622
www.ymca.net

## YWCA (YOUNG WOMEN'S CHRISTIAN ASSOCIATION) OF THE USA

Established in 1859, the YWCA is the oldest and largest multicultural women's organization in the world, with more than 300 local associations in the nation. To accomplish its mission of empowering women and eradicating racism, each chapter provides a variety of services, which may include child care, domestic violence shelters, rape crisis intervention, career counseling, health and fitness, and social justice programs. Aside from its programs, the YWCA advocates for women's rights and civil rights in Congress.

### Volunteer Opportunities

Contact the organization for details.

### Contact Information

**Headquarters:** 2025 M Street, NW, Suite 550
Washington, DC 20036

(202) 467-0801
E-mail: info@ywca.org
www.ywca.org

# VIOLENCE PREVENTION AND PEACE

## AMERICAN FRIENDS SERVICE COMMITTEE (AFSC)

Established in 1917, AFSC is a faith-inclusive Quaker organization that is committed to humanitarian service, social justice, and peace programs throughout the world. AFSC applies a nonviolent approach in their programs and efforts, which currently include the elimination of nuclear weapons, immigrants' rights, withdrawing U.S. troops from Iraq and Afghanistan, and providing disaster relief to Haiti, among other global issues.

### Volunteer Opportunities

Contact the organization for details.

### Contact Information

1501 Cherry Street
Philadelphia, PA 19102

(215) 241-7000
www.afsc.org

## BRADY CAMPAIGN TO PREVENT GUN VIOLENCE AND BRADY CENTER TO PREVENT GUN VIOLENCE

The Brady Campaign strives to regulate the purchase and acquisition of guns in an effort to fight gun violence. The campaign applies grassroots activism to help pass and enforce federal and state gun laws, regulations, and public policies. Its sister organization, The Brady Center, provides legal representation to victims of gun violence and educates the public through litigation, grassroots mobilization, and outreach. These organizations were established in 1974 and 1983, respectively.

### Volunteer Opportunities

The organization relies heavily on volunteers to do research, make phone calls to legislative offices at the state and federal level, represent the organization in speaking to local groups and school groups, attend rallies and press conferences, and many other activities. A one-hour-per-week time commitment is required.

Volunteers work in the organization's national office in Washington, D.C., and in many offices of its affiliated chapters in thirty-six states. The largest numbers of volunteers work in New York City and Albany, New York; Los

Angeles and Sacramento, California; Philadelphia, Pennsylvania; Chicago, Illinois; Denver, Colorado; and Seattle, Washington.

**Contact Information**

1225 Eye Street, NW, Suite 1100
Washington, DC 20005
Brady Campaign: (202) 898-0792

www.bradycampaign.org
Brady Center: (202) 289-7319
www.bradycenter.org

## COUNCIL FOR A LIVABLE WORLD (CLW)

Founded in 1962 by nuclear physicist Leo Szilard and other scientists, CLW is an organization that advocates for the reduction of nuclear weapons and the increase of national security. CLW provides members of Congress with scientific and technical information about topics of importance, including weapons of mass destruction and nuclear nonproliferation. It also employs legislation, lobbying, media, and online outreach to find peaceful solutions to international conflict.

**Volunteer Opportunities**

Supporters of nuclear disarmament and progressive national security policies are encouraged to become a member of Council for a Livable World and sign up for its e-mail alerts, which include opportunities to sign petitions, participate in action alerts (such as calling your senator about a policy issue), and make contributions to support candidates for Congress who also represent these values.

Full-time internships are available through CLW's sister organization, The Center for Arms Control and Non-Proliferation in Washington, D.C., and are geared toward students of political science, international relations, the sciences, peace studies, or related fields.

**Contact Information**

322 4th Street, NE
Washington, DC 20002

(202) 543-4100
www.livableworld.org

## FAIR FUND

FAIR Fund, a D.C.-based international nonprofit organization, works to prevent human trafficking and sexual violence in the lives of youth, especially girls, around the world. FAIR Fund builds the capacity of communities to better identify and assist youth ages eleven to twenty-four who are at high risk or have been exploited via human trafficking and sexual violence. FAIR Fund has active programs in Bosnia; Chicago, Illinois; Serbia; Russia; Washington, D.C.; and Uganda.

**Volunteer Opportunities**
Contact the organization for details.

**Contact Information**

| | |
|---|---|
| P.O. Box 21656 | E-mail: info@fairfund.org |
| Washington, DC 20009 | www.fairfund.org |
| (202) 265-1505 | |

---------------------------------- ★ ----------------------------------

## MOVEON.ORG

Established in 1998, MoveOn.org is comprised of two organizations: MoveOn .org Civic Action (formerly known just as MoveOn.org), a nonprofit that primarily focuses on education, advocacy, and media, and MoveOn.org Political Action (formerly known as MoveOn PAC), a federal PAC that mobilizes people across the country to engage with Congress to bring about change and to help elect desired candidates. In 2002 and 2003, MoveOn.org Civic Action conducted several important campaigns, including one to stop the Iraq war, and one that called to reduce America's dependence on oil.

**Volunteer Opportunities**
Contact the organization for details.

**Contact Information**
www.moveon.org

---------------------------------- ★ ----------------------------------

## NUCLEAR AGE PEACE FOUNDATION (NAPF)

Established in 1982, NAPF has a vision of a world free of violent conflict and weapons of mass destruction. It cites its core mission as one that helps "advance initiatives to eliminate the nuclear weapons threat to all life, to foster the global rule of law, and to build an enduring legacy of peace through education and advocacy." The foundation provides research and education, and has created a national and international network of affiliates, associates, and representatives on several continents and in the United Nations.

**Volunteer Opportunities**
NAPF has many projects to which volunteers can lend their skills and time. Opportunities exist in NAPF's Santa Barbara, California, office, but the organization can also utilize volunteers who are willing to work remotely from anywhere. Interested individuals are instructed to e-mail NAPF's director of programs, Rick Wayman, by completing a form at www.wagingpeace.org.

VIOLENCE PREVENTION AND PEACE

**Contact Information**

**Physical address:**
1622 Anacapa Street
Santa Barbara, CA 93101
(805) 965-3443

**Mailing address:**
Nuclear Age Peace Foundation
1187 Coast Village Road, Suite 1,
  PMB 121
Santa Barbara, CA 93108-2794
www.wagingpeace.org

★

## PEACE ACTION

Established in 1957, Peace Action is the largest grassroots network working for peace and nuclear abolition, with over a hundred chapters in thirty-four states. It applies practices such as protest, direct action, congressional lobbying, and voter education to bring issues of peace and security and human rights to the forefront of U.S. foreign and domestic policy. The organization provides education on the effects of politics and current events on the global community through its quarterly newsletter, monthly e-newsletter, and weekly Action Alerts. Peace Action also organizes a student network, SPAN, which provides opportunities for high school and college youth to meet like-minded mentors and participate in regional conferences.

### Volunteer Opportunities

Volunteers can lend help to five different departments in the Maryland office:

- Development / fund-raising: database work and mailings
- Office of the executive director: research and writing
- Finance: accounting and filing
- Program: writing, attending meetings, and helping with lobbying
- Communications: assisting with the website, writing blogs and press releases, and calling the media

Individuals living outside Maryland can contact any of the organization's many chapters and affiliates to learn of opportunities in their area.

**Contact Information**

8630 Fenton Street, Suite 524
Silver Spring, MD 20910

(301) 565-4050
www.peace-action.org

★

## RAPE, ABUSE, AND INCEST NATIONAL NETWORK (RAINN)

RAINN is the nation's largest anti–sexual violence organization. Among its programs, RAINN created and operates the National Sexual Assault Hotline at (800) 656-HOPE. This nationwide partnership of more than 1,100 local rape crisis centers provides victims of sexual assault with free, confidential services around the clock. The hotline has helped more than 1.4 million people since it began in 1994. In 2006, RAINN launched the National Sexual Assault *Online* Hotline, the nation's first secure web-based hotline. In addition, RAINN uses its community partnerships to put critical information into the hands of young women and men at concerts, on campuses, and in communities. Through these efforts, RAINN educates more than 120 million Americans each year about sexual assault. RAINN also publicizes the hotlines' free, confidential services and leads national efforts to improve services to victims and ensure that rapists are brought to justice.

### Volunteer Opportunities

There are many ways to volunteer for RAINN: staff a hotline, volunteer at your local rape crisis center, raise money to support programs, and raise awareness through public education efforts like RAINN Day, the organization's college campaign on over a thousand campuses nationwide.

### Contact Information

2000 L Street, NW, Suite 406
Washington, DC 20036
(202) 544-3064

E-mail: info@rainn.org
www.rainn.org

VIOLENCE PREVENTION AND PEACE

# WILDLIFE AND ANIMAL RIGHTS

## AMERICAN SOCIETY FOR THE PREVENTION OF CRUELTY TO ANIMALS (ASPCA)

In 1866, the American Society for the Prevention of Cruelty to Animals (ASPCA) was the first humane society to be established in North America, and is, today, one of the largest in the world. The organization was founded on the belief that animals are entitled to kind and respectful treatment at the hands of humans, and must be protected under the law (ASPCA is granted legal authority to investigate and make arrests for crimes against animals). It provides local and national leadership in three key areas: caring for pet parents and pets, providing positive outcomes for at-risk animals, and serving victims of animal cruelty. Headquartered in New York City, the ASPCA maintains a strong local presence, and with programs that extend its anticruelty mission across the country, it is recognized as a national animal welfare organization.

### Volunteer Opportunities

Opportunities are available at the organization's administrative office and its shelter, both in New York City. Volunteers walk dogs or socialize (play) with them, assist in obedience and behavior modification training, or help socialize with cats and kittens. Volunteers can also help young, ill, or frightened animals recuperate in foster homes and help find ASPCA's dogs and cats loving homes through its adoptions counselor training. Additionally, volunteers can perform clerical duties or assist with special projects or events. All volunteers receive training in each specific area of interest (dog, cat, adoptions, foster, etc.), and volunteers are required to perform eight hours of volunteer service per month and sign up for a minimum of six months.

The ASPCA encourages anyone outside of the New York City area to volunteer at their local animal shelter or rescue group.

### Contact Information

424 E. 92nd Street
New York, NY 10128-6804

www.aspca.org

**Name: Diane Wilkerson**

**Location: New York City**

**Organization: ASPCA**

# Director of the ASPCA's Adoption Center Volunteer Program

### How did you get involved with the ASPCA?

When we moved to New York City four years ago for my husband's job, I wanted to do something with my time. Knowing that the ASPCA was nearby, I walked over one day. I adopted a kitten, and as a result of my positive experience, started volunteering as an adoption counselor; this eventually led to getting my dream job!

### What about working with volunteers and running a volunteer program appealed to you?

It was the perfect blend of the two things I love the most: people and animals.

### What's a typical day at your job?

One of the things I like most about my job is that every day is different! But a typical day is making sure the adoptions center is appropriately staffed with volunteer adoptions counselors; being available for questions; scheduling classes; and helping to respond to the different requests that come in for volunteers, etc.

### Can you recall a particularly memorable experience you had while working at the ASPCA?

To be honest, there are so many wonderfully memorable experiences, but if I had to pick one, it would be the example of one of our newest volunteers who started volunteering while she was on break from her teaching job. She so enjoyed her experience volunteering in the adoption center—working with our dogs, cats, and adopters—that she decided to make a career change and was recently hired.

**Do you find your work rewarding?**

I consider myself truly blessed to have a job where I really feel I am making a difference in the lives of the wonderful animals here at the ASPCA. The volunteer program is essential in helping make our dogs and cats more adoptable, whether through socialization, training, or presenting the animals and their specific characteristics to potential adopters through the adoption counseling process.

**What advice would you give to someone considering doing volunteer work? How about someone specifically interested in volunteering to help animals?**

Volunteering provides that wonderful combination of doing something that makes you feel good while you are making a difference in the lives of people and animals!

## HUMANE FARMING ASSOCIATION (HFA)

Founded in 1985, HFA's goals are to protect farm animals from cruelty; to protect the public from the dangerous misuse of antibiotics, hormones, and other chemicals used on factory farms; and to protect the environment from the impact of industrialized animal factories. The association's programs include: anticruelty investigations and exposés; national media and ad campaigns; and direct, hands-on emergency care and refuge for abused farm animals.

**Volunteer Opportunities**
Contact the organization for details.

**Contact Information**
P.O. Box 3577
San Rafael, CA 94912
(415) 771-CALF

E-mail: hfa@hfa.org
www.hfa.org

★

## HUMANE SOCIETY OF THE UNITED STATES (HSUS)
Established in 1954, the HSUS seeks a humane and sustainable world for all animals. It works to reduce suffering and to create meaningful social change for animals by advocating for public policies, investigating cruelty and working to enforce existing laws, educating the public about animal issues, joining with corporations on behalf of animal-friendly policies, and conducting hands-on programs to make the world more humane. HSUS is also the lead disaster-relief agency for animals, and it provides direct care for thousands of animals at its sanctuaries and rescue facilities, wildlife rehabilitation centers, and mobile veterinary clinics. The HSUS publishes *All Animals*, a membership magazine, and *Animal Sheltering*, a bimonthly magazine for animal sheltering professionals.

**Volunteer Opportunities**
Volunteers work in emergency response, gather signatures for campaigns, and serve as online ambassadors who help spread the word about HSUS through the web. HSUS stresses that there are numerous ways for volunteers to get involved with the organization, but it also urges individuals to consider volunteering at local shelters for hands-on opportunities. People can sign up for action alerts through HSUS's website.

**Contact Information**
2100 L Street, NW
Washington, DC 20037

(202) 452-1100
www.humanesociety.org

★

## NATIONAL WILDLIFE FEDERATION (NWF)
The National Wildlife Federation is America's largest conservation organization. It works with more than 4 million members, partners, and supporters in communities across the country to protect and restore wildlife habitat, confront global warming, and connect with nature.

## Volunteer Opportunities

NWF provides a host of different opportunities, but warns that its volunteers do not directly handle wildlife. Interested parties should complete an online registration form at www.nwf.org. Positions include:

- **Habitat volunteers** work with their community member to learn about how to create, install, and maintain wildlife-friendly backyards, schools, and other locations. There are three different types of opportunities:
  - *Hosts* serve as trainers for other volunteer opportunities in their community. Hosts need to be able to commit to at least six weeks of training and to volunteer for at least six hours a week.
  - *Stewards* are hands-on skilled volunteers who are trained to assist community members with projects such as creating a wildlife garden. Stewards' opportunities are more physically demanding.
  - *Ambassadors* talk with community members and share information about how they can engage in programs or make a difference in their community. Ambassadors are on-the-ground spokespersons for NWF.
- **Wildlife advocates** volunteer in their communities to promote changes in laws or other policies. Virtual opportunities are available, or volunteers can work in one of NWF's offices to help staff members with a variety of projects, ranging from research, marketing, and writing to making phone calls or handling data entry (varies by location and need).
- **Special events volunteers** staff a table or help with a one-time event. Events are seasonal, and held mainly in the spring, early summer, or fall. Event volunteers give time to a specific event and are more generalist, helping in many different ways. Volunteers help during a short span of time, such as a few days or months. Volunteers need to be committed for the duration of the event.
- **Behind-the-scenes volunteers** work with NWF staff members to help with office projects ranging from research to data entry. Volunteers can work either in an NWF office or in a virtual capacity (from home). Volunteers need to be able to give at least four hours a week for a year.
- **Special situation volunteers** are on-call volunteers that can help with a variety of activities depending on their skills. Situation volunteers will be active as needed, and may have an intense volunteer experience for a shorter term.

- **Corporate employee volunteers** are employees that can volunteer under their employer. Visit www.nwf.org for details.
- **"Be Out There" volunteers** work with parents and kids to get outside and enjoy the outdoors.

### Contact Information

11100 Wildlife Center Drive
Reston, VA 20190-5362

(800) 822-9919
www.nwf.org

★

## PEOPLE FOR THE ETHICAL TREATMENT OF ANIMALS (PETA)

Founded in 1980, PETA focuses its attention on the four areas in which the largest numbers of animals suffer the most intensely for the longest periods of time: on factory farms, in laboratories, in the clothing trade, and in the entertainment industry. It also works on a variety of other issues, including the cruel killing of beavers, birds, and other "pests," and the abuse of backyard dogs. PETA strives to achieve its mission through public education, cruelty investigations, research, animal rescue, legislation, special events, celebrity involvement, and protest campaigns.

### Volunteer Opportunities

PETA provides opportunities at its Norfolk, Virginia, headquarters. Volunteers can get involved by attending outreach activities, including local tabling events at fairs and festivals and leafleting; critiquing medical and scientific research proposals; conducting online and library research; performing various types of office work, such as data entry, preparation of mailings, and faxing; and participating in PETA's weekly work party on Wednesday nights.

Individuals outside the Virginia area can join PETA's Action Team by completing an online form at www.peta.org. Participants receive information on upcoming events and demonstrations in their area, breaking news, urgent alerts, and tips on how to improve the lives of animals every day.

### Contact Information

501 Front Street
Norfolk, VA 23510

www.peta.org

★

WILDLIFE AND ANIMAL RIGHTS

## PETCONNECT RESCUE AND WELLNESS

PetConnect Rescue was founded in 2005, in the wake of Hurricane Katrina, and has evolved into an all-breed animal rescue organization. Its mission is to save the lives of dogs and cats that have been abandoned and place them in loving and permanent homes. On a daily basis, PetConnect responds to e-mail and phone pleas for help for dogs and cats imminently slated for euthanasia. The organization pulls these animals into rescue from overextended local shelters as well as rural shelters from West Virginia to Georgia. In the fall of 2009, PetConnect Rescue joined forces with The Kyra Macy Foundation, a nonprofit animal rescue organization.

### Volunteer Opportunities

Opportunities are offered in Maryland and Virginia, and include transporting animals, fostering, conducting home visits, and assisting at adoption events, as well as participating in the care of the rescues at PetConnect's two properties. In addition, those who wish to get involved can help with public relations, fund-raising, and administrative support. PetConnect asks potential volunteers to complete an online application on its website.

### Contact Information

**Virginia:**
PetConnect Rescue and Wellness
The Kyra Macy Foundation
12054 North Shore Drive
Reston, VA 20190

**Maryland:**
PetConnect Rescue and Wellness
P.O. Box 60714
Potomac, MD 20859
(877) 838-9171
E-mail: info@petconnectrescue.org
www.petconnectrescue.org

---★---

## THE STUDENT CONSERVATION ASSOCIATION (SCA)

Founded in 1957, SCA provides college- and high school–aged members with hands-on conservation service opportunities in virtually every field imaginable, from tracking grizzlies through the Tetons to restoring desert ecosystems and teaching environmental education at Washington, D.C.'s, Urban Tree House. SCA's members protect and restore national parks, marine sanctuaries, cultural landmarks, and community green spaces in all fifty states.

### Volunteer Opportunities

SCA is looking for members who are motivated to serve the environment, and eager to get their hands dirty while gaining real-world job experience and making a difference for our planet. There are virtually no limits to the services and experiences offered by SCA. From wildlife management, habitat restoration, forestry, fisheries, and hydrology, to archaeology, trail construction, cultural interpretation, environmental education, and visitor services—if it is practiced within the conservation field, there's a related position available at SCA.

Some specific examples of opportunities include: SCA members restoring areas of Angeles National Forest that were devastated by last year's Station Fire (they are preventing erosion by revegging burned-out areas and reconstructing trails and campsites); SCA interns at Yellowstone compiling an online database of all the park's geothermal features (information is being used by medical professionals seeking to develop new cures in answer to NASA's research regarding how life may exist under extreme conditions); interns working on climate change/sustainability outreach at the Field Museum.

SCA annually places thousands of members nationwide, covering all fifty states. It collaborates with partners including the National Park Service, the U.S. Forest Service, and the Bureau of Land Management; numerous state and local resource management offices; and private organizations such as The Nature Conservancy and the Audubon Society. Members do not ordinarily work at the New Hampshire headquarters, but the organization's regional offices (Boise, Houston, Oakland, Pittsburgh, Seattle, and Washington, D.C.) not only conduct local conservation programs for urban, often underrepresented populations, but also often host interns in a variety of outreach and support positions.

As for specific terms, SCA's crew program for high school students operates each summer, and the obligations run from three to six weeks in length, depending upon the project. For individuals age eighteen and over, it offers internships that run from anywhere between thirteen and fifty-two weeks (this also varies by project).

All SCA programs are tuition-free and most are expenses-paid, including transportation to and from the site, housing, a cost-of-living stipend, insurance, and, upon completion of service, an AmeriCorps education award of up to $5,000.

**Contact Information**

| | |
|---|---|
| 689 River Road | (603) 543-1700 |
| P.O. Box 550 | www.thesca.org |
| Charlestown, NH 03603 | |

★

## THE WILDERNESS SOCIETY

Since its founding in 1935, The Wilderness Society has led the effort to permanently protect as wilderness nearly 110 million acres in forty-four states. From the 1964 Wilderness Act to the landmark 2009 bill that permanently protected

WILDLIFE AND ANIMAL RIGHTS

more than 2 million acres of wilderness across the country, The Wilderness Society has been at the forefront of nearly every major public lands victory over the past seventy-five years.

## Volunteer Opportunities

Duties typically include research to answer questions from staff members, legal and policy memos on technical issues, letters to federal agencies such as the Forest Service, and short updates for the organization's website. The Wilderness Society also has opportunities for office assistance.

Most volunteers work in the organization's national office in Washington, but sometimes there are opportunities in the largest regional offices, located in Seattle, San Francisco, Anchorage, Denver, Boise, and Bozeman (Montana). Smaller offices are less likely to have volunteers.

Internships for school credit or stipends are also available.

## Contact Information

1615 M Street, NW
Washington, DC 20036

(202) 833-2300
www.wilderness.org

★

# WORLD WILDLIFE FUND (WWF)

WWF works in hundred countries and is supported by close to 5 million volunteers globally in its mission of protecting nature. The conservation organization combines global reach with a foundation in science, involves action at every level from local to global, and ensures the delivery of innovative solutions that meet the needs of both people and nature to preserve the diversity and abundance of life on Earth and the health of ecological systems. WWF focuses on three areas: protecting natural areas and wild populations of plants and animals (including endangered species); promoting sustainable approaches to the use of renewable natural resources and supporting more efficient use of resources and energy; and the maximum reduction of pollution. Its goal for the year 2020 is to conserve nineteen of the world's most important natural places and significantly change global markets to protect the future of nature.

## Volunteer Opportunities

WWF offers a volunteer program for people between the ages of twenty and twenty-seven. Participants work with WWF for several months in such countries as Madagascar, India, Paraguay, South Pacific, and Bhutan.

For people outside the age requirements, WWF suggests contacting one's local county parks and recreation department for opportunities such as cleaning up local parks, monitoring stream quality, or censusing migratory birds.

WWF also encourages interested individuals to join its online Conservation Action Network, to subscribe to its e-newsletter, and to regularly visit its website for information on how to support its mission.

**Contact Information**

1250 Twenty-Fourth Street, NW

P.O. Box 97180

Washington, DC 20090-7180

www.worldwildlife.org

★

# WOMEN'S RIGHTS

## CHOICE USA

Renowned activist and author Gloria Steinem founded Choice USA in 1992, along with other feminist leaders. As a national pro-choice organization, Choice USA gives emerging leaders the tools they need to organize, network, and exchange ideas to build a youth-centered pro-choice agenda and mobilize communities for reproductive justice. Choice USA helps students and young activists build leadership and organizing skills through its institutes, trainings, and internships; mobilize their communities for reproductive justice by providing effective strategies for education and outreach; and win victories to increase the availability of reproductive and social justice information and services.

### Volunteer Opportunities

Contact the organization for details.

### Contact Information

**Headquarters:** 1317 F Street, NW, Suite 501
Washington, DC 20004

(202) 965-7700 or (888) 784-4494
www.choiceusa.org

## EQUALITY NOW

Equality Now was founded in 1992 to work for the protection and promotion of the human rights of women around the world. Working with national human rights organizations and individual activists, Equality Now documents violence and discrimination against women and mobilizes international action to support their efforts to stop these human rights abuses. Through its Women's Action Network of concerned groups and individuals around the world, Equality Now distributes information about human rights violations, takes action to protest these violations, and brings public attention to human rights violations against women. Issues of urgent concern to Equality Now include rape, domestic violence, reproductive rights, trafficking of women, female genital mutilation, and the denial of equal access to economic opportunity and political participation.

### Volunteer Opportunities

Equality Now has research and campaign internships, media and outreach internships, and fund-raising and accounting internships. Opportunities are available in London, New York, and Nairobi. Research and campaign interns generally conduct legal and fact-finding research and draft Women's Actions and campaign correspondence as the work requires. Media and outreach interns help out with media outreach, including assisting with drafting columns for newspapers and targeting other local media outlets. Outreach may also involve assisting in growing the Women's Action Network membership. Fund-raising and accounting interns generally do research, draft reports, prepare spreadsheets, work special events, and handle filing and other office duties as assigned. Interns may also attend meetings at the United Nations and participate in other advocacy efforts to further Equality Now's work.

Summer interns spend eight to ten weeks full-time with Equality Now, and semester interns spend approximately ten hours a week with Equality Now. Please note that internships are unpaid and no arrangements can be made for housing or visas.

Application details can be found at www.equalitynow.org.

**Contact Information**

P.O. Box 20646
Columbus Circle Station
New York, NY 10023

E-mail: info@equalitynow.org
www.equalitynow.org

★

## GLOBAL FUND FOR WOMEN (GFW)

The Global Fund for Women is a nonprofit grant-making foundation that advances women's human rights worldwide. GFW is a network of women and men who believe that ensuring women's full equality and participation in society is one of the most effective ways to build a just, peaceful, and sustainable world. It raises funds from a variety of sources and makes grants to women-led organizations that promote the economic security, health, safety, education, and leadership of women and girls.

**Volunteer Opportunities**

Opportunities are available in GFW's San Francisco office. Volunteers work regular business hours and occasionally help staff events. Volunteers handle basic administrative tasks, including mailing, filing, and data entry, assisting with global fund events, and translation.

**Contact Information**

222 Sutter Street, Suite 500
San Francisco, CA 94108
(415) 248-4800

E-mail: gfw@globalfundforwomen
.org
www.globalfundforwomen.org

★

## NARAL PRO-CHOICE AMERICA

Established in 1966, NARAL Pro-Choice America is committed to protecting a woman's right to choose, and to electing candidates who will promote policies to prevent unintended pregnancy. In its goal to protect women's reproductive freedom, NARAL Pro-Choice America educates and mobilizes voters, provides information about state bills, the enactment of new laws, and decisions handed down by state and federal courts related to reproductive rights, and works to stop anti-choice legislation.

### Volunteer Opportunities

Contact the organization for details.

### Contact Information

1156 15th Street, NW, Suite 700
Washington, DC 20005

(202) 973-3000
www.prochoiceamerica.org

## NATIONAL NETWORK OF ABORTION FUNDS (NNAF)

Established in 1993, NNAF is a network of over a hundred grassroots groups in more than forty states that help women pay for abortion services. Some of the network's initiatives include providing intensive training and support to its member funds across the country, supporting the emergence of new abortion funds in underserved areas, advocating on the state and national level for increased access to abortion, emergency contraception, and full reproductive health care for all women, coordinating funding for women needing financial assistance from more than one member fund, and providing direct funding to women in need.

### Volunteer Opportunities

Although there are not many volunteer opportunities at the network's national office in Boston, NNAF is made up of over a hundred funds, many of which are completely volunteer-run. Volunteers respond to calls from women in need, raise money, put on educational events, and in many cases do everything that makes a grassroots abortion Fund function. Opportunities range in terms of time commitment and skill set required. NNAF encourages interested individuals to visit its website, www.nnaf.org, to learn more.

### Contact Information

42 Seaverns Avenue
Boston, MA 02130-2865
(617) 524-6040

E-mail: info@nnaf.org
www.nnaf.org

## NATIONAL ORGANIZATION FOR WOMEN FOUNDATION (NOW FOUNDATION)

The NOW Foundation, established in 1986, is devoted to furthering women's rights through education and litigation. The NOW Foundation is affiliated with the National Organization for Women, the largest women's rights organization in the United States, with a membership of over 500,000 contributing women and men dedicated to legal, political, social, and economic equality for women. NOW works on issues such as violence against women, racial and ethnic diversity, economic equality, welfare rights, health-care and reproductive rights, lesbian and gay rights, and the Equal Rights Amendment. NOW urges activists to strive for equality and justice through mass action, lobbying, nonviolent civil disobedience, and direct action.

### Volunteer Opportunities

For those interested in taking an active role in the women's rights movement, NOW provides both daytime and evening opportunities. Volunteer projects fall into several areas, including office support, public relations/communications, and field organizing. Volunteers work under the direct supervision of national officers and staff members. Tasks vary depending on the needs and the skills of the volunteer, but can include selecting and preparing materials to be archived at a library for women's history; office support, such as bookkeeping or database entry; phoning members with information about an event, issue, or action; helping with mailings; responding to inquiries from the public; writing communications; or organizing events. Opportunities are available at the national office and local chapter. NOW asks daytime volunteers to work at least two to three hours per week. Interested parties can complete the online form at www.now.org/organization/volunt.html.

### Contact Information
1100 H Street, NW, Third Floor
Washington, DC 20005

(202) 628-8669
www.nowfoundation.org

★

## NATIONAL WOMEN'S POLITICAL CAUCUS (NWPC)

The National Women's Political Caucus is a multipartisan, multicultural, grass-roots organization dedicated to increasing women's participation in the political field and creating a political power base designed to achieve equality for all women. Founded in 1971, the NWPC prides itself on increasing the number of pro-choice women elected and appointed into office every year. Through recruiting, training, and financial donations, the NWPC provides support to women candidates running for all levels of office, regardless of political affiliation. In addition, hundreds of state and local chapters reach out to women in communities across the country to better assist them in achieving their dream of being elected into office.

## Volunteer Opportunities

NWPC is open to volunteers of all ages who share the goals of the organization. Opportunities abound at the local level, but volunteers can also work at NWPC's national office in Washington, D.C. At the state or local level, volunteers can help plan and staff events, assist on campaigns of endorsed candidates, and fund-raise. At the national office, volunteers assist staff with research, writing, and administrative tasks.

There are also opportunities to become directly involved on NWPC's board. All of its national board members are elected to serve, but in a volunteer capacity.

## Contact Information

P.O. Box 50476
Washington, DC 20091
(202) 785-1100

E-mail: info@nwpc.org
www.nwpc.org

★

# Organizations by Type

If you're not sure where to start, or what exactly you have to offer, you can contact one of these organizations; staff members will be happy to steer you in the right direction. In this section, you'll learn where to go if you're interested in advocacy or policy and issues. Faith-based organizations are a great place to explore if you belong to a church or synagogue (or simply have an affinity for a specific faith). The general resources are listed here, as well as organizations operating near or on college campuses.

# ADVOCACY ORGANIZATIONS

## CORPORATE ACCOUNTABILITY INTERNATIONAL

Since 1977, Corporate Accountability International (formerly Infact) has waged—and won—campaigns that challenge irresponsible and dangerous actions by corporate giants. From bringing about significant reforms in the life-threatening marketing of infant formula in economically poor countries to pushing GE out of nuclear weapon-making, to being a major contributing factor in the adoption of the world's first corporate accountability treaty, the Framework Convention on Tobacco Control, its work has influenced the way corporations are held accountable for the last thirty years.

### Volunteer Opportunities
To receive action alerts, visit www.stopcorporateabuse.org to join the organization's online activist network.

### Contact Information
**Campaign Headquarters:** 10 Milk Street, Suite 610
Boston, MA 02108
(800) 688-8797 or (617) 695-2525

E-mail: info@stopcorporateabuse.org
www.stopcorporateabuse.org

★

## DEMOCRACY FOR AMERICA (DFA)

Democracy for America, the people-powered PAC, has over 1 million members nationwide. DFA is a grassroots powerhouse working to change our country and the Democratic Party from the bottom up. It provides campaign training, organizing resources, and media exposure so that its members have the power to support progressive issues and candidates up and down the ballot.

### Volunteer Opportunities
Contact the organization for details.

### Contact Information
**Mailing Address:** P.O. Box 1717
Burlington, VT 05402
**Physical Address:** 38 Eastwood Drive, Suite 300

South Burlington, VT 05403
(802) 651-3200
www.democracyforamerica.com

★

## JOBS WITH JUSTICE (JWJ)

JwJ engages workers and allies in campaigns to win justice in workplaces and in communities where working families live. JwJ was founded in 1987 with the vision of lifting up workers' rights struggles as part of a larger campaign for economic and social justice.

### Volunteer Opportunities

Contact the organization for details.

### Contact Information

1325 Massachusetts Avenue, NW, Suite 200
Washington, DC 20005

(202) 393-1044
E-mail: jwjnational@jwj.org
www.jwj.org

---

## NATIONAL LABOR COMMITTEE (NLC)

The mission of the National Labor Committee is to help defend the human rights of workers in the global economy. The NLC investigates and exposes human and labor rights abuses committed by U.S. companies producing goods in the developing world. It undertakes public education, research, and popular campaigns that empower U.S. citizens to support the efforts of workers to learn about and defend their rights.

### Volunteer Opportunities

Student and recent graduate interns help with conducting corporate and trade research, updating NLC's donor database, and maintaining its website and social media network pages. NLC welcome volunteers and provides opportunities on a case-by-case basis, depending on its project needs.

### Contact Information

5 Gateway Center, 6th Floor
Pittsburgh, PA 15222
(412) 562-2406

E-mail: nlc@nlcnet.org
www.nlcnet.org

---

## PUBLIC CAMPAIGN

Public Campaign is a nonprofit, nonpartisan organization dedicated to sweeping campaign reform that aims to dramatically reduce the role of big special interest money in American politics. Public Campaign is laying the foundation for reform by working with a broad range of organizations (including local community groups) around the country that are fighting for change, and with national organizations whose members are not fairly represented under the current campaign finance system. Together they are building a network of national and state-based efforts to create a powerful national force for federal and state campaign reform.

## Volunteer Opportunities

Public Campaign is always looking for people who want to support its efforts. Volunteers help with a variety of activities, including phone banking, letter-writing campaigns, and rallies, to name a few. Public Campaign deeply values the commitment of their supporters, and eagerly welcomes others who want to be involved in promoting Fair Elections policy.

## Contact Information

1133 19th Street, NW, Suite 900
Washington, DC 20036
(202) 293-0222

E-mail: info@pcactionfund.org
www.publicampaign.org

★

# RESULTS AND RESULTS EDUCATIONAL FUND (REF)

RESULTS and RESULTS Educational Fund (REF) are sister organizations that, together, are a leading force in ending poverty in the United States and around the world. They create long-term solutions to poverty by supporting programs that address its root causes: lack of access to medical care, education, or opportunity to move up the economic ladder. They do this by empowering ordinary people to become extraordinary voices, working together to end poverty by spreading the word in their communities, the media, and the halls of government. The collective voices of these passionate grassroots activists, coordinated with grass-tops efforts driven by the organizations' staff, leverage millions of dollars for programs and improved policies that give low-income people the tools they need to move out of poverty.

## Volunteer Opportunities

The RESULTS website lists activist how-tos about engaging your elected official, working with your local media, and building a community coalition. The guidelines encompass the simple to the advanced, and provide direction on how to move decision makers toward becoming champions for the end of poverty. Available internships are also posted at www.results.org.

Volunteers can also join a local RESULTS advocacy group or start a new group in their area if one does not already exist. Volunteers meet monthly to become educated on the issues, train on how to best advocate for them, and then take action. RESULTS has about a hundred groups nationwide, with approximately 800 active volunteers.

## Contact Information

RESULTS / RESULTS Educational
Fund
750 First Street, NE, Suite 1040
Washington, DC 20002
**RESULTS:** (202) 783-7100

**RESULTS Educational Fund:** (202)
783-4800
E-mail: results@results.org
www.results.org

-----------------------------------  ★  -----------------------------------

## TRUEMAJORITY

TrueMajority was founded by Ben Cohen, cofounder of Ben and Jerry's. It is a grassroots education and advocacy joint project of USAction and USAction Education Fund.

### Volunteer Opportunities

Once you register as a member with TrueMajority via its website, you will receive e-mail alerts about electoral campaign issues, activities, events, and critical topics. With one click of a button you can either send TrueMajority's suggested letters and petitions to local representatives or edit them yourself (and the organization will still send them for you).

## Contact Information

TrueMajority.org / USAction: 1825 K
Street, NW, Suite 210
Washington, DC 20006

(202) 263-4520
E-mail: info@truemajority.org
www.truemajority.org

-----------------------------------  ★  -----------------------------------

# CAMPUS ORGANIZATIONS

## AMNESTY INTERNATIONAL (AI)

Established in 1961, Amnesty International is a worldwide movement of people who campaign for internationally recognized human rights for all. Among its areas of focus, AI takes action to stop violence against women, defend the rights and dignity of those trapped in poverty, regulate the global arms trade, and abolish the death penalty. AI has more than 2.8 million members and supporters in more than 150 countries and regions.

### Volunteer Opportunities

Becoming a member of AI gains you entry into local activist volunteer groups. Groups may work on freeing prisoners of conscience, economic justice, or the abolition of the death penalty, as well as other human rights campaigns. They also fund-raise and organize meetings with members of Congress. Volunteering in one of AI's local offices as an activist is also an option. Visit www.amnestyusa.org to search for groups or opportunities in your area, or to view the AI activist tool kit.

### Contact Information

5 Penn Plaza, 16th Floor
New York, NY 10001
(212) 807-8400

E-mail: admin-us@aiusa.org
www.amnesty.org

★

Name: Becky Farrar

Location: Arlington, Virginia

Organization: Amnesty International

**Can you describe what you do as a volunteer for Amnesty International?**

I wear different hats with Amnesty International. I have a fantastic volunteer position as a Legislative Coordinator (LC). There are LCs around the country who work with Amnesty members and activists on lobbying members of Congress on human rights issues. I was the LC for Florida during law school, and have been LC for Washington, D.C., since I moved to D.C. last summer. I particularly enjoy leading lobbying trainings. I am also a member of a local Amnesty group, and we are involved in several exciting projects. These have included taking part in rallies; hosting evening events and happy hours that raise awareness (and some funds); tabling at Eastern Market (to explain specific human rights abuses); and volunteering at arts festivals. And finally, I sit on one of the strategic member committees, which has allowed me to participate in some of the strategic planning for our Demand Dignity campaign.

**So you don't work in an Amnesty office?**

Much of my volunteer work is done from my home (sending e-mails, making phone calls), but I also attend meetings as a member of a local Amnesty group, and with other members on projects I am working on. I like the combination of things I can do from home and being in meetings and group gatherings.

**How did you learn about this opportunity?**

I decided to go to law school after several years in the workforce, in part because I wanted to figure out how to make a bigger difference in the world on a global level. Years before, while living in Canada, I wrote letters on prisoners of conscience as an Amnesty member. But my law school didn't have an Amnesty chapter. Two of my fellow law students and I started one and I served as president. I became LC for Florida when my friend from the chapter graduated.

**What appealed to you about volunteering with Amnesty?**

I wanted to learn more about human rights from a credible source (and I knew Amnesty was that), and I wanted to give others the same information and awareness, and encourage them to get involved in human rights work.

**What impact has volunteering had on your life?**

It's important for me as a volunteer to feel passionate about what I'm working on, and it's also important to feel that what I give is valued and appreciated. Volunteering with Amnesty fulfills both of those needs. My personal goal is to do something for human rights every day, and with my Amnesty activities, that hasn't been a problem. The other key aspect in my volunteering is feeling appreciated. I have been very fortunate to work with staffers at Amnesty who have valued my contributions and that's been great.

Another huge joy for me is harder to put into words. I feel "akin" to the people involved in Amnesty. I've described that to people in the past by saying "This is my tribe." I feel that with my fellow LCs, and I feel it when I attend Amnesty meetings, conferences, and gatherings and meet other Amnesty members from around the country. It means I feel a part of a larger group—part of a community—that I identify with. That's very important to me as well.

**What advice would you give to someone who wanted to volunteer in their community?**

First, do it! Pick something you care about, something you really love or are passionate about, or something you think would be fun. Make sure there's an intrinsic joy in it—that's what keeps you going.

And then, research—figure out who does the kind of thing you want to do and do some research on the group itself. Make sure you're comfortable with what they do and how they operate, and see if they have a good opportunity for you. There's some chemistry involved, so if you don't feel comfortable, look for another group. Every nonprofit organization can use help and needs talented and passionate volunteers!

## CAMPUS PROGRESS

Campus Progress is a national organization that works with and for young people to promote progressive solutions to key political and social challenges. Through programs in activism, journalism, and events, Campus Progress engages a diverse group of young people nationwide, inspires them to embrace progressive values, provides them with essential training, and helps them to make their voices heard—and to push policy outcomes in a strongly progressive direction.

### Volunteer Opportunities

The organization's campus and local activism work is done through the action alliance program. Action alliances consist of grants or help in executing an activism campaign, or both. Visit the website to apply for a grant (recipients receive up to $1,500 a year to help with websites, flyers, and other materials), or to apply for a progressive partnership (Campus Progress provides guidance, networking, strategic planning, and training for youth-led efforts). Campus Progress's national advocacy team works in Washington, D.C., and with young people around the country to promote and protect progressive solutions to key national policy challenges. The organization also offers funding, training, and editorial guidance to a diverse network of print, online, and broadcast media on college campuses across the country. Interested individuals can also write for CP.org (stipends are provided) or sign petitions and contact public officials through the Campus Progress website. Contact the organization for more information on these opportunities.

### Contact Information

Campus Progress
Center for American Progress
1333 H Street, NW, 10th Floor
Washington, DC 20005

(202) 682-1611
E-mail: campus@campusprogress.
  com
www.campusprogress.com

★

## DEMOCRACY MATTERS

Democracy Matters was founded in 2001 by NBA basketball player, poet, and activist Adonal Foyle and his parents, Joan and Jay Mandle, both of whom are Colgate University professors and lifelong organizers. Its mission is to strengthen democracy by training young people how to be effective grassroots organizers and advocates, and by supporting public financing of election campaigns ("fair elections") and other pro-democracy reforms. Democracy Matters is a nonpartisan campus-based national student organization in partnership with Common Cause. Offering paid internships to undergraduates and affiliate internships to high school students, Democracy Matters mentors the next generation of leaders dedicated to strengthening democracy.

**Volunteer Opportunities**

Volunteers serve as liaisons between the organization and their own college campuses. Internships are offered to undergraduates to do political organizing on their campuses. In addition, interested individuals can download resources from the Democracy Matters website to start a campus action campaign (www.democracymatters.org also posts petitions and letters to local representatives that can be signed).

**Contact Information**

P.O. Box 157

Hamilton, NY 13346

(315) 824-4306

www.democracymatters.org

★

## ENERGY ACTION COALITION

Energy Action Coalition is a coalition of fifty youth-led environmental and social justice groups working together to build the clean energy and climate movement. Working with hundreds of campus and youth groups, dozens of youth networks, and hundreds of thousands of young people, Energy Action Coalition and its partners have united a burgeoning movement behind winning local victories and coordinating on state, regional, and national levels in the United States and Canada.

**Volunteer Opportunities**

There are a wide range of activity engagements through the coalition's partner organizations. Visit the Energy Action Coalition website to search the list of organizations.

**Contact Information**

1850 M Street, Suite 1150

Washington, DC 20036

(202) 631-1992

E-mail: Theteam@energyaction.net

www.energyactioncoalition.org

★

## IDEALIST.ORG

Idealist is a project of Action Without Borders, a nonprofit organization founded in 1995 with offices in the United States and Argentina. Idealist is an interactive site where people and organizations can exchange resources and ideas and locate opportunities and supporters.

### Volunteer Opportunities

Idealist.org offers an extensive search to help connect individuals with programs of interest.

### Contact Information

302 Fifth Avenue, 11th Floor
New York, NY 10001
1220 SW Morrison, 10th Floor

Portland, OR 97205
(503) 227-0803
www.idealist.org

★

## NATIONAL STUDENT CAMPAIGN AGAINST HUNGER AND HOMELESSNESS

The Campaign is committed to ending hunger and homelessness in America by educating, engaging, and training students to directly meet individuals' immediate needs while advocating for long-term systemic solutions.

### Volunteer Opportunities

Students who join the Campaign's network receive information on hunger and homelessness issues and updates about upcoming events. The Campaign also provides advice and resources for students to help them organize on campus. Visit the organization's website to sign up or to view posted events.

### Contact Information

**National Organizing Office:** 407 S.
  Dearborn, Suite 701
Chicago, IL 60605
(312) 291-0349 x302

E-mail: info@studentsagainsthunger
  .org
www.Studentsagainsthunger.org

★

## OXFAM AMERICA

Oxfam America is an affiliate of Oxfam International, a relief and development organization established in 1970. Oxfam America strives to create lasting solutions to poverty, hunger, and injustice. Current campaigns focus on helping poor communities who are vulnerable to climate change and unfair practices by international oil, gas, and mining companies, and on ensuring U.S. foreign aid is effective in fighting global poverty. Oxfam America also provides emergency relief around the world and helps communities rebuild and establish lasting change.

### Volunteer Opportunities

Founded by a group of volunteers in response to a humanitarian crisis, Oxfam America offers a long list of opportunities for interested volunteers. One way to get involved is by joining the Oxfam Action Corps. Volunteers work to improve national legislation and to fight poverty on a local level by collecting signatures, organizing petition drives, planning events, or joining a delegation to a lawmaker's local office. Other opportunities are regularly posted on the organization's website. To apply, Oxfam America requests a cover letter and résumé e-mailed to internsandvolunteers@oxfamamerica.org with the name of the desired position in the subject line.

**Contact Information**

**Headquarters:** 26 Causeway Street, 5th Floor
Boston, MA 02114-2206

(800) 77-OXFAM or (800)-776-9326
www.oxfamamerica.org

## SIERRA STUDENT COALITION (SSC)

The Sierra Student Coalition (SSC) is a broad network of high school– and college-aged youth from across the country working to protect the environment. The SSC is the youth-led chapter of the Sierra Club, the nation's oldest and largest grassroots environmental organization. The mission of the SSC is to "train, empower, and organize youth to run effective campaigns that result in tangible environmental victories and that develop leaders for the environmental movement."

**Volunteer Opportunities**

Check out the SSC website to sign up for the organization's monthly newsletter, *SSC Update*, which provides details on SSC campaigns and highlights. Interested individuals can also join the SSC Energy Forum to receive e-mails about energy campaigns and new opportunities and events.

In addition, the website provides information on becoming a campus organizer or community coordinator, registering a group as an SSC affiliate, and joining one of the organization's national committees. Internships are also available.

**Contact Information**

E-mail: info@ssc.org

www.ssc.sierraclub.org

## STUDENT COALITION FOR ACTION ON LITERACY EDUCATION (SCALE)

SCALE supports campus-based literacy programs locally, statewide, and nationally through its Literacy Action Networks. In these programs, college students serve as literacy tutors or teachers in their community. It works with all types of program models, including America Reads, Family Literacy, Youth

Literacy and Mentoring, and GED Preparation. The college students serving in these programs include volunteer/paid tutors or coordinators, AmeriCorps members, VISTA members, and service-learning students.

**Volunteer Opportunities**

Volunteers can get involved through the North Carolina Literacy Corps (a state AmeriCorps program). Through the Corps, Volunteers work for a one-year term beginning August 1 and concluding on July 31. They are placed in community- and college-based literacy programs where they provide tutoring, train other volunteers to become tutors, and, depending on experience, work in program management. Part-time (900 hours) and full-time (1,700 hours) participants receive a living allowance. Training is provided.

Volunteers can also get involved through Project Literacy, a program that connects students from the University of North Carolina with community-based literacy organizations, or find opportunities through SCALE's partner organizations.

**Contact Information**

101 E. Weaver Street, Carr Mill Mall,    E-mail: scale@unc.edu
Suite 201    www.readwriteact.org
Carrboro, NC 27510
(919) 962-1542

★

## STUDENT ENVIRONMENTAL ACTION COALITION (SEAC)

SEAC is a student- and youth-run national network of progressive organizations and individuals whose aim is to uproot environmental injustices through action and education. It defines the environment to include the physical, economic, political, and cultural conditions in which we live. By challenging the power structure which threatens these conditions, students in SEAC work to create progressive social change on both the local and global levels.

**Volunteer Opportunities**

Joining SEAC puts you in contact with SEAC resources and adds you to the organization's activist lists. Local groups can become affiliated with SEAC and individuals can become regional coordinators—meaning, the point people for their state or region. Regional coordinators are in regular communication with the SEAC National Office, as well as participating in and encouraging strategy and action among youth in their region. Another option is to become a chapter point person; each SEAC chapter is encouraged to have a point person who keeps in touch regularly with SEAC National and learns strategy and skills for their group. Internships are available in fund-raising and graphic design, and one can also become a SEAC blog contributor. Visit the organization's website to register.

**Contact Information**

2206 Washington Street E
Charleston WV 25311

(304) 414-0143
www.seac.org

------------------------------------ ★ ------------------------------------

## STUDENT PUBLIC INTEREST RESEARCH GROUPS (PIRGS)

PIRGs are independent statewide student organizations that work on issues like environmental protection, consumer protection, and hunger and homelessness.

### Volunteer Opportunities

You can get involved with a variety of programs, including community service events, environmental campaigns, voter registration drives, and local research projects. Visit the organization's website to complete a volunteer form. The website also discusses internships and features an activist tool kit for download.

**Contact Information**

407 S. Dearborn, Suite 701
Chicago, IL 60605
(312) 291-0349

E-mail: info@studentpirgs.org
www.studentpirgs.org

------------------------------------ ★ ------------------------------------

## UNITED STATES STUDENT ASSOCIATION (USSA) / UNITED STATES STUDENT ASSOCIATION FOUNDATION (USSF)

The United States Student Association, the country's oldest, largest, and most inclusive national student-led organization, develops current and future leaders and amplifies the student voice at the local, state, and national levels by mobilizing grassroots power to win concrete victories on student issues.

The United States Student Association Foundation ensures the pipeline of effective student leadership by facilitating education, training, and other development opportunities at national, state, and local levels in advocating for issues that affect students.

### Volunteer Opportunities

USSA offers several internships each year that primarily focus on one of its two yearly conferences. USSA also helps coordinate student voter coalitions, which are groups of students who work on nonpartisan get-out-the-vote efforts in a volunteer capacity on college campuses.

**Contact Information**

1211 Connecticut Avenue, NW, Suite 406
Washington, DC 20036

(202) 640-6570
E-mail: ussa@usstudents.org
www.usstudents.org

------------------------------------ ★ ------------------------------------

## UNITED STUDENTS AGAINST SWEATSHOPS (USAS)

United Students Against Sweatshops is a grassroots organization of youth and students who fight for the rights of working people, particularly garment workers who make collegiate licensed apparel. USAS organizes campaigns protecting the right of workers to form unions, stopping tuition hikes, and advocating for workers in higher education and in garment factories. Another focus of theirs, the Sweat-Free Campus Campaign, forces schools to require basic workers rights of corporations producing collegiate apparel.

### Volunteer Opportunities

Opportunities are available at USAS's national office in D.C. Tasks vary from research to helping keep accounting records to calling supporters for donations. There are no time commitments or age restrictions.

**Contact Information**

**Headquarters:** 1150 17th Street, NW
Washington, DC 20036
(202) NO-SWEAT

E-mail: staff@usas.org
www.usas.org

------------------------------------ ★ ------------------------------------

211

# GENERAL RESOURCE ORGANIZATIONS

## AMERICA'S PROMISE ALLIANCE

Founded in 1997 with General Colin Powell as chairman and chaired today by Alma Powell, America's Promise Alliance is a cross-sector partnership of more than 300 corporations, nonprofits, faith-based organizations, and advocacy groups that are passionate about improving lives and changing outcomes for children. The Alliance has made a top priority of ensuring that all young people graduate from high school ready for college, work, and life. Its work involves raising awareness, encouraging action, and engaging in advocacy to provide children the key supports the Alliance calls the Five Promises: Caring Adults, Safe Places, A Healthy Start, An Effective Education, and Opportunities to Help Others.

### Volunteer Opportunities

America's Promise Alliance encourages interested individuals to visit its website to view the full list of Alliance Partners (corporations, nonprofit service organizations, foundations, policymakers, advocacy organizations, and faith groups) and contact those of interest to learn of their volunteer opportunities. The Alliance also offers unpaid internships year-round.

### Contact Information

1110 Vermont Avenue, NW,
Suite 900
Washington, DC 20005

(202) 657-0600
www.americaspromise.org

## CORPORATION FOR NATIONAL & COMMUNITY SERVICE (CNS)

The Corporation is the nation's largest grant maker supporting service and volunteering. Through its Senior Corps, AmeriCorps, and Learn and Serve America programs, it provides opportunities for Americans of all ages and backgrounds to express their patriotism while addressing critical community needs.

### Volunteer Opportunities

Visit the CNS website to search for opportunities in your area. See also "AmeriCorps" (page 112) and "Volunteers in Service to America" (page 118) in chapter 6, Community Development and Economic Justice.

**Contact Information**

1201 New York Avenue, NW
Washington, DC 20525
(202) 606-5000 or TTY:
  (202) 606-3472

E-mail: info@cns.gov
www.nationalservice.org

★

## EARTHSHARE

Founded by its member charities in 1988, EarthShare is an opportunity for employees and workplaces to support hundreds of environmental charities through workplace-giving campaigns. A workplace-giving campaign is an annual, employer-sponsored program that lets employees contribute a few dollars per paycheck as their charitable donation.

**Volunteer Opportunities**

EarthShare's website lists volunteer and event opportunities offered by EarthShare member charities and state affiliates across the country. It also provides a list of year-round volunteer opportunities offered by its members.

**Contact Information**

7735 Old Georgetown Road,
  Suite 900
Bethesda, MD 20814

(800) 875-3863 or (240) 333-0300
E-mail: info@earthshare.org
www.earthshare.org

★

## NETWORK FOR GOOD

Network for Good helps nonprofit organizations (NPOs) raise money on their own websites and on social networks with free and low-cost fund-raising tools. It also enables giving to any charity registered in the U.S. at www.networkforgood.org, through fund-raising widgets on social networks, and via partners' websites. Its "SixDegrees.org" initiative links people with celebrity philanthropists.

**Volunteer Opportunities**

At www.networkforgood.org, users can research any charity and search from among more than 40,000 volunteer opportunities. Individuals can also search for volunteer opportunities through Network for Good's state Volunteer Network sites: California, Louisiana, and New York.

**Contact Information**

7920 Norfolk Avenue, Suite 520
Bethesda, MD 20814

(888) 284-7978
www.networkforgood.org

★

## OPPORTUNITY KNOCKS

Opportunity Knocks is a national online job site, HR resource, and career development destination focused exclusively on the nonprofit community. It is committed to lead and support efforts that help further nonprofit careers and promote a robust workforce that enables organizations to complete their missions.

### Contact Information

50 Hurt Plaza, Suite 845
Atlanta, GA 30303
888-OKNOCKS

E-mail: support@opportunityknocks
.org
www.opportunityknocks.org

## POINTS OF LIGHT INSTITUTE AND HANDSON NETWORK

Points of Light Institute inspires, equips, and mobilizes people to take action that changes the world. The Institute has a global focus to redefine volunteerism and civic engagement for the twenty-first century, putting people at the center of community problem-solving. It is organized to innovate, incubate, and activate new ideas that help people act upon their power to make a difference. Points of Light Institute operates three business units that share its mission: HandsOn Network, MissionFish, and the Civic Incubator.

HandsOn Network, the volunteer-focused arm of Points of Light Institute, is the largest volunteer network in the nation and includes more than 250 HandsOn Action Centers in sixteen countries. HandsOn includes a powerful network of more than 70,000 corporate, faith, and nonprofit organizations that are answering the call to serve and creating meaningful change in their communities. Annually, the network delivers approximately 30 million hours of volunteer service valued at about $600 million.

### Volunteer Opportunities

The HandsOn Network action centers connect volunteers with projects in their geographical areas. Visit www.handsonnetwork.org to search opportunities in your area or to find a local HandsOn Action Center.

### Contact Information

**Atlanta Office, Headquarters:** 600
Means Street, Suite 210
Atlanta, GA 30318
(404) 979-2900

**Washington, D.C. Office:** 1875 K
Street, NW, 5th Floor
Washington, DC 20006
Volunteer Info: 1-800-Volunteer

## PROGRESSNOW

Since 2003, ProgressNow has been developing its network of state partner organizations to fill a unique and critical role in the progressive infrastructure of key states. ProgressNow state partners serve as nonstop, multi-issue advocacy organizations. Year-round, ProgressNow promotes progressive ideas and causes with creative earned media strategies, targeted e-mail campaigns, and cutting-edge new media. Working with its allies, the organization has significantly improved the communications effort of the entire progressive community in its states.

### Volunteer Opportunities

ProgressNow is located in about thirteen states. To get involved, visit www.progressnow.org and find the link to your state to view action items.

### Contact Information

1536 Wynkoop Street, Suite 203
Denver, CO 80202
(303) 991-1900

E-mail: info@progressnow.org
www.progressnow.org

★

## PROGRESSIVE FUTURE

Progressive Future promotes progressive values through grassroots action. It is a nonprofit organization advocating for core progressive principles such as community, fairness, and security; and working for progress on critical issues, such as providing health care for all Americans, promoting a clean-energy economy, and ending the war in Iraq.

### Volunteer Opportunities

Progressive Future lists actions, such as contacting local representatives, on its website.

### Contact Information

218 D Street SE, Suite 250
Washington, DC 20003
(202) 543-3332

E-mail: info@progressivefuture.org
www.progressivefuture.org

★

## VOLUNTEERMATCH

VolunteerMatch strengthens communities by making it easier for good people and good causes to connect. The organization offers a variety of online services to support a community of nonprofit, volunteer, and business leaders committed to civic engagement. Its popular service, www.volunteermatch.org, welcomes millions of visitors a year and has become the preferred Internet recruiting tool for more than 73,000 nonprofit organizations.

### Volunteer Opportunities

The organization is best known for its public website, www .volunteermatch.org, which makes it possible for volunteers to search through a variety of volunteer roles and projects based on skills, cause, time commitment, and other requirements. VolunteerMatch also has opportunities available in its San Francisco office, which are posted in the organization's own account on its website.

**Contact Information**
717 California Street, 2nd Floor
San Francisco, CA 94108

(415) 241-6868
www.volunteermatch.org

# FAITH-BASED ORGANIZATIONS

## AMERICAN JEWISH CONGRESS (AJC)

Established in 1918, the AJC is an association of Jewish Americans organized to defend Jewish interests at home and abroad through public policy advocacy, using diplomacy, legislation, and the courts.

### Volunteer Opportunities

Contact the organization for details.

### Contact Information

**National Headquarters:** 115 East 57th Street, Suite 11 New York, NY 10022

(212) 879-4500
E-mail: contact@ajcongress.org
www.ajcongress.org

---

★

## ASSOCIATION OF JEWISH FAMILY AND CHILDREN'S AGENCIES (AJFCA)

AJFCA is a membership organization comprised of over 130 Jewish Family and Children's Agencies and specialized Jewish human service agencies in the United States and Canada. Member JF&CS agencies provide social services to children, adults, and the elderly in the Jewish and general community. Tracing their roots back to the nineteenth century, JF&CS agencies began by assisting Jewish refugees and immigrants, orphans, and the poor and needy. Today, JF&CS agencies continue to provide preventative as well as social services to people of all ages and to those with special needs.

### Volunteer Opportunities

Contact the organization for more information.

### Contact Information

5750 Park Heights Avenue
Baltimore, MD 21215

(800) 634-7346
www.ajfca.org

---

★

## CATHOLIC CAMPAIGN FOR HUMAN DEVELOPMENT

Founded in 1969, the Catholic Campaign for Human Development is the domestic antipoverty, social justice program of the U.S. Catholic bishops. Its mission is to address the root causes of poverty in America through promotion and support of community-controlled self-help organizations and through transformative education.

**Volunteer Opportunities**
Visit the website to learn about supporting the campaign's mission.

**Contact Information**

3211 Fourth Street, NE
Washington, DC 20017
(202) 541-3210

E-mail: cchdpromo@usccb.org
www.usccb.org/cchd

★

## CATHOLIC NETWORK OF VOLUNTEER SERVICE (CNVS)

The CNVS, established in 1963, is a nonprofit membership organization of 200 domestic and international volunteer and lay mission programs. Currently, more than 10,000 volunteers and lay missioners serve in these programs throughout the U.S. and in 108 other countries.

CNVS publishes and distributes *Response,* a comprehensive handbook of lay-mission volunteer opportunities. The network also provides its member programs with recruitment services, training, and technical-assistance resources, including its national conference, formation workshops, renewal workshops, and its web-based resource library.

**Volunteer Opportunities**
Catholic and Christian volunteer programs can be found by using the CNVS *Response* directory. It allows individuals to search all volunteer opportunities offered by CNVS's 200 member programs by type of placement; region, state, or country; length of service; financial arrangements; living arrangements; size of program; and participation in the AmeriCorps Education Awards Program (AEAP).

CNVS also seeks volunteer associates to provide administrative and project support in its national office in Takoma Park, Maryland. Long- and short-term opportunities are available annually to help with team projects, assist in various administrative tasks, maintain databases and resource materials, support projects, and assist with mailings, writing reports, and recordkeeping. Applicants must be at least twenty-one years old, and have some understanding of mission and the role of the laity and a commitment to Christian values. Desirable qualities include excellent interpersonal, organizational, computer, and writing skills; ability to work independently; and previous volunteer experience. Housing and stipend is available for yearlong volunteers and handled on a case-by-case basis for short-term volunteers. Applicants should contact Jim Lindsay at jlindsay@cnvs.org for more information.

**Contact Information**

6930 Carroll Avenue, Suite 820

Takoma Park, MD 20912-4423

(301) 270-0900 or (800) 543-5046

E-mail: cnvsinfo@cnvs.org

www.cnvs.org

---

## CATHOLIC WORKER MOVEMENT

The Catholic Worker Movement began on May 1, 1933, when a journalist named Dorothy Day and a philosopher named Peter Maurin teamed up to publish and distribute a newspaper called *The Catholic Worker.* This radical paper promoted the biblical promise of justice and mercy.

Grounded in a firm belief in the God-given dignity of every human person, their movement was committed to nonviolence, voluntary poverty, and the Works of Mercy as a way of life. It wasn't long before Dorothy and Peter were putting their beliefs into action, opening a "house of hospitality" where the homeless, the hungry, and the forsaken would always be welcome.

Over many decades the movement has protested injustice, war, and violence of all forms. Today there are some 185 Catholic Worker communities in the United States.

### Volunteer Opportunities

All Catholic Worker communities welcome volunteers to work in many capacities, including helping with gardening, letter writing, and bookkeeping. Contact a local community for details, or visit www.catholicworker.org to learn of specific opportunities.

### Contact Information

www.catholicworker.org lists communities by state.

## CENTER FOR COMMUNITY ACTION FOR B'NAI B'RITH INTERNATIONAL

Established in 1843, the B'nai B'rith International (BBI) Center for Community Action (CCA) helps BBI serve individual Jewish communities and the world, providing disaster relief and services to those in need, promoting respect for others and celebrating diversity, and offering a helping hand.

### Volunteer Opportunities

The center provides activities (such as food distributions for Hanukkah and Passover) for individuals who wish to get involved in programs that assist those in need. Activities are locally based in communities across the U.S. and the world. Many of the programs are part of an annual calendar and are coordinated by local chairpersons who also run the programs. Other examples of possible opportunities include working with a daily food rescue program in Los Angeles, California, or participating in Christmas Eve or Christmas Day hospital visits. The center also provides opportunities through some of its partnerships with other organizations. For more information about getting involved with B'nai B'rith programs, e-mail cca@bnaibrith.org, or call (212) 490-3290.

## Contact Information

**Headquarters:** B'nai B'rith
International
2020 K Street, NW, 7th Floor
Washington, DC 20006
(202) 857-6600 or (888) 388-4224

www.bnaibrith.org
**Center for Community Action:**
(212) 490-3290
E-mail: cca@bnaibrith.org
www.bnaibrith.org/centers/cca.cfm

------------------------------------ ★ ------------------------------------

## CHRISTIAN RELIEF SERVICES (CRS)

Incorporated in 1985, Christian Relief Services was founded on the belief that community partnerships are the best way to solve problems related to poverty, both here in the United States and around the world. The mission of Christian Relief Services is to work through partnerships and in collaboration with grassroots charitable organizations to connect the vast resources of the United States with communities in need, to enable the people of these communities to help themselves.

### Volunteer Opportunities

Opportunities are available on Indian reservations in South Dakota and Montana, working with Native American youth. CRS asks volunteers for a three- to four-week commitment, and housing is provided.

Volunteers can also perform general clerical work in the CRS office in Alexandria, Virginia.

### Contact Information

2550 Huntington Avenue, Suite 200
Alexandria, VA 22303
(703) 317-9086 or (800) 33-RELIEF

E-mail: info@christianrelief.org
www.christianrelief.org

------------------------------------ ★ ------------------------------------

## CITYTEAM MINISTRIES

CityTeam Ministries is a nonprofit organization serving the poor and homeless in San Jose, San Francisco, Oakland, Portland, and Philadelphia, and actively training church planters and planting churches in eighty-two other countries around the world. Since 1957, CityTeam has provided lifesaving food, shelter, clothing, recovery programs, youth outreach, camp for at-risk inner city kids, discipleship, and other essential care 365 days a year.

## Volunteer Opportunities

Volunteers are vital to the heartbeat of CityTeam Ministries. Visit the organization's website to learn more about volunteer events, and to find contact information for volunteer coordinators in CityTeam Ministries' offices.

## Contact Information

**Headquarters:** 2304 Zanker Road
San Jose, CA 95131
(408) 232-5600

E-mail: sanjose@cityteam.org or
info@cityteam.org
www.cityteam.org

★

# CRISTA MINISTRIES

CRISTA describes its mission as "to love God by serving people—meeting practical and spiritual needs so that those we minister to will be built up in love, united in faith and maturing in Christ."

## Volunteer Opportunities

There are many opportunities for volunteers. Ministries include senior living, world concern, Seattle Urban Academy, broadcasting, veterinary missions, CRISTA camps, and King's Schools. Visit the organization's website or contact CRISTA for details.

## Contact Information

19303 Fremont Avenue N
Seattle, WA 98133
(206) 546-7200

E-mail: info@crista.net
www.crista.org

★

# FELLOWSHIP OF RECONCILIATION (FOR)

The FOR seeks the company of people of faith who will respond to conflict nonviolently, searching for reconciliation through compassionate action. Its campaigns include abolishing nuclear weapons, ending U.S. Military aid in Colombia, opposing any future military drafts, and promoting nonviolence in Iran.

## Volunteer Opportunities

FOR has several dozen local chapters and affiliates across North America, so one way to become active in FOR's work is by participating in those local expressions of activism. FOR also coordinates campaigns on various issues toward peace, justice, human rights, and interfaith engagement, and regularly invites all of its members and supporters to participate.

**Contact Information**

521 N. Broadway
Nyack, New York 10960

(845) 358-4601
www.forusa.org

★

## GENERAL BOARD OF CHURCH AND SOCIETY, THE UNITED METHODIST CHURCH (GBCS)

The General Board of Church and Society (GBCS) is one of four international general program boards of the United Methodist Church. The General Board is defined by its five areas of ministry: public witness and advocacy, administration, ministry of resourcing congregational life, United Nations ministry, and communications.

**Volunteer Opportunities**

Contact the organization for details.

**Contact Information**

100 Maryland Avenue, NE
Washington, D.C. 20002

(202) 488-5600
www.umc-gbcs.org

★

## LUTHERAN SERVICES IN AMERICA (LSA)

Lutheran Services in America creates opportunities for people in thousands of communities throughout the United States and the Caribbean as an alliance of the Evangelical Lutheran Church in America, The Lutheran Church–Missouri Synod, and their over 300 health and human service organizations. Working neighbor to neighbor through services in health care, aging, and disability supports; community development; housing; and child and family strengthening, these organizations together touch the lives of one in fifty Americans each year, and have aggregated annual incomes of over $16.6 billion.

**Volunteer Opportunities**

LSA seeks people who want to be partners in supporting social ministry and social change, people who can help create relationships, work groups, think tanks, and innovation sessions with philanthropists, universities, corporations, and social entrepreneurs. It looks for volunteers to help it leverage the Lutheran social ministry network to create better communities and more opportunities for all people. If you are interested in how your experience and interests can intersect with those of Lutheran social ministry at the national level, contact Cynthia Osborne at cosborne@lutheranservices.org or (410) 230-3546.

Individuals can also volunteer with one of LSA's member organizations. Volunteers have many opportunities to work with member organizations, from working with clients to offering management expertise or support behind the scenes. Similarly, LSA's denominational members, the Evangelical Lutheran Church in America and the Lutheran Church–Missouri Synod, have multiple volunteer options. Visit LSA's website for more information.

**Contact Information**
**National Headquarters:** 700 Light
   Street
Baltimore, MD 21230-3850

(800) 664-3848
E-mail: lsa@lutheranservices.org
www.lutheranservices.org

★

## MISSIONS DOOR

Missions Door exists to assist local churches and Christ followers in their efforts to evangelize, disciple, and plant churches around the world.

### Volunteer Opportunities

For short- or long-term mission work around the world, visit the Missions Door website to complete an online form.

### Contact Information

2530 Washington Street
Denver, CO 80205-3142
(303) 308-1818

E-mail: info@missionsdoor.org
www.missionsdoor.org

★

## NATIONAL BENEVOLENT ASSOCIATION OF THE CHRISTIAN CHURCH (NBA) / DISCIPLES BENEVOLENT SERVICES (DBS)

NBA—which is now doing business as Disciples Benevolent Services (DBS), but holds on to NBA as its legal name—is a nonprofit organization headquartered in the St. Louis suburb of Maryland Heights, Missouri. The organization has programs and facilities in nine states. Included in its services are chaplaincy care ministry for residents of older adult facilities, as well as alcohol and drug treatment facilities; residential facilities and programs for at-risk children and youth; family unification programs; and community-based supportive-living programs for developmentally disabled adults.

### Volunteer Opportunities

Opportunities vary by location. The organization asks that interested individuals e-mail the headquarters office to be put in contact with a representative at the appropriate location.

### Contact Information

149 Weldon Parkway, Suite 115
Maryland Heights, MO 63043-3103
(314) 993-9000

E-mail: grp-nba@nbacares.org
www.nbacares.org

------------------ ★ ------------------

## PRESBYTERIAN HUNGER PROGRAM (PHP)

The Presbyterian Hunger Program is a ministry of the Presbyterian Church working with congregations and partners around the globe to alleviate hunger and eliminate its causes. To achieve this mission of the church, PHP provides grants to programs addressing hunger and its causes in the United States and around the world. It also provides special educational, mission, and action programs and campaigns for Presbyterians.

### Volunteer Opportunities

One way of offering volunteer service to the hunger program is through creative events that raise funds for PHP, that in turn allow the organization to give more grants to organizations doing direct food relief. A list of the organisation's grantees from 2008 and 2009 (for 2010 work) are listed here: http://gamc.pcusa.org/ministries/hunger/grants. Contacting the local congregation or a grantee in their area would be a good way of making contact.

In addition, PHP encourages individuals to get involved with local bodies doing work surrounding hunger issues, such as local presbytery hunger committees. Also through its work with the Campaign for Fair Food, there are opportunities to support the work of some of PCP's partners, like the CIW. Its international work is done through a program called Joining Hands, and those networks have opportunities to get connected locally and internationally. Visit http://gamc.pcusa.org/ministries/fairfood to learn more about the work PHP does with the Campaign for Fair Food and CIW. Contact the organization for further details.

### Contact Information

100 Witherspoon Street
Louisville, KY 40202

http://archive.pcusa.org/hunger

------------------ ★ ------------------

## SOJOURNERS

Sojourners—publisher of a monthly magazine of the same name—is a voice and vision for social change. Founded in 1971 as a faith-based organization, Sojourners provides an alternative perspective on faith, politics, and culture through its magazine, website, e-mail services, media commentaries, and public events. It nurtures community by bringing together people from the various traditions and streams of the church, and also hosts an annual program of voluntary service.

## Volunteer Opportunities

Sojourners strives to provide an internship program of Christian discipleship, with a focus on life and faith, prayer and formation, and work and mission.

*Life and Faith:* Participants live together as a community in Washington, D.C. Together, the interns design the structures for maintaining their shared household. Through weekly house meetings, the interns worship, conduct business, pray, and experience city life as a community.

*Prayer and Formation*: Interns receive a structured curriculum and monthly educational seminars on a wide range of topics designed to provoke and challenge their perspectives on personal and social issues of faith. Interns are matched with mentors to provide spiritual and vocational guidance during their yearlong experience. Time for personal reflection, contemplation, and community building is offered at retreats given throughout the year.

*Work and Mission*: Participants develop skills by working full-time in the ministry of Sojourners. Skilled staff members challenge interns as supervisors in a variety of departments, including editorial, marketing, and circulation and development. Also, volunteer opportunities are encouraged to enhance interns' experience of Washington, D.C.'s, diverse activities and culture.

The program is open to anyone twenty-one years or older who is single or married without dependents. Room, board, health insurance, city transportation, and a $100 monthly stipend for clothing, travel, and recreation are provided. Sojourners interns commit themselves to one year of service, starting in early September and ending in mid-August the following year.

In addition, actions (such as signing petitions) are posted on the website.

## Contact Information

3333 14th Street, NW, Suite 200
Washington, DC 20010
(202) 328-8842 or (800) 714-7474

E-mail: sojourners@sojo.net
www.sojo.net

★

FAITH-BASED ORGANIZATIONS

## UNITARIAN UNIVERSALIST ASSOCIATION (UUA)

The Unitarian Universalist Association (UUA) is a religious organization that combines two traditions: the Universalists, who organized in 1793, and the Unitarians, who organized in 1825. They consolidated into the UUA in 1961. Unitarian Universalism is a liberal religion with Jewish-Christian roots. It has no creed. Among other things, Unitarian Universalists have been at the forefront of the same-sex marriage debates, advocating for the right of each person to marry the partner of his or her choice.

### Volunteer Opportunities

Congregations are self-governing, and volunteer opportunities are based on the interests and needs of local chapters. Visit the UUA website to find local congregations to contact for more information.

### Contact Information

25 Beacon Street
Boston, MA 02108
(617) 742-2100

E-mail: info@uua.org
www.uua.org

★

## UNITARIAN UNIVERSALIST SERVICE COMMITTEE (UUSC)

UUSC, the activist arm of the Unitarian Universalist church, is a nonsectarian organization that advances human rights and social justice in the United States and around the world. Through a combination of advocacy, education, and partnerships with grassroots organizations, UUSC promotes economic rights, advances environmental justice, defends civil liberties, and preserves the rights of people in times of humanitarian crisis. It also engages local communities through two experiential-learning programs, JustWorks and Just-Journeys, which introduce participants to the work of its domestic and overseas partners—who are often on the front lines of addressing social justice issues.

### Volunteer Opportunities

The most popular way for individuals to engage with UUSC's work is through its experiential learning, or JustWorks, program. Through JustWorks camps, participants work directly with people in local communities on direct-service projects, learning about human rights issues firsthand.

These camps included projects such as helping to rebuild the homes and lives of survivors of the 2005 Gulf Coast hurricanes, rebuilding African American churches in the South that were destroyed by racially motivated arson, renovating schools and community facilities on Native American reservations, and working on local service projects in migrant farm worker communities.

JustWorks camps generally are short-term (usually weeklong) projects that help participants examine and understand the root causes and damaging effects of injustice, with an eye toward promoting intercultural understanding. Participants are taught advocacy skills for addressing issues of poverty, discrimination, and racism in their own communities.

In addition to JustWorks camps, UUSC has a limited number of opportunities for volunteers interested in its human rights mission, including those who have expertise in the organization's specific program focus areas. These individuals contribute their time and efforts to helping UUSC in many valuable ways, from basic data entry to research and analysis of human rights issues.

Individuals interested in volunteering their time and skills to further UUSC's mission are invited to e-mail employment@uusc.org with a résumé and a short description of interests and availability.

## Contact Information

**National Headquarters:** 689 Massachusetts Avenue Cambridge, MA 02139-3302

(617) 868-6600 or (800) 388-3920
www.uusc.org

FAITH-BASED ORGANIZATIONS

# POLICY AND ISSUES ANALYSIS ORGANIZATIONS

## ALLIANCE FOR RETIRED AMERICANS

Established in 2001, the mission of the Alliance for Retired Americans is to ensure social and economic justice and full civil rights for all citizens so that they may enjoy lives of dignity, personal and family fulfillment, and security. The Alliance believes that all older and retired persons have a responsibility to strive to create a society that incorporates these goals and rights, and that retirement provides them with opportunities to pursue new and expanded activities with their unions, civic organizations, and their communities.

**Contact Information**

815 16th Street, NW, 4th Floor
Washington, DC 20006

(202) 637-5399
www.retiredamericans.org

## AMERICAN ASSOCIATION OF PEOPLE WITH DISABILITIES (AAPD)

The American Association of People with Disabilities (AAPD), the country's largest cross-disability membership organization, organizes the disability community to be a powerful voice for change—politically, economically, and socially. AAPD was founded in 1995 to help unite the diverse community of people with disabilities, including their families, friends, and supporters, and to be a national voice for change in implementing the goals of the Americans with Disabilities Act (ADA).

**Contact Information**

1629 K Street, NW, Suite 950
Washington, DC 20006

(202) 457-0046 (V/TTY) or (800) 840-8844 (Toll-Free V/TTY)

## AMERICAN FEDERATION OF TEACHERS (AFT)

The American Federation of Teachers, an affiliate of the AFL-CIO, was founded in 1916 and represents nearly 3,000 local affiliates nationwide, forty-three state affiliates, and 1.5 million members.

Five divisions within the AFT represent the broad spectrum of the AFT's membership: pre-K through twelfth-grade teachers; paraprofessionals and other school-related personnel; higher-education faculty and professional staff; federal, state, and local government employees; and nurses and other health-care professionals. In addition, the AFT represents approximately 80,000 early childhood educators and nearly 250,000 retiree members.

The mission of the American Federation of Teachers includes improving the lives of its members and their families; giving voice to its members' legitimate professional, economic, and social aspirations; bringing together all members to assist and support one another; and promoting democracy, human rights, and freedom throughout the world.

**Contact Information**

555 New Jersey Avenue, NW
Washington, DC 20001

(202) 879-4400
www.aft.org

★

## AMERICAN PSYCHOLOGICAL ASSOCIATION (APA)

Based in Washington, D.C., and established in 1892, the American Psychological Association (APA) is a scientific and professional organization that represents psychology in the United States. With 150,000 members, APA is the largest association of psychologists worldwide. The mission of the APA is to advance the creation, communication, and application of psychological knowledge to benefit society and improve people's lives.

**Contact Information**

750 First Street, NE
Washington, DC 20002-4242

(800) 374-2721 or (202) 336-5500
www.apa.org

★

## AMERICANS FOR FINANCIAL REFORM

Americans for Financial Reform is a coalition of more than 250 national, state, and local consumer, labor, investor, civil rights, community, small business, and senior citizen organizations that have come together to spearhead a campaign for reform. Together, they are fighting for a banking and financial system based on accountability, fairness, and security. The organizations that make up Americans for Financial Reform bring together expertise in policy, advocacy, mobilization, public outreach, media relations, and legislative strategy.

**Contact Information**

1825 K Street, NW, Suite 210
Washington, DC 20006
(202) 263-4533

E-mail: info@ourfinancialsecurity.org
www.ourfinancialsecurity.org

★

POLICY AND ISSUES ANALYSIS ORGANIZATIONS

## CAMPAIGN FOR AMERICA'S FUTURE

Established in 1996, the Campaign for America's Future is the strategy center for the progressive movement. Its goal is to "forge the enduring progressive majority needed to realize the America of shared prosperity and equal opportunity that our country was meant to be."

To attain its ultimate goal, the campaign spearheads a progressive agenda that addresses the kitchen-table issues working families face. It regularly convenes and educates progressive thinkers, organizers, and community activists so their voices will be coordinated, cogent, and potent. And it incubates national campaigns on the critical issues that will define America for generations to come.

### Contact Information

1825 K Street, NW, Suite 400         (202) 955-5665
Washington, DC 20006                 www.ourfuture.org

## CENTER FOR AMERICAN PROGRESS

Founded in 2003, the Center for American Progress is dedicated to improving the lives of Americans through progressive ideas and action. Building on the achievements of progressive pioneers such as Teddy Roosevelt and Martin Luther King, its work addresses twenty-first-century challenges such as energy, national security, economic growth and opportunity, immigration, education, and health care. The center develops new policy ideas, critiques the policy that stems from conservative values, and challenges the media to cover issues that truly matter and shape the national debate.

### Contact Information

1333 H Street, NW, 10th Floor        (202) 682-1611
Washington, DC, 20005                www.americanprogress.org

## CENTER FOR AUTO SAFETY

Consumers Union and Ralph Nader founded the Center for Auto Safety (CAS) in 1970 to provide consumers a voice for auto safety and quality in Washington, and to help "lemon" owners fight back across the country. Among its accomplishments, the organization has achieved numerous legal victories over government agencies that have saved vital consumer, safety, and environmental laws under assault by industry.

**Contact Information**

1825 Connecticut Ave, NW, Suite 330
Washington, DC 20009-5708

(202) 328-7700
www.autosafety.org

★

## CENTER FOR COMMUNITY CHANGE (CCC)

The mission of the Center for Community Change (CCC) is to build the power and capacity of low-income people, especially low-income people of color, to change their communities and public policies for the better. CCC strengthens, connects, and mobilizes grassroots groups to enhance their leadership, voice, and power. It works to amplify community efforts and ensure that grassroots voices are heard in Washington, so that they can help shape the national conversation about building a better America. Founded in 1968 to honor the life and values of Robert F. Kennedy, the Center is one of the longest-standing champions for low-income people and communities of color.

**Contact Information**

**Main Office:** 1536 U Street, NW
Washington, DC 20009
(202) 339-9300

E-mail: info@communitychange.org
www.communitychange.org

★

## CENTER FOR SCIENCE IN THE PUBLIC INTEREST (CSPI)

The Center for Science in the Public Interest (CSPI) is a consumer advocacy organization whose twin missions are to conduct innovative research and advocacy programs in health and nutrition, and to provide consumers with current, useful information about their health and well-being. Its award-winning newsletter, *Nutrition Action Healthletter*, with some 900,000 subscribers in the United States and Canada, is the largest-circulation health newsletter in North America.

**Contact Information**

1875 Connecticut Avenue, NW, Suite 300
Washington, DC 20009

(202) 332-9110
www.cspinet.org

★

## CENTER ON BUDGET AND POLICY PRIORITIES (CBPP)

Established in 1981, the Center on Budget and Policy Priorities (CBPP) is a policy organization working at the federal and state levels on fiscal policy and public programs that affect low- and moderate-income families and individuals. It conducts research and analysis to help shape public debates over proposed budget and tax policies, and to help ensure that policymakers consider the needs of low-income families and individuals in these debates. CBPP also develops policy options to alleviate poverty.

In addition, the Center examines the short- and long-term impacts of proposed policies on the health of the economy and the soundness of federal and state budgets. Among the issues it explores are whether federal and state governments are fiscally sound and have sufficient revenue to address critical priorities, both for low-income populations and for the nation as a whole.

**Contact Information**

820 First Street, NE, Suite 510
Washington, DC 20002
(202) 408-1080

E-mail: center@cbpp.org
www.cbpp.org

★

## CITIZENS FOR TAX JUSTICE (CTJ)

Citizens for Tax Justice, founded in 1979, is a public interest research and advocacy organization focusing on federal, state, and local tax policies and their impact upon our nation. CTJ's mission is to give ordinary people a greater voice in the development of tax laws. Against special interest lobbyists for corporations and the wealthy, CTJ fights for:

- Fair taxes for middle- and low-income families
- Requiring the wealthy to pay their fair share
- Closing corporate tax loopholes
- Adequately funding important government services
- Reducing the federal debt
- Taxation that minimizes distortion of economic markets

**Contact Information**

1616 P Street, NW, Suite 200
Washington, DC 20036
(202) 299-1066

E-mail: ctj@ctj.org
www.ctj.org

★

## COALITION ON HUMAN NEEDS (CHN)

Established in 1981, the Coalition on Human Needs (CHN) is an alliance of national organizations working together to promote public policies that which address the needs of low-income and other vulnerable populations. The Coalition's members include civil rights, religious, labor and professional organizations, and those concerned with the well-being of children, women, the elderly, and people with disabilities.

## Contact Information

1120 Connecticut Avenue, NW, Suite 312
Washington, DC 20036
(202) 223-2532

E-mail: djohnson@chn.org or info@chn.org
www.chn.org

★

## CONSUMER FEDERATION OF AMERICA (CFA)

The Consumer Federation of America (CFA) is an association of nonprofit consumer organizations that was established in 1968 to advance the consumer interest through research, advocacy, and education. Today, nearly 300 of these groups participate in the federation and govern it through their representatives on the organization's board of directors.

## Contact Information

1620 I Street, NW, Suite 200
Washington, DC 20006
(202) 387-6121

E-mail: cfa@consumerfed.org
www.consumerfed.org

★

## CORPORATION FOR SUPPORTIVE HOUSING (CSH)

Established in 1991, the Corporation for Supportive Housing (CSH) is a national nonprofit organization and community development financial institution that helps communities create permanent housing with services to prevent and end homelessness. CSH advances its mission by providing advocacy, expertise, leadership, and financial resources to make it easier to create and operate supportive housing. The organization is committed to a ten-year plan of creating 150,000 new units of supportive housing by 2012. CSH has offices in eleven states and provides limited assistance to many other communities.

## Contact Information

**Headquarters:** 50 Broadway, 17th Floor
New York, NY 10004

(212) 986-2966
E-mail: info@csh.org
www.csh.org

★

## CORPWATCH

Established in 1997, CorpWatch provides nonprofit investigative research and journalism to expose corporate malfeasance and to advocate for multinational corporate accountability and transparency. It works to foster global justice, independent media activism, and democratic control over corporations. The organization seeks to expose multinational corporations that profit from war, fraud, and environmental, human rights, and other abuses; and to provide critical information to foster a more informed public and an effective democracy.

**Contact Information**

2958 24th Street

San Francisco, CA 94110

(415) 641-1633

www.corpwatch.org

★

## DEMOS

Demos is a nonpartisan public policy research and advocacy organization founded in 2000. Headquartered in New York City, Demos works with advocates and policymakers around the country in pursuit of four overarching goals:

- A more equitable economy with widely shared prosperity and opportunity
- A vibrant and inclusive democracy with high levels of voting and civic engagement
- An empowered public sector that works for the common good
- Responsible U.S. engagement in an interdependent world

**Contact Information**

**National Office:** 220 Fifth Avenue,

    5th Floor

New York, NY 10001

(212) 633-1405

E-mail: info@demos.org

www.demos.org

★

## DISABILITY RIGHTS ADVOCATES (DRA)

Established in 1993, DRA is a nonprofit legal center whose mission is to ensure dignity, equality, and opportunity for people with all types of disabilities throughout the United States and worldwide.

DRA's national advocacy work includes high-impact class-action litigation on behalf of people with all types of disabilities, including mobility, hearing, vision, learning, and psychological disabilities. Through negotiation and litigation, DRA has made thousands of facilities throughout the country accessible and has enforced access rights for millions of people with disabilities in many key areas of life, including access to technology, education, employment, transportation, and health care. DRA also engages in nonlitigation advocacy throughout the country, including research and education projects focused on opening up access to schools, the professions, and health care. DRA publishes a variety of reports that provide information and guidance on disability rights and obligations of entities, as well as statistics that address the status of people with disabilities.

**Contact Information**

2001 Center Street, 4th Floor
Berkeley, CA 94704-1204
(510) 665-8644 or
TTY: (510) 665-8716

E-mail: general@dralegal.org
www.dralegal.org

★

## DO SOMETHING (DOSOMETHING.ORG)

Established in 1993, DoSomething.org is one of the largest organizations in the U.S. that helps young people rock causes they care about. A driving force in creating a culture of volunteerism, DoSomething.org is on track to activate 2 million young people in 2011. By leveraging the web, television, mobile, and pop culture, DoSomething.org inspires, empowers, and celebrates a generation of doers: teenagers who recognize the need to do something, believe in their ability to get it done, and then take action.

**Contact Information**

24-32 Union Square East, 4th Floor
New York, NY 10003
Contact: Mike Fantini
(212) 254.2390 x232

E-mail: mfantini@dosomething.org
www.dosomething.org
6399 Wilshire Boulevard, #600
Los Angeles, CA 90048

★

## ECONOMIC POLICY INSTITUTE (EPI)

EPI is an independent, nonprofit, and nonpartisan research institute founded in 1986 on the belief that every working family deserves a better future: a good job, fair pay, affordable health care, and access to a quality education. To that end, its staff of PhD economists and policy analysts conducts rigorous research on the economic issues that impact working families, and works to promote policies that are good for working Americans. EPI was the first organization to focus on these issues, and remains the premier institute publishing research on the economic condition of low- and middle-income American families.

**Contact Information**

1333 H Street, NW, Suite 300, East
  Tower
Washington, DC 20005-4707

(202) 775-8810
E-mail: epi@epi.org
www.epi.org

★

## FAMILIES USA

Established in 1982, Families USA is a national nonprofit, nonpartisan organization dedicated to the achievement of high-quality, affordable health care for all Americans. Working at the national, state, and community levels, it has earned a national reputation as an effective voice for health-care consumers for twenty-five years. Along with other tasks, the organization manages a grassroots advocates' network for organizations and individuals working for the consumer perspective in national and state health policy debates, produces healthy policy reports, acts as a watchdog over government actions affecting health care, and conducts public information campaigns.

**Contact Information**

1201 New York Avenue, NW,
Suite 1100
Washington, DC 20005

(202) 628-3030
E-mail: info@familiesusa.org
www.familiesusa.org

## FAMILY VIOLENCE PREVENTION FUND (FVPF)

Established in 1980, the Family Violence Prevention Fund (FVPF) has worked for more than three decades to end violence against women and children around the world. Instrumental in developing the landmark Violence Against Women Act passed by Congress in 1994, the FVPF has continued to break new ground by reaching new audiences, including men and youth, promoting leadership within communities to ensure that violence prevention efforts become self-sustaining, and transforming the way health-care providers, police, judges, employers, and others address violence.

**Contact Information**

**Main Office:** 383 Rhode Island
    Street, Suite #304
San Francisco, CA 94103-5133

(415) 252-8900 or TTY:
    (800) 595-4889
E-mail: info@endabuse.org
www.endabuse.org

## FOOD RESEARCH AND ACTION CENTER (FRAC)

Established in 1970, the Food Research and Action Center (FRAC) is a national nonprofit organization working to improve public policies and public-private partnerships to eradicate hunger and undernutrition in the United States. FRAC works with hundreds of national, state, and local nonprofit organizations, public agencies, corporations, and labor organizations to address hunger, food insecurity, and their root cause—poverty.

**Contact Information**
1875 Connecticut Avenue, NW,
Suite 540

Washington, DC 20009
(202) 986-2200
www.frac.org

------------------------------------ ★ ------------------------------------

## HOUSING ASSISTANCE COUNCIL (HAC)

A nonprofit corporation headquartered in Washington, D.C., the Housing Assistance Council (HAC) has been helping local organizations build affordable homes in rural America since 1971. HAC emphasizes local solutions, empowerment of the poor, reduced dependence, and self-help strategies. HAC assists in the development of both single- and multifamily homes, and promotes home ownership for working low-income rural families through a self-help, "sweat equity" construction method. The Housing Assistance Council offers services to public, nonprofit, and private organizations throughout the rural United States. HAC also maintains a special focus on high-need groups and regions: Indian country, the Mississippi Delta, farm workers, the Southwest border *colonias,* and Appalachia.

**Contact Information**
**National Office:** 1025 Vermont
 Avenue, NW, Suite 606
Washington, DC 20005

(202) 842-8600
E-mail: hac@ruralhome.org
www.ruralhome.org

------------------------------------ ★ ------------------------------------

## INDEPENDENT SECTOR

Independent Sector serves as the premier meeting ground for the leaders of America's charitable and philanthropic sector. Since its founding in 1980, it has sponsored groundbreaking research, fought for public policies that support a dynamic, independent sector, and created unparalleled resources so staff, boards, and volunteers can improve their organizations and better serve their communities.

**Contact Information**
1602 L Street, NW, Suite 900
Washington, DC 20036
(202) 467-6100

E-mail: info@independentsector.org
www.independentsector.org

------------------------------------ ★ ------------------------------------

## INSIGHT CENTER FOR COMMUNITY ECONOMIC DEVELOPMENT

Established in 1969 as the National Economic Development and Law Center, the Insight Center for Community Economic Development is a national research, consulting, and legal services organization dedicated to building economic health in vulnerable communities. It develops and promotes innovative solutions that help people and communities become and remain economically secure. Program work includes legal services, savings and asset building, early care and education, and workforce development.

**Contact Information**

| | |
|---|---|
| 2201 Broadway, Suite 815 | (510) 251-2600 |
| Oakland, CA 94612-3024 | E-mail: info@insightcced.org |
| 3701 Wilshire Boulevard, Suite 208 | www.insightcced.org |
| Los Angeles, CA 90010-2826 | |

## INSTITUTE ON RACE AND POVERTY (IRP)

Established in 1993, the Institute on Race and Poverty (IRP) investigates the ways that policies and practices disproportionately affect people of color and the disadvantaged. A core purpose for IRP's work is to ensure that people have access to opportunity. Another is to help the places where people live develop in ways that both promote access to opportunity and help maintain regional stability. The Institute is directed by Myron Orfield, associate professor of law at the University of Minnesota Law School.

**Contact Information**

| | |
|---|---|
| Institute on Race and Poverty, | Minneapolis, MN 55455 |
| University of Minnesota | (612) 625-8071 |
| N150 Walter Mondale Hall | www.irpumn.org |
| 229 South 19th Avenue | |

## LEADERSHIP CONFERENCE ON CIVIL AND HUMAN RIGHTS (LCCHR) AND LEADERSHIP CONFERENCE ON CIVIL RIGHTS EDUCATION FUND (LCCREF)

The Leadership Conference on Civil and Human Rights (formerly called the Leadership Conference on Civil Rights) is a coalition charged by its diverse membership of more than 200 national organizations to promote and protect the civil and human rights of all persons in the United States. Through advocacy and outreach to targeted constituencies, the Leadership Conference works toward the goal of a more open and just society. It was founded in 1950 and has coordinated national lobbying efforts on behalf of every major civil rights law since 1957.

The Leadership Conference on Civil Rights Education Fund was founded in 1969 as the education and research arm of the Leadership Conference, and builds public will for federal policies that promote and protect the civil and human rights of all persons in the United States. The Education Fund's campaigns empower and mobilize advocates around the country to push for progressive change in the United States.

**Contact Information**

LCCR/LCCREF:
1629 K Street, NW, 10th Floor
Washington, DC 20006

★

**LCCR:** (202) 466-3311
**LCCREF:** (202) 466-3434
www.civilrights.org

## LEAGUE OF WOMEN VOTERS OF THE UNITED STATES (LWV)

Established in 1920, the League of Women Voters, a nonpartisan political organization, encourages informed and active participation in government, works to increase understanding of major public policy issues, and influences public policy through education and advocacy.

**Contact Information**

1730 M Street, NW, Suite 1000
Washington, DC 20036-4508

★

(202) 429-1965
www.lwv.org

## MEDIA MATTERS FOR AMERICA

Media Matters for America is a web-based, not-for-profit, progressive research and information center dedicated to comprehensively monitoring, analyzing, and correcting conservative misinformation in the U.S. media.

Launched in May 2004, Media Matters for America put in place, for the first time, the means to systematically monitor a cross section of print, broadcast, cable, radio, and Internet media outlets for conservative misinformation—news or commentary that is not accurate, reliable, or credible, and that forwards the conservative agenda—every day, in real time.

Using the website MediaMatters.org as the principal vehicle for disseminating research and information, Media Matters posts rapid-response items as well as longer research and analytic reports documenting conservative misinformation throughout the media. Additionally, Media Matters works daily to notify activists, journalists, pundits, and the general public about instances of misinformation, providing them with the resources to rebut false claims and to take direct action against offending media institutions.

**Contact Information**

455 Massachusetts Avenue, NW,
Suite 600
Washington, DC 20001

★

(202) 756-4100
www.mediamatters.org

## NAACP LEGAL DEFENSE AND EDUCATIONAL FUND, INC. (LDF)

Established in 1940, the NAACP Legal Defense and Educational Fund, Inc. is America's premier legal organization fighting for racial justice. Through litigation, advocacy, and public education, LDF seeks structural changes to expand democracy, eliminate disparities, and achieve racial justice in a society that strives to fulfill the promise of equality for all Americans. LDF also defends the gains and protections won over the past seventy years of civil rights struggle and works to improve the quality and diversity of judicial and executive appointments.

**Contact Information**
**National Headquarters:** 99 Hudson
Street, Suite 1600
New York, NY 10013

(212) 965-2200
www.naacpldf.org

## NATIONAL ASSOCIATION FOR COMMUNITY HEALTH CENTERS (NACHC)

Established in 1970, NACHC works with a network of state health centers and primary care organizations to serve health centers in a variety of ways:

- Provide research-based advocacy for health centers and their clients
- Educate the public about the mission and value of health centers
- Train and provide technical assistance to health center staff and boards
- Develop alliances with private partners and key stakeholders to foster the delivery of primary health-care services to communities in need

**Contact Information**
7200 Wisconsin Avenue, Suite 210
Bethesda, MD 20814

(301) 347-0400
www.nachc.org

## NATIONAL CENTER FOR BICYCLING AND WALKING (NCBW)

Established in 1977, the NCBW is the major program of the Bicycle Federation of America, Inc. (BFA), a national, nonprofit corporation. The NCBW works with local, state, and national bicycle, pedestrian, and transportation advocates to bring about changes in government policies, programs, and procedures to help create more bicycle-friendly and walkable communities.

Several of NCBW's many activities include providing specialized community-based workshops, consulting services in the areas of long-range planning, policy development, public involvement, and route selection.

**Contact Information**

E-mail: info@bikewalk.org

www.bikewalk.org

------------------------------------- ★ -------------------------------------

## NATIONAL CONGRESS FOR COMMUNITY ECONOMIC DEVELOPMENT (NCCED)

Founded in 1970, the National Congress for Community Economic Development is the trade association for community development corporations (CDCs) and the community economic development (CED) industry. Its mission is to promote, support, and advocate for CDCs and the CED industry, whose work creates wealth, builds healthy and sustainable communities, and achieves lasting economic viability.

**Contact Information**

1030, 15th Street, NW, Suite 325       or

Washington, DC 20005                   (877) 44-NCCED (62233)

(202) 289-9020                         www.ncced.org

------------------------------------- ★ -------------------------------------

## NATIONAL CONSUMER LAW CENTER

The National Consumer Law Center is a nonprofit advocacy organization that seeks to build economic security and family wealth for low-income and other economically disadvantaged Americans. It promotes access to quality financial services and protects family assets from unfair and exploitative transactions that wipe out resources and undermine self-sufficiency. For over forty years NCLC has used its expertise to write the rules of a fair marketplace.

**Contact Information**

**Headquarters:** 7 Winthrop Square    www.nclc.org

Boston, MA 02110-1245                  E-mail: consumerlaw@nclc.org

(617) 542-8010

------------------------------------- ★ -------------------------------------

## NATIONAL COUNCIL OF CHURCHES (NCC)

Since its founding in 1950, the National Council of the Churches of Christ in the USA has been the leading force for ecumenical cooperation among Christians in the United States. The NCC's member faith groups—from a wide spectrum of Protestant, Anglican, Orthodox, evangelical, historic African American, and

Living Peace churches—include 45 million persons in more than 100,000 local congregations in communities across the nation. Among its working groups/ task forces, the NCC has an eco-justice program, health task force, special commission for the Gulf Coast, and living wage campaign.

**Contact Information**

475 Riverside Drive, 8th Floor
New York, NY 10115

E-mail: info@ncccusa.org
www.nccusa.org

★

## NATIONAL EDUCATION ASSOCIATION (NEA)

Established in 1857, the mission of the NEA is to advocate for education professionals and to unite the organization's members and the nation to fulfill the promise of public education to prepare every student to succeed in a diverse and interdependent world.

**Contact Information**

1201 16th Street, NW
Washington, DC 20036-3290

(202) 833-4000
www.nea.org

★

## NATIONAL ENERGY ASSISTANCE DIRECTORS' ASSOCIATION (NEADA)

Established in 1990, NEADA is the primary educational and policy organization for the state and tribal directors of the Low-Income Home Energy Assistance Program (LIHEAP). LIHEAP is a federal program providing formula grants to states to help low-income families pay their heating and cooling bills.

**Contact Information**

1232 31st Street, NW
Washington, DC 20007

(202) 333-5915
E-mail: info@neada.org
www.neada.org

★

## NATIONAL HEAD START ASSOCIATION (NHSA)

Established in 1965, the National Head Start Association is a private not-for-profit membership organization dedicated exclusively to meeting the needs of Head Start children and their families. (Head Start is the longest-running national school readiness program in the United States. It provides comprehensive education, health, nutrition, and parent involvement services to low-income children and their families.)

NHSA represents more than 1 million children, 200,000 staff, and 2,600 Head Start programs in the United States. The Association provides support for the entire Head Start community by advocating for policies that strengthen services to Head Start children and their families; by providing extensive training and professional development to Head Start staff; and by developing and disseminating research, information, and resources that enrich Head Start program delivery.

**Contact Information**

1651 Prince Street
Alexandria, VA 22314

(703) 739-0875
www.nhsa.org

★

## NATIONAL RESOURCES DEFENSE COUNCIL (NRDC)

Established in 1970, NRDC uses law, science, and the support of 1.3 million members and online activists to protect the planet's wildlife and wild places, and to ensure a safe and healthy environment for all living things. It works to foster the fundamental right of all people to have a voice in decisions that affect their environment, and also aims to solve pressing environmental issues, including: curbing global warming, getting toxic chemicals out of the environment, moving America beyond oil, reviving our oceans, and helping China go green.

**Contact Information**

**Headquarters:** 40 West 20th Street
New York, NY 10011
(212) 727-2700

E-mail: nrdcinfo@nrdc.org
www.nrdc.org

★

## PHYSICIANS FOR SOCIAL RESPONSIBILITY (PSR)

Established in 1961, Physicians for Social Responsibility is a nonprofit advocacy organization that is the medical and public health voice for policies to prevent nuclear war and proliferation, and to slow, stop, and reverse global warming and toxic degradation of the environment. PSR's 50,000 health professionals and concerned citizen members and e-activists, thirty-one PSR chapters, and forty-one student PSR chapters at medical and public health schools, along with national and chapter staff, form a unique nationwide network committed to a safer and healthier world.

**Contact Information**

1875 Connecticut Avenue, NW, Suite 1012
Washington, DC, 20009

(202) 667-4260
E-mail: psrnatl@psr.org
www.psr.org

★

## PLOUGHSHARES FUND

Established in 1981, Ploughshares Fund works to create a safe, secure, and nuclear-weapon-free world. Combining high-level advocacy, an enhanced grant-making capacity, and the organization's own expertise, Ploughshares Fund is helping to fundamentally change nuclear weapons policy.

**Contact Information**

**Headquarters:** Fort Mason Center
  B-330
San Francisco, CA 94123

(415) 775-2244
www.ploughshares.org

## POLICYLINK

Established in 1999, PolicyLink is a national research and action institute advancing economic and social equity. It connects the work of people on the ground to the creation of sustainable communities of opportunity that allow everyone to participate and prosper. The organization shares its findings and analysis through its publications, website, and online tools, convenings, and national summits, and in briefings with national and local policymakers.

**Contact Information**

**Headquarters:** 1438 Webster Street,
  Suite 303
Oakland, CA 94612

(510) 663-2333
E-mail: info@policylink.org
www.policylink.org

## POPULATION ACTION INTERNATIONAL (PAI)

Established in 1965, Population Action International uses advocacy and research to improve access to family planning and reproductive health care across the world. PAI believes that by ensuring couples are able to determine the size of their families, poverty and the depletion of natural resources are reduced, improving the lives of millions across the world.

**Contact Information**

1300 19th Street, NW, Suite 200
Washington, DC 20036-1624
(202) 557-3400

E-mail: pai@popact.org
www.populationaction.org

## PUBLIC EDUCATION NETWORK (PEN)

Established in 1983, PEN is a national association of local education funds (LEFs) and individuals working to advance public school reform in low-income communities across the country. PEN and its members are building public demand and mobilizing resources for quality public education on behalf of 12 million children in thirty-two states, the District of Columbia, and Puerto Rico. It has expanded its work internationally to include members in Mexico, Peru, the Philippines, South Africa, and Tanzania.

### Contact Information

601 Thirteenth Street, NW, Suite 710 South
Washington, DC 20005-3808

(202) 628-7460
E-mail: PEN@PublicEducation.org
www.publiceducation.org

★

## TRUTHDIG

Truthdig is a news website that provides expert coverage of current affairs as well as a variety of thoughtful, provocative content assembled from a progressive point of view. The site is built around reports by authorities in their fields who conduct in-depth exploration of contemporary topics. To offer frequent change and surprise, the site also presents a diversity of original reporting and aggregated content culled by the site's editors and staff.

### Contact Information

1158 26th Street, No. 443
Santa Monica, CA 90403-4698

E-mail: info@truthdig.com
www.truthdig.com

★

## USACTION

Established in 1999, USAction builds power by uniting people locally and nationally, on the ground and online, to win a more just and progressive America. It promotes a guarantee of quality, affordable health coverage for everyone in the U.S., an end to the war in Iraq, and new commitments to strengthen public education and promote safe, clean energy to end America's dependence on oil.

### Contact Information

1825 K Street NW, Suite 210
Washington, DC 20006
(202) 263-4520

E-mail: usaction@usaction.org
www.usaction.org

★

# SERVICE ORGANIZATIONS

## CENTER FOR GLOBAL EDUCATION (CGE)

Established in 1982, the Center for Global Education collaborates with colleges, universities, and other organizations around the world to promote international education and raise cross-cultural awareness. CGE works to create and enhance existing study abroad programs, integrate international perspectives in the U.S. education system, increase the ethnic diversity of study abroad participants, and encourage research in the area of international education.

### Volunteer Opportunities
Contact the organization for details.

### Contact Information
Loyola Marymount University
1 LMU Drive
University Hall, Suite 1840
Los Angeles, California 90045-2659

(310) 980-6971
E-mail: globaled@lmu.edu
www.globaled.us

## KIWANIS INTERNATIONAL

Established in 1915, Kiwanis is a global organization of volunteers dedicated to changing the world, one child and one community at a time. Its members develop youth as leaders, build playgrounds, and raise funds for pediatric research. In addition, Kiwanis helps shelter the homeless, feed the hungry, mentor the disadvantaged, and care for the sick.

### Volunteer Opportunities
Visit the Kiwanis website to find a club in your area.

### Contact Information
3636 Woodview Trace
Indianapolis, IN 46268-3196
(317) 875-8755 [dial 411]

or (800) 549-2647 [dial 411]
www.kiwanis.org

## LIONS CLUB INTERNATIONAL

Established in 1917, Lions Club International is the world's largest service club organization, with 1.35 million members in more than 45,000 clubs worldwide. The organization is best known for fighting blindness, but it also volunteers for many different kinds of community projects, including caring for the environment, feeding the hungry, and aiding seniors and the disabled. Its community projects often support local children and schools through scholarships, recreation, and mentoring. Along with the Lions Club International Foundation (which helps to fund Lions humanitarian projects), Lions Club International helps communities following natural disasters by providing for immediate needs, such as food, water, clothing, and medical supplies, and also aiding in long-term reconstruction.

### Volunteer Opportunities

Lions Club International has community clubs that meet in person, cyber clubs that meet online, and special interest clubs that can be based on a member's profession or hobby. Each club matches the needs of its members to help them support their community. Membership is by invitation, but it is also possible to start a new club. Visit the Lions Club website to find a club near you, or to learn more about starting a club. To learn more about becoming a Lion, contact the club's membership team at memberops@lionsclubs.org.

### Contact Information

**International Headquarters:**
    300 W. 22nd Street
Oak Brook, IL 60523-8842

(630) 571-5466
www.lionsclubs.org

## NATIONAL ASSOCIATION OF JUNIOR AUXILIARIES (NAJA)

Junior Auxiliary is a national nonprofit organization that encourages members to render charitable services which are beneficial to the general public, with particular emphasis on children. NAJA has more than 14,000 active, associate, and life members in 101 chapters located in Alabama, Arkansas, Florida, Louisiana, Mississippi, Missouri, Tennessee, and Texas. Junior Auxiliaries are all-women organizations.

### Volunteer Opportunities

Opportunities vary by chapter, so contact your local chapter.

### Contact Information

**Headquarters / Mailing Address:**
P.O. Box 1873
Greenville, MS 38702-1873
**Physical Location Address:**
845 South Main Street

Greenville, MS 38701
(662) 332-3000
E-mail: najanet@bellsouth.net
www.najanet.org

## ROTARY INTERNATIONAL

Established in 1905, Rotary International is the world's first service club organization, with more than 1.2 million members in 33,000 clubs worldwide. Rotary club members are volunteers who work locally, regionally, and internationally to combat hunger, improve health and sanitation, provide education and job training, promote peace, and eradicate polio under the motto "Service Above Self."

### Volunteer Opportunities

Rotary club membership is by invitation, and club members must hold or be retired from a professional, proprietary, executive, or managerial position and live or work within the locality of the club or surrounding areas. Visit the website to complete a Prospective Member form and find a club near you.

### Contact Information

**Headquarters:** One Rotary Center
1560 Sherman Ave.
Evanston, IL 60201

(847) 866-3000
www.rotary.org

★

## YOUTH SERVICE AMERICA (YSA)

Youth Service America (YSA) seeks to improve communities by increasing the number and the diversity of young people, ages five to twenty-five, serving in important roles. Founded in 1986, YSA is an international nonprofit resource center that partners with thousands of organizations in more than a hundred countries to expand the impact of the youth service movement with families, communities, schools, corporations, faith-based organizations, nonprofits, the media, and governments. Through this network, it works to increase the quality and quantity of service opportunities and to make service and service-learning the common expectation and common experience of all young people. YSA also operates Servenet.org, a website that includes a searchable database of local volunteer opportunities.

### Volunteer Opportunities

YSA provides grants to help individuals coordinate their own volunteer projects. Volunteers can also check out www.servenet.org to find opportunities that match their needs.

### Contact Information

1101 15th St NW, Suite 200
Washington, DC, 20005

E-mail: info@ysa.org
www.ysa.org

★

# PART THREE

# ON YOUR

# OWN

Any level of community involvement—whether a daily commitment or simply starting a book club in your neighborhood, as described in this section—is good for you, vital to those being served, and healthy for your communities and our nation. There is a postscript to this story that is worth thinking about: My fifteen years of working with volunteers has confirmed what my intuition told me—volunteering for community service could well be the quickest, most rewarding, and least expensive way of gaining self-esteem. ★

# The Reading Cure:
## How to Organize a Book Group with a Social Conscience

I f, for whatever reason, you do not want to volunteer to do community service, there is one other important role you can perform in your neighborhood or community. It is to help organize—with friends, neighbors, or colleagues—a socially conscious book group. This chapter lists all the essential elements that go into setting one up. ★

It also has a suggested reading list of novels that deal with social, environmental, political, and economic justice. And, if you are willing to volunteer for community service, you might very well want to read some of the books recommended, as quite often, volunteers are not familiar with the issues and problems facing neighborhoods or groups different form their own.

> In a democratic society, where every individual opinion counts, [literature's] incomparable ability to instruct, to make alternatives intellectually and emotionally clear, to spotlight falsehood, insincerity, and foolishness—[literature's] incomparable ability, that is, to make us understand—ought to be a force bringing people together, breaking down the barriers of prejudice and ignorance, and holding up ideals worth pursuing. Literature in America does fulfill these obligations.

The novelist John Gardner wrote these words in his essay collection, *On Moral Fiction*, and he is absolutely correct. Novels offer genuine hope for learning how to handle our daily personal problems—and those political issues of our communities and our country—in a moral and human way. They can help us to understand the relationship between our inner lives and the outer world, and the balance between thinking, feeling, and acting. They can give us awareness of place, time, and condition—about ourselves and about others. As our great Nobel Prize–winner William Faulkner said, the best literature is far more true than any journalism.

Throughout history, the imaginations of young people have been fired by characters that function as role models. Yet when we look around us today, we find role models who are less than healthy and truths that are far from self-evident. We find troubling and false symbols of success, fantasy, or celebrity. All the while, we are surrounded by a technology of speed and efficiency that neither questions its means nor knows its ends. In the past thirty years, mass-marketing and advertising techniques have created an entirely new moral climate in America. The superficiality, the alienation, the escapism, and the hollowness are a result of a steady bombardment of confusing and deadening messages designed to reduce us to passive consumers. And we have paid a heavy price: a sharp decline in both civic participation and meaningful public discourse. We have become serious about frivolous issues and frivolous about serious ones.

How curious: While people around the world are risking their lives for American democratic ideals, we're voting in underwhelming numbers and telling pollsters that we're alienated from our political system. For the past thirty years, the acquisition of more and more material goods has become our highest form of endeavor. Terminal consumerism has become a way of life. However, as novelist John Nichols puts it, "Thirty-six flavors doth not a democracy make." How has it come to pass that our founding fathers gave us a land of political and economic opportunity, and we have become a nation of political and economic opportunists? As we have come to worship the idols of power, money, and success, we have neglected the core political principles of justice, equality, community, and democracy.

## POLITICS AND THE MEDIA

The decline in our political culture has occurred in direct proportion to the increase in TV-driven soft news, celebrity scandal-mongering, and superficial political coverage. Every day the electronic media feverishly compete to hype news into entertainment. And when they get a Michael Jackson, Mark Sanford, Elliot Spitzer, or O.J. trial or scandal—especially if it has a sex angle—they stage extravaganzas that would make Barnum and Bailey blush.

With the attention span of viewers decreasing with each generation, and with the networks and cable competing for a large audience, what counts is who can make the fastest and the most enjoyable images. Faster images may tickle the pleasure centers of viewers and achieve higher ratings and more money for media owners, but they make America stupid. TV news turns democracy into "duh-mocracy." Television actress Kristen Johnston put it this way: "TV can really suck the brain right out of your body." And suck the life out of our democracy.

Politics has become a business-game of manipulating symbols and perpetuating myths to conform to the media's mass-marketing techniques and needs. As with so many other aspects of modern living, the process itself has become kingmaker. The process is politics as entertainment—a curious combination of hype and palliation. We know our dependence on mindless, endless, irrelevant TV commercials—and evening news sound bites—creates the illusion that we are learning something. But we are not. In the process we lose our freedom to make genuine choices based on coherent, rational ideas. As T. S. Eliot asked, "Where is the wisdom in knowledge? Where is the knowledge in information?" We might add, where is the knowledge in a thirty-second decontextualized political news sound bite? Hype has impoverished our political debate. It has undermined the very idea that political discourse can be educational and edifying—or that national public policy can grow out of reflective discussion and shared political values. This MacNews approach has undercut our moral values and civic traditions. We have sought simplistic answers to complex problems without even beginning to comprehend the consequences of our loss. We desperately need a commonsense prescription for change. My practical and modest solution is a four-step remedy for reviving our ailing civic culture:

1.  Pull the plug on television news and stick with serious print media.
2.  Get active in the organizations and political campaigns that support the same issues and causes you do.
3.  Read good political novels.
4.  Organize a political reading group.

The last two steps may seem tangential, but they are indispensable to the cure. A good novel serves as a conscience and a guide to action. It revives passionate and thoughtful political debate, providing in-depth exploration of values and political problems marginalized by the media circus.

## ORGANIZING A BOOK GROUP

The number of book clubs and reading groups is growing across the country. Individual readers, booksellers, and librarians are organizing new groups and facilitating the introduction of new members into ongoing groups in record numbers. These active readers are following in the American historical tradition of the women's literary discussion groups of the colonial era, the literary and study clubs of the late-1800s "progressive era," and the Great Books groups of the mid-1900s. So, if you're interested in a stimulating, pleasurable, and democracy-building literary exercise, why not organize a reading group yourself? Here are some basic guidelines.

### The Logistics: Who and When

Look for eight to twelve people who are thoughtful, interesting, and curious. If they already enjoy reading, so much the better. A group needs people who can articulate their ideas and who are good listeners. Those who are enthusiastic, sensitive, and have a sense of humor are a real plus to any discussion. Start with your friends, relatives, and acquaintances who enjoy reading. Ask them to make suggestions. Branch out to those at work and your social, professional, or neighborhood organizations. Put up a sign in your local bookstore or advertise in a community newspaper. Although groups may be homogeneous, such as those composed of women (a majority of existing groups), some of the most successful groups are quite diverse. They have men and women, a variety of cultural backgrounds, and a wide range of ages. While some groups shy away from structure, most groups do have some rules. You might consider adopting guidelines that address issues related to attendance and tardiness, the presence of children and animals, and methods for accepting new members and choosing appropriate books.

Most groups also have facilitators. The facilitator is often the group member who suggested the book, but it could be any participant or a professional leader hired by the group. One good way to find a facilitator is to make inquiries or put up an ad at your local university, community college, or high school. A good facilitator encourages active participation and listening, and ensures that each member is listened to and respected. He or she influences the ambience by making members comfortable in voicing unpopular opinions. By keeping the discussion on track and making sure no one dominates, the facilitator provides the background for a successful discussion.

The goal for facilitation is to encourage the flow of discussion as subtly as possible, in the style of a free-flowing, informed, spirited direction, while assisting the group to move from one topic to another in a timely manner. There is no formula for assuring lively and insightful discussion, but each member of the group might think about the following issues while reading the book: What do you think is the central theme? What are the underlying themes? Did the author raise any emotional conflicts you may have had . . . or resolve any? Did the author challenge any political, economic, social, or cultural beliefs that you may have held with regard to race, sex, gender, class, or ethnicity?

## The Books

Finding appropriate books can be challenging. Many reading groups adopt an annual reading list, while others select books a month or two in advance. Suggestions come from the group's members, their friends, librarians, and booksellers.

One process for book selection that works well is to designate one person each month to bring a selection of books and introduce them to the group. Anyone who has read the books can veto them. The group then narrows the selection down to three, and votes. As a reading group participant, you will find yourself involved in a perpetual search for stimulating books. So I've provided a balanced list of fifty novels by contemporary authors that I believe will enliven the mind and nourish the soul. The novels I recommend are a healthy antidote to living in Entertainment Nation—and reflect that the best in our character is carried in our literature.

We depend on our fiction for metaphoric news of who we are, or who we think we ought to be. The writers of today's political and social realism are doing no less than reminding us of our true, traditional American values—the hope, the promises, and the dreams. When we read these novels, we learn about who we are as individuals and as a nation. They inform us, as no other medium does, about the state of our national politics and character—of the difference between what we say we are and how we actually behave. They offer us crucial insights into the moral, social, and emotional conflicts that are taking place in communities across America. We need such exploration today more than ever.

### *Recommended Reading List*

Dorothy Allison, *Bastard Out of Carolina* (Dutton). An unsparing, passionate, and gritty work about a young girl growing up in poverty. Resonates with integrity and empathy.

Lisa Alther, *Original Sins* (Knopf). Set in the South, this intelligent and absorbing story details the challenges, dreams, and follies of the 1960s. Transcends the differences between races in an insightful and generous manner.

Harriette Arnow, *The Dollmaker* (Avon). A family moves from the hills of Kentucky to industrial Detroit. This epic novel tests the strength of the human heart against the bitterest odds.

James Baldwin, *Another Country* (Dell). A magnificent, tumultuous, and disturbing work about racism that rings with authenticity.

Russell Banks, *Continental Drift* (Ballantine). An absorbing story about a frost-belt family that moves to Florida to find the good life. Instead, they find a nightmare.

Charles Baxter, *Shadow Play* (Norton). The assistant city manager of a small, depressed town in Michigan sees his life fall apart when the chemical plant he lured to town turns out to be an environmental disaster.

Saul Bellow, *Herzog* (Penguin). Keen insights into what it takes to maintain one's individuality and civility while corporations dominate our culture and politics, and critical thinking gives way to the demands of social conformism and consumerism.

Wendell Berry, *The Memory of Old Jack* (Harvest). Remarkable and graceful; explores the life of an aging Appalachian farmer amid America's changing values.

Dorothy Bryant, *Confessions of Madame Psyche* (Ata). The twentieth century as experienced by a Chinese American woman. This moving account of Mei-li Murrow's saga is a metaphor for California's and our nation's multicultural experience.

Sandra Cisneros, *The House on Mango Street* (Knopf). A poignant coming-of-age novel, with unforgettable characters, set in the Latino section of Chicago.

E. L. Doctorow, *The Book of Daniel* (Plume). The most important political novel about the Cold War, the arms race, Red-baiting, and McCarthyism.

Michael Dorris, *A Yellow Raft in Blue Water* (Warner). Compassionate and psychologically complex, this novel spans three generations of Native

American women in the Pacific Northwest—on and off the reservation—who share a fierce independence and a love of family.

Gretel Ehrlich, *Heart Mountain* (Penguin). Explores the experience of Japanese Americans exiled to a World War II relocation camp in Wyoming, and their relationship with local ranchers.

Ralph Ellison, *Invisible Man* (Vintage). A powerful classic about race, individuality, and identity. A Southern black man moves to New York and learns the many ways whites are unable to see him.

Louise Erdrich, *Love Medicine* (Harper Perennial). Presents stunning and haunting insight into life for Native Americans today.

Denise Giardina, *The Unquiet Earth* (Ivy). From the devastation of the Depression to the hope of the War on Poverty, a moving story of a West Virginia community's struggle for survival.

Kaye Gibbons, *Ellen Foster* (Algonquin). An exhilarating and endearing tale of an eleven-year-old orphan who calls herself "old Ellen," and who moves from one woebegone situation to another with spirit and determination.

Davis Grubb, *Shadow of My Brother* (Zebra). Perfectly paced; a dramatic tale of a Tennessee town in the 1950s caught in a moral crisis over racial violence.

Ernest Hebert, *The Dogs of March* (New England Press). Brilliant, sensitive, and funny. Captures what it was like to be unemployed in the 1980s. Set in New England, it's the American dream gone belly-up.

Ursula Hegi, *Stones from the River* (Scribner). In a small German town, the ordinary and secret lives of people and their relationship to politics disclose the quandaries and conflicts that allowed the greatest crime of the twentieth century.

Linda Hogan, *Mean Spirit* (Ivy). A magical and compelling story about whites robbing the Osage Indian tribe of their oil wealth in Oklahoma.

John Irving, *The Cider House Rules* (Bantam). A fine writer brings his incisive storytelling gifts to fruition with this excellent novel about choice, class, and Yankee common sense.

Arturo Islas, *The Rain God* (Avon). A Southwestern classic set in a fictional small town on the Texas-Mexico border. Examines the spirit of Mexican American life—faith, family, and culture—and how it conflicts with the Anglo drive to "make it."

William Kennedy, *Ironweed* (Penguin). A Pulitzer Prize winner's shrewd study of the diceyness of fate. This modern Dante's *Inferno* about life on skid row is especially poignant as homelessness continues to cast a shadow across our land.

Sue Monk Kidd, *The Secret Life of Bees* (Penguin). A stunning and lush story of race and gender set in South Carolina. In the struggle between bigotry and love, the latter wins out.

Barbara Kingsolver, *Animal Dreams* (Harper Perennial). A wonderful tale of multiculturalism in Arizona. Explores themes of authenticity, community, integrity, and truth.

Maxine Hong Kingston, *The Woman Warrior: Memoirs of a Girlhood Among Ghosts* (Vintage). A brilliant portrayal of the Chinese American experience. Kingston's account of growing up Asian and poor adds a cultural richness to the landscape.

Ella Leffland, *Rumors of Peace* (Harper Perennial). A fierce California girl comes of age during World War II, making her own sense of racism, Nazism, the bombings of Pearl Harbor and Hiroshima, and the coming of peace.

Alan Lightman, *The Diagnosis* (Vintage). A Kafkaesque tale that questions America's compulsive love affair with modern technology, efficiency, speed, money, and "making it."

Thomas Mallon, *Henry and Clara* (Ticknor & Fields). Clara and Henry, the young couple in the box with Lincoln when he was shot, are the focus of this riveting account of the political and cultural conflicts of the Civil War era.

Carson McCullers, *The Heart is a Lonely Hunter* (Bantam). This enduring masterpiece, set in small-town Georgia, is a compassionate study of how people confront the problems of poverty, race, class, and gender—and how they handle the conflicts of the human condition.

Toni Morrison, *Beloved* (Plume). Winner of a Pulitzer Prize, this is a powerful story of the legacy of slavery. The central theme—the relationship between slave and master—illuminates the tragic complications underlying our historical experience.

Bharati Mukherjee, *The Middleman* (Fawcett). Winner of the National Book Critics Circle Award, this is a profound, intelligent, and often funny book about recent immigrants to America and their struggle to survive.

Faye Ng, *Bone* (Harper Perennial). In a clear and emotionally powerful novel, Ng takes us into the heart and inner secrets of a family in San Francisco's Chinatown.

John Nichols, *The Milagro Beanfield War* (Ballantine). Reveals how the economic and political "shell game" is being run on ordinary Americans. Part of the author's New Mexico trilogy, it is a contemporary *Grapes of Wrath*, leavened with Mark Twain's down-home humor.

Joyce Carol Oates, *Them* (Vanguard). A poignant account of the hopes, strategies, and chaos of urban community organizing during the time of the 1960s riots.

Tillie Olsen, *Yonnondio* (Laurel). A remarkable, poetic, and timeless book about a young family's struggle to overcome poverty during the Great Depression.

Ruth Ozeki, *My Year of Meats* (Penguin). A feisty Japanese American filmmaker takes on the beef industry, chemical corporations, and commercial advertising. Muckraking, witty, and provocative.

Jayne Anne Phillips, *Machine Dreams* (Dutton). A chronicle of middle-American family life, from the Depression to Vietnam, about identity, shifting values, and the ironies of a rapidly changing America.

Marge Piercy, *Gone to Soldiers* (Fawcett). A sweeping epic about women's lives during World War II that seamlessly blends political, social, and economic issues on the home front.

Chaim Potok, *Davita's Harp* (Fawcett). A compassionate coming-of-age novel about a young girl in 1930s New York developing a social, moral, and political consciousness.

E. Annie Proulx, *Postcards* (Collier). Winner of the PEN/Faulkner Award. A remarkable story of the struggle of New England farmers to confront the loss of home and place in economic hard times.

Philip Roth, *American Pastoral* (Vintage). An unsparing story of the political excesses of the 1960s. How youthful idealism led to romantic, out-of-control, anti-liberal activism, which in turn laid the groundwork for the reactionary policies of Nixon and Reagan.

Richard Russo, *Empire Falls* (Vintage). A passionate and rich examination of the working-class heart of small-town America, and the consequences of inequitable distribution of wealth in a deindustrialized society.

May Sarton, *Kinds of Love* (Norton). Three generations celebrate the American bicentennial in a small New Hampshire town. About truth, honesty, integrity—all those traditional virtues that have become unfashionable.

Danzy Senna, *Caucasia* (Riverhead). Birdie Lee's black father flees in the seventies, and her white, activist mother is forced to take the girl underground, where Birdie copes with adolescence and the complexities of her racial identity.

Mary Lee Settle, *The Scapegoat* (Ballantine). A stirring account of a historic strike in the coal fields, depicting a real-life struggle between immigrants (Italian, Greek, Polish, and Slavic, among others) and robber barons. You won't find this in most history texts.

Jane Smiley, *Moo* (Random House). The financial, academic, sexual, and political scandals of a Midwestern university are laid bare in this satire of higher education.

John Steinbeck, *The Grapes of Wrath* (Penguin). This classic novel of farmers forced to move West during the Great Depression electrified the nation and reminded us of our historical commitment to compassion, opportunity, and social justice.

Kurt Vonnegut, *Jailbird* (Dell). Hilarious tale about Nixon's social policies of "benign neglect" and the Watergate era. An unflinching mix of wit, politics, and class that should be required reading.

Alice Walker, *Meridian* (Fawcett). A powerful novel about civil rights activism in the South of the 1960s. Warm, generous, and complex, it challenges each of us to examine what it is to become a decent, responsible, and honorable person.

# Acknowledgments

Any book is, to some extent, a collaboration among author, editor, and publisher. In this respect I have been fortunate, as Ann Treistman and Tony Lyons could not have been more supportive and generous at each stage of the development of this project. Helen Matatov has done a superb job of researching the list of volunteers organizations in the book, and it would be incomplete without her efforts.

Judy MacLean's editorial suggestions and commonsense insights have been invaluable. Marla Wilson and Lee Patterson have provided exceptional technological and word-processing support. Stan and Sidney Shuman and Mary-Ann and Philip Hobel provided friendship and gracious hospitality that gave me the space to reflect upon and design this project.

I am also deeply appreciative of the time and effort that the following individuals have put forth to write reflective and insightful essays about their personal volunteer experiences. They are, in alphabetical order: Sam Beard, Sabrina Bornstein, Juan Cruz, John Garamendi, Sophia Bracy Harris, Sara Hobel, Paul Marienthal, Martine Makower, Anna McCorvey, Julie Claire Morial, Elliot Naishtat, Susan Patricof, Matthew Piepenburg, Laura Polacheck,

Tom Powers, Bruce Reeves, William Stacy Rhodes, Casey Rogers, Michael Roth, Rosemary Shahan, Megan Voorhees, Ashley Wiltshire, and Susan Ford Wiltshire.

I also want to thank Robert Bellah and William M. Sullivan for their contribution to the Final Report of the National Advisory Council on Economic Opportunity, which is the basis for chapter 3 of this book.